How to Write for
TELEVISION

How to Write for

TELEVISION

Madeline DiMaggio

A FIRESIDE BOOK
Published by Simon & Schuster
New York London Toronto Sydney Tokyo Singapore

FIRESIDE

Rockefeller Center
1230 Avenue of the Americas
New York, New York 10020

Manufactured in the United States of America

10 9 8 7 6

First Fireside Edition 1993

Library of Congress Cataloging-in-Publication Data

DiMaggio, Madeline.
   How to write for television / Madeline DiMaggio.
     p. cm.
    1. Television authorship. 2. Television plays—Technique.
  I. Title.
  PN1992.7.D5 1990
  808'.066791—dc20   89-37579
                                           CIP

ISBN 0-671-76641-1

To my mother and silent partner, Mary Marsh DiMaggio
To my daughter, Jordan, my greatest accomplishment
And to Joyce Barkeley, who put the whole thing in motion

Acknowledgments

With many thanks . . .

To my wonderful typist, a writer in her own right, Barbara Whitworth Taylor, for all the good advice.

To my students who turned me on to writing again. For their inspiration, the joy, and the great learning experience.

To Earl Wallace and to Pamela Wallace for who they are and for the great experience I've had working with them. Thank you for allowing me to use excerpts from some of our shared material, and thanks Earl for the interview.

To Kathy Donnell for permission to use excerpts of the scripts we wrote during our eight-year partnership. To the good times and the rough times, and to all the work.

To my agent, Mitchel Stein, for his faith in me and for the interview he gave over that great lunch he bought.

To Jay Tarses for sharing his experiences on the creation of "The Days and Nights of Molly Dodd."

To Alene Terasaki, director of development for movies and series for Think Entertainment, for her interview and vast knowledge of the new cable television markets.

To DLT Entertainment Ltd. for permission to use excerpts from "Three's Company," "Coffee, Tea or Jack."

To MTM for permission to use excerpts from "The Bob Newhart Show," "A Day in the Life."

To Columbia Pictures for permission to use excerpts from "Starsky and Hutch," and "Fantasy Island."

To the Writers Guild of America, west, for permission to reprint guild documents and periodical literature. And to Chuck Slogen, director of industrial analysis, for all those helpful statistics.

A Special Thanks . . .

To my family, who for some reason still love and support me,
To my friends, who after this ordeal have not written me off,
To Gurumayi Chidvilasananda, my meditation teacher, who keeps chipping away at my stubbornness.

Contents

1

How I Broke In, Got Hot, Burned Out . . . and Why I Came Back for More

I never intended to become a television writer. Had I known what the years had in store, I might have paid more attention in English Comp., or at least shown up for some typing classes. Essentials such as these that would later prove invaluable were far from my mind.

My training was as an actress. I lived acting, ate it, slept it, received my degree in it, knocked around for years, and never got that much-needed break. And I was good. But I've learned in this industry that good isn't always enough. I was carrying around a belief system that was deadly—in fact, I might as well have taken a bath with Jaws. Why? I bought the Catch 22—you can't get a job unless you're a member of the Screen Actors Guild; you can't get into the Guild unless you have a job; and you can't get an agent without either. So, no matter who I trained with or what auditions I may have had, I went in search of these insurmountable obstacles, and since the universe seems to provide us with what we're looking for, I found them.

And then one day I met a television writer. I hadn't met any scriptwriters before, so it was my good fortune to be completely naive to the difficulties of breaking into this field. My friend Joyce Barkeley, who operated a shop on the Universal lot, introduced me to Rod Baker, of the writing team Olsen and Baker. Rod was new to the industry, fresh out of college, and had just completed his first assignment, a script for "Hawaii Five-O." I read the script in hopes of auditioning for the show. The audition never came but something else happened—something was set in motion, though I was not aware of it yet.

Once television writers deliver a good teleplay, the producers of the show will almost always invite them back the following season, provided the show remains on the air. Rod and his partner, Glen, wrote two more "Hawaii Five-O" scripts. I studied each in hope that I'd have a shot at reading for one of the parts. But something more interesting was happening along the way. I was beginning to recognize elements that each script had in common. No matter how original or unique the material, they were identical in their style, mood, and structure. Suddenly it hit me! What if I could do this! What if I could write a script! Maybe I could make my entrance as an actress through the back door! Why hadn't I thought of it before? I'd write a script and then cleverly write in a part for myself!

At about this time I discovered another unemployed actress who was living in my apartment complex. We teamed up and decided to write a "Kojak," which is called writing on "spec," or speculation—that is, writing and delivering a completed script in hopes that the "Kojak" producers would want to buy it.

Naive? Perhaps, but looking back, that naivete turned out to be our strongest attribute, along with our enthusiasm and the three "Hawaii Five-O" scripts we were using as examples.

Unfortunately, it wasn't enough. Four or five months into the project we had to scrap it. Although we had a hot idea, and knew the show extremely well, our story was so complex that we wrote ourselves into an inevitable hole. Neither a crane nor a devout religious experience could pull us out.

At this juncture we had a choice—one that every writer makes: We could forget writing altogether, or we could attempt writing something else. Not jaded by disappointment—it was second nature to me as an actress—we turned our attention to the half-hour comedy. After all, if we were not destined to write cop shows, perhaps our futures were in making people laugh. We decided to tackle a "Rhoda."

By some miracle we were able to complete the script. I thought it was good. I even took it to my mother and she told me it was good. My partner's grandmother said it was good. What more do you need than the complete honesty of your relatives? I was certain of a sale. It was now just a matter of time before I had my parking space on the studio lot. I could see myself driving through the gate in my Mercedes, waving nonchalantly to the guards!

As luck would have it, I learned there was a man in my apartment complex who knew a man, who knew another man, who played tennis with an agent. I invited my contact over. I filled him with wine and pasta and threatened his life if he didn't read our script. Threats of this nature seem to work better if your last name is Italian. I don't know if it was a miracle or just plain fear that prompted this gentleman to give our script to the man who knew the other man who played tennis with the agent. Somehow our script landed at Shapiro-Lichtman, writers representatives.

The agent who had our hot little script in his hands was going to love it—some things you just know. He was going to call up and say, "I need you as my clients. Come in right now. I have to sign you up!"

So I waited by the phone. And I waited, and I waited, and I waited! Finally I called him. I was scared to death as I introduced myself as one of the writers of the "Rhoda" script. The dialogue went something like this:

INTERCUT TELEPHONE CONVERSATION

> AGENT
> . . . Yeah . . . un huh . . . oh, right.
> The script had some good stuff in it.
> Keep writing, you've got some talent.

> MYSELF
> Thank you . . .

A long, uncomfortable pause. I was waiting for him to say more.

> MYSELF (continuing)
> We're looking for representation . . .
> and we thought

> AGENT (cutting me off)
> I'm not looking for new clients.

Another pause.

> MYSELF
> Oh . . . well . . . do you think
> we could come in and meet you?

> AGENT
> Why do you want to meet me when
> I'm not taking new clients?

> MYSELF
> . . . We really appreciate your
> reading our script. I promise
> it'll only take a minute. We
> just want to shake your hand.

And so began my fifteen years of creative lying. We met with the agent and the meeting was indeed short. Though he still had no intention of signing us, we did have a great rapport. I think quite honestly he got a kick out of us. We were aggressive, not obnoxious, overly enthusiastic, and ridiculously hopeful. Before we left, I asked him for just one more favor. Though he had no intention of handling us, wouldn't he please submit the "Rhoda" script on our behalf, just so somebody—anybody—would read it. At this point all he wanted was to get us out of his office. He agreed.

The producer of "Rhoda" called me a few weeks later. She felt the script was gimmicky and clichéd. Rhoda didn't act that way, Brenda didn't talk that way, the story was forced, and in so many words the "Rhoda" staff was a tight little family and they were not looking for new writers. This circumstance was not one where I could ask to come in and shake the producer's hand. I thanked her for reading the script and politely hung up. Obviously our destiny did not lie in half-hour comedy.

So, my partner and I promptly returned to crime and murder and picked up the unfinished "Kojak." The holes that seemed so impossible before weren't impossible after all. Perhaps all we needed were those few months to air them out. This time we completed the script.

Since we still didn't have an agent, I submitted the script to the story editor whose name appeared on the credits each week. Why we chose this particular show to write for, or how it happened that Gene Kearney was working on staff at the time, is serendipity. "Kojak" was bought. Gene, an incredible writer and Emmy nominee, gave us time and expertise far beyond the call of any story editor. He painstakingly stepped us through rewrites until the script worked, which was no small task for a writer of his caliber working with two novices.

The agent who we had met with earlier sent us formal contracts. We now had representation. I officially became a member of the Writers Guild with a credit to my name.

My dream of acting began to pale. I liked carrying an attaché case onto the lot. Story editors were actually offering me a seat in their office. They wanted to know if I took cream in my coffee. Producers who had never given me a second glance now seemed genuinely interested in what I had to say. Maybe the door hadn't opened where I had intended, but I was no fool, either. This was not an industry in which one could be picky! Through writing, I was stepping inside.

I no longer envisioned a star on the door. Instead I envisioned my name on-screen under writing credits. I bought a VCR so I could hit the pause button every time my credit rolled. When people asked me what I did for a living, I would modestly mention that I was a television writer. The effect was bigger if I downplayed it. Almost everyone was fascinated by what I did and my ego was loving it.

Knowing my Mercedes was getting closer, I quit my job leasing apartments. I was absolutely certain my next big assignment was just around the corner. Okay, so I miscalculated a little!

It was a year before we got another script commitment, a "Petrocelli." With this second television credit I felt we were out of the gate. Finally our careers would get rolling. Six more months passed before we were able to land a "Bionic Woman."

During that time I was constantly on the phone calling various shows, asking their status and for an opportunity to come in with ideas. This job is usually the agent's, but in all fairness to my agents, 10 percent of nothing was still nothing. The agency had a big name and successful clients. Though it was actively doing little for us, just using the agency's name on the phone became an entree.

We received story money for "Bionic Woman" but were eventually cut off due to budget problems. The producers liked us and they decided to give us a shot at another episode. After turning in the treatment (the story synopsis), I received a call from the story editor. Though we had impressed him the first time, this time he found the material a great disappointment and we were cut off again.

Two years after we had sold the "Kojak," my now-former husband told me I had to start contributing to the family income. We had just bought our first fixer-upper and could only survive on two salaries. I was at the end. Unless I could somehow manage to derive a reliable income from script writing, I would have to quit and find some other kind of job.

Perhaps it was this realization that turned the tide, because a month later we got a commitment for a "Starsky and Hutch." The producers were so happy with the script that the following season we were asked back for a three-script commitment, but by then we were too busy with other assignments. We had suddenly unplugged a dam. All the calls I had made in the two previous years began paying off.

To this day, I believe those two years of unemployment was possibly the most productive time of my life! Why? Because I never stopped. I never let up, and it was this perseverance, more than it was talent, that led to the jackpot.

Looking back, I've learned a valuable lesson. It is totally ludicrous to judge your successes by what is materializing at the moment. Rather it's what you put in beforehand that creates the payoff.

In Hollywood, as the old saying goes, "When you're hot, you're hot, and when you're not your agent doesn't call." Our agent was calling. The jobs began rolling in, sometimes two at a time. After a year of cop shows and other one-hour episodes, we managed to break into half-hour comedies, Movies of the Week, pilots for television, and finally development deals at both NBC and Paramount studios. In six years, we sold twenty-seven consecutive shows. The gratification was incredible, and the money was exceptional. Just as I had imagined, I was driving a Mercedes, and I waved nonchalantly to the Paramount guards as I passed the gates and parked in a spot with my name on it.

Seven years later I had a classic case of burnout. We had worked nonstop. If I wasn't writing, I was thinking about writing. Or, I was trying to think up a new idea for another assignment. There was never a day off. I had tried a trip to Europe with my husband once, but I was called back by an executive for rewrites on a pilot.

The negatives of the profession started to get to me: the pressures of deadlines, having little or no control over my own material, and working with demanding executives who I was too timid to challenge. Instead of excitedly anticipating the next job, I secretly began dreading it, knowing how much work was involved. The relationship with my partner was becoming increasingly more difficult and the stress was beginning to affect the quality of our work.

The money that I had earned in television up to this point had been invested in my husband's business. Now the company, which initially had done well, was on the verge of financial collapse. I was also juggling my time between writing and a six-month-old daughter. And then the 1982 Writers Guild strike hit.

Though I was a big supporter of the strike, financially it could not have come at a worse time. My life was falling apart. A year earlier, I had gone to a meditation teacher who asked me what I wanted. I told him spiritual awareness. I was hoping this wasn't it. If it was, I wanted to take back my request. There is truth in the old saying, "Be careful what you ask for." You may get it.

A year later, I arrived on the Monterey Peninsula divorced, bankrupt, split from my writing partnership, and a single parent. I meditated, took walks along the beach, contemplated my life, and spent the next few years living on unemployment and my diminishing television residuals.

I tried to write during this time, but no longer was Big Daddy Producer waiting for the pages. No longer did I have the luxury of deadlines. Whatever I began I had trouble completing. Every time I picked up *Daily Variety* or a trade journal a certain panic would set in. The thought of rejection or even returning to Hollywood terrified me. I was suffering from a tremendous block and had no idea what to do.

One day a friend asked me to speak to a high school video class. He wanted me to play some tapes of my television shows and talk about my career. It felt so good being there that I returned several times to help the students prepare scripts for their senior class projects.

I had never considered teaching before but I discovered I absolutely loved it, and this crowd couldn't walk out on me—they were a captive audience. The students were energetic and receptive. They had an enthusiasm for writing that helped rekindle my own.

I started speaking at colleges and universities, and eventually conducted my own workshops in television and screen writing throughout the country. It was gratifying and had rewards, but after a while I discovered that I needed to *do* what I was talking about. I missed the industry, the pitching sessions, the adrenaline rush of driving onto the studio lot. I missed seeing my name on the television screen, and quite honestly, I missed the lucrative income. But most of all, I missed writing. I was beginning to realize how much I really loved it.

I wanted to go for it again. But how? I hadn't had a credit in years. Once I left Hollywood, I made no attempt to keep in touch with my contacts. I no longer even had an agent. It would be like starting over.

I went to work on a screenplay entitled, "Belly Up." It is a comedy based on my experiences in bankruptcy. I submitted it to my old agency, which had dropped me three years earlier, and they signed me to a new two-year contract. The script acted as a calling card, and I was soon actively involved again in pitching sessions. Three of the "Movie of the Weeks" I pitched found producers and went to the networks.

During this time I met Pamela and Earl Wallace, Academy Award-winning writers of the motion picture *Witness*. My friendship with Pam turned into an exciting collaboration, the result of which was a screenplay entitled, "If the Shoe Fits," which was optioned in early 1988. We are now at work developing a pilot for television under Earl's banner, Wallace Communications.

Why did I come back for more? Because I love it. I like the rush that happens with an exciting idea, the butterflies that happen before a pitching session, the bouncing of ideas from creative minds, the accomplishment of completing a good script, the money that comes with a sale, the excitement of the unknown, and always, the possibility of hitting it really big. But then, I like to use hot sauce on my food, and for some people it burns a hole in their stomach. So there you have it!

Now, About This Book . . .

I make no false promises, nor am I telling anyone they can simply run out and pick up a fast buck as a television writer. Let's face it, deciding to make a living by writing television scripts is not a practical career choice. Therefore, you have to be driven. Your passion is the sole, or should I say soul, prerequisite. You *must* see your name listed as a credit. Life will have little meaning unless you join the Writers Guild of America. And somewhere along the line, if you're nominated for an Emmy, it will all have been worth it. You are a person who never bought into the negative statistics, and besides, somewhere inside you have the unwavering feeling that you are the exception.

Consider this:

- There are 7,000 film, television, and radio writers in the Writers Guild of America, west.
- In general, in any given year, half of the Guild members will work. About half of this half will derive their sole income from writing.
- Out of this group, 25 percent of the writers will make a substantial living—that is, $50,000 or more per year.
- There are approximately 2,000 episodic television assignments available per season and approximately 100 Movies for Television. The majority of these assignments are given to writers already in the Writers Guild. About half of these shows are staff-written (these are writers employed solely by a certain show). The other half are written by free-lancers.
- The Guild brings in about 400 to 450 new writers a year. These are writers breaking in from outside who have made a sale.

Now for the Good News

It can be done: You can break into television writing. It happened to me and it's happened to some of my students. The industry is full of writers who have somehow managed to buck the odds. These writers weren't all related to somebody, nor did they all have contacts. Some of them lived or are still living outside the Los Angeles area. These success stories are as diverse as the personalities of the individuals, but the writers did have one thing in common: a good idea, a well-written script, and some knowledge of marketing. The script was their calling card. If it didn't sell, the quality of the writing opened doors for an eventual sale.

Consider the story of Kevin Falls. Kevin was one of my students when I began teaching about four years ago. He had a look in his eye, a kind of determination that, as a teacher, I couldn't help but recognize.

I read his first screenplay and it was quite good. I could tell that he had talent. The script didn't sell but Kevin found an agent. He kept writing. He completed his second screenplay and that also didn't sell. But he kept writing.

One day I got a call from Kevin. He was angry and distraught. He now had three completed screenplays to his credit and still no bites. I completely understood his frustration. Such moments are difficult. I wondered as a teacher if I was doing Kevin a grave disservice by giving him a pep talk. But I knew, as down as Kevin was, he wouldn't give up.

About six months later I heard from him again. He called to tell me he had just signed a four-picture deal with Disney Studios. An executive there, a woman who I came to know later, read one of his scripts. She was not interested in buying the script but she loved the way it was written. She called Kevin's agent and asked to read more. The agent sent down the other two scripts. Again, for various reasons, she didn't buy the scripts, but she found the writing wonderful. It was not only consistent but Kevin's style was perfect for the Disney genre. He was placed under contract and he had not even sold a script!

What would have happened if Kevin had stopped writing after completing his first script? The executive who called his agent and asked for more would have been told there was no more. Today, Kevin would still be employed in retail clothing!

It Can Be Done

The only question is, Do you want it badly enough to work that hard? If you do, be assured that there are producers, agents, and studio executives who are constantly searching for new talent.

A Note from the Author

There are two ways you can learn to write for television. One is to read television scripts and the other is to write them. "How to" books are helpful, and I certainly hope you buy this one. But when you get right down to it, there is no text better than the actual script. For this reason, I have included in this book excerpts of scripts I have collaborated on or written in the half-hour, one-hour, and two-hour

Movie for Television formats. I use these examples to facilitate stepping you through the developmental process. They make it easier because you have actual pages of narrative and dialogue in front of you.

Many books on script writing begin with structure. Structure is the single most important element of all scripts. I have chosen to take another avenue, however, the one by which I learned, and the one I teach. There are basic steps in all art forms. To successfully create requires a recipe. The correct ingredients must be known and located at one's fingertips. We will begin by studying the ingredients of the script.

Television relies on hooks. Its sole purpose is to grab the audience and keep them from changing the channel. We will analyze these hooks: They are what producers want and what they will be looking for in your scripts.

My goal is that you will never view television in the same way again. If you know what to look for, then every time you turn on your set you'll be in the classroom. Your education will be perennial, not just a one-time read.

Once we have studied the mechanics of the script writing and the tenets on which television rests, we will move into structure. Together, we will walk through the necessary steps in developing a script. Finally, we will cover marketing. What is the point of crafting something sensational unless you know how to get it out there and get it read?

In my lecturing and various workshops, I have found that I can best instruct through my personal experiences in the industry. These include the horror stories as well as the victories. I've made mistakes and I am bluntly honest about them. I point out these errors to educate you—from the voice of a writer who faces the blank page every day, not a Hollywood hotdog with spotless credits and all the answers.

This book is intended to be a "how to" as well as a "what not to do" in the industry. My intention is to instruct and to entertain. What's the point of all this work unless we can have a little fun along the way? I hope I've succeeded. I'm a month late turning in this book and I've already spent my advance!

2

The Tools of Teleplay Writing

Writing for television, or teleplay writing as it is referred to in the industry, is an "art of less," the Zen of writing. Unlike the novel, the script is not "complete." It is a series of visual impressions giving the illusion of completeness. Here, the writer's perception must shift from the word to the picture. The goal is to show, not to talk about, to indicate or to suggest rather than to explain. Since the teleplay writer is working with terrific time limitations (that is, half-hour, one-hour, or the two-hour Movie for Television), his or her purpose is to select the right fragments and pictures that most effectively tell the story, and to eliminate all the other fragments and pictures that don't directly contribute to the story.

When you read television scripts—and it is absolutely essential that you read them—you will be amazed at how simple they appear. This simplicity is an illusion simply because in good scripts the writing is so economical. There is truly an art in less. What television writers choose to leave out of the script is just as important as what they choose to put in. Often, the picture is enough. Silence, or no words, speak more loudly than dialogue.

Television is a *visual* art form. Therefore, writing for television requires more than literary skills. To write for television, you must think in pictures. A good visual sense is absolutely crucial. Timing and rhythm are also important, as well as your ability to identify with the viewing masses. Certainly, if you have no sense of what the viewing masses like or can identify with, your stories will not be marketable.

Last, but certainly not least, you need a flair for the dramatic. You must recognize and work with what is "theatrical," because first and foremost your job is to entertain.

In executing the script, the television writer has only four tools with which to work, or progress the story forward. These are:

LOCALES: Choosing the picture
NARRATIVE: Describing what is taking place in the picture
DIALOGUE: What is being said in the picture

Together these tools combine and create:

THE SCENE: The unit of action that moves the action forward

Locales

Choosing Your Pictures

Imagine yourself sitting in front of the television set. You are watching your favorite one-hour series. In this scene the main character returns home and discovers his house has been ransacked. There is another shot as he walks through the room to assess the damage. Suddenly, a sound emanates from the kitchen and there is another camera shot as he swings around. What you are witnessing is the work of the director. The director is responsible for the various angles or shots within a given locale.

When the character, however, follows the noise and walks into the kitchen, you are watching the work of the scriptwriter. The scriptwriter creates the locale; the director decides how to shoot it.

Count how often the locales change in a given one-hour episode and you will understand the medium of "moving" pictures. Choosing locales is my favorite part of script writing. Each picture becomes your canvas, and the pictures you choose can change the entire feeling of a scene or even the mood of the entire show.

Let's suppose that you are crafting a scene in which a man and a woman profess their love for each other. You decide the locale should be a steel mill and they will have to yell over the grinding industrial noise to try to communicate their feelings to each other. Take the same dialogue and now imagine placing the lovers on the beach in Malibu. What you will have will be two very different scenes, two very different moods.

Good scriptwriters use interesting and unique locales. They bring the very best visuals they can to a script because they understand the rule of film—that is, the viewer would rather watch than listen. When the television audience turns on the tube, what they want to see are pictures. Remember, if they only wanted words, they'd buy novels.

In the "Starsky and Hutch" script, which I use later as an example of a one-hour episode, I had to script one of those annoying yet necessary expositional (explanatory) cop scenes. You can't get around them. If the cop's investigation doesn't take them to point "A," then Starsky and Hutch won't get the information they need to get to point "B."

The locale for this particular scene could have been anywhere in L.A. where the show took place. I decided it would be an outdoor market in a very bad section of town. The man Starsky and Hutch needed to get the information from was a butcher. His white apron had blood smeared on it, and he was chopping a chunk of raw meat while listening to the horse race returns on a transistor radio. There was a cigarette in the butcher's mouth with an ash that was about ready to drop onto the meat, and there were flies buzzing around.

This particular locale allowed for interesting visuals. The audience was kept occupied while they were being fed the necessary information. Read the scene (page 99) and see how the locale not only lended itself to interesting visuals but how it literally created the dialogue.

Good locales are crucial for the television script. Play with them. They make for a good read and a good script, as well as making the writing process fun. Look around you; perceive your world as a filmmaker. Everything you look at is a backdrop for your script. Locales are everywhere.

Narrative

Narrative is description. It describes what is taking place in the locale. In order to generate interest a script must first be a good read, one in which the movie or television episode visually plays in the reader's head. Much of this visualizing happens in the narrative. Good narrative is what makes the pictures come alive. If we equate choosing the locale to choosing the canvas, then we can equate writing the narrative to filling the canvas with a paintbrush. Every word in the narrative, every stroke, matters.

Some locales require more narrative than others. For example, if you are describing a foreign environment, such as Subic Bay in the Philippines, more words will be required than when describing a new housing development somewhere in suburbia. Most of us have never been to Subic Bay, but we are all familiar with housing developments. The only narrative needed would be the price range of the houses and how near they are to completion.

Again, *lean* is the name of the game. Words should be kept to a bare minimum. They should suggest the picture without getting too detailed or tedious.

In "Belly Up," a Movie of the Week I scripted that I use later as an example of the seven-act structure, I needed to establish where Alex Holman, my protagonist, worked. Holman, a successful California businessman, had offices in the very high-rent, glitzy Century City. I wanted more, however, than just to establish Century City. I wanted to convey a feeling for the town and for the acquisitive type A personalities, who in their expensive cars, surge into the streets every day.

Writing good narrative is a challenge. The writer must always ask, What are the words that most descriptively or metaphorically get my message across? The wonderful thing about writing is that no two writers will ever choose the same words.

In "Belly Up," the narrative I chose was the following:

EXT. CENTURY CITY—DAY

We're at the height of midday traffic. HORNS are honking, and Mercedes are battling for underground parking like pitbulls going for the jugular. Looming high above us are the Century City Twin Towers.

Certainly there is more going on in Century City than what I described, but adding more words would have been unnecessary. Your narrative should indicate; it should give an overall impression of a bigger picture.

Narrative Tells a Story

While at a speaking engagement in Denver, I went downstairs to use a pay phone. On the phone counter in front of me was an ash tray with a burning cigarette, a hotel room key, a half-filled mug of beer, and a telephone calling card.

What do the objects in this picture tell us? At the time, I remember thinking if this were a painting or a photograph, an appropriate title would have been, "On the Road." Suddenly, a man rushed up with a pad and pen, and grabbed the receiver. He eyed me suspiciously, wondering why I was so fascinated and what I was about to take.

Try this exercise: Choose a locale. Your narrative within the chosen locale must be revealing. You cannot use people in this locale, only objects that tell a story.

We have great fun with this exercise in my workshops. Writers weave amazing and rich scenarios. They are forced to think visually. How many words is a picture worth?

Narrative Reveals Character

A novelist can reveal the inner monologue or thoughts in a character's head; this is not so for the scriptwriter. On film, the only way we can indicate what characters are thinking is by what they say, by what they do, and in some situations by what they do not do. An exception is the Voice-over (V.O.), a film technique where the character's thoughts are heard over the picture. An example of a voice-over occurs in the television show "The Wonder Years," in which an adult narrates thoughts and memories of himself as a child. Another example of an effective voice-over is in the former series "Magnum, P.I." We heard Magnum's thoughts strategically woven throughout the show. It is important that writers use voice-overs only if the show utilizes them week after week on the show.

How can a scriptwriter reveal externally who the character is internally? You are writing a teleplay. In it, you have created a character with a compelling characteristic. How can you convey this characteristic in the narrative? Perhaps this character is a multimillionaire. He pulls his Masserati up to a very posh Manhattan restaurant. As the valets take his car, he notices a quarter on the sidewalk. He makes sure no one is looking and then bends down and picks it up. Inside the restaurant, before the waiter approaches, he removes the sugar and artificial sweeteners from a silver bowl on the table, then discreetly slides them into the pocket of his $2,500 jacket.

What do we know about this character? *Actions speak louder than words.* This is a man who, when he opens the menu, will scan the prices first. So who is he? An eccentric? A man who's had to struggle for everything he has or a person who's spent his last dime? Whatever his story, he's interesting and we, the audience, are caught in the discovery process.

A friend and successful career woman told me a funny story that she said I could share. It was about her first significant date after the breakup of a ten-year marriage. He was threatened by her position, so she wanted to appear soft and feminine. She invited the man over for a casual gourmet dinner, carefully making the dinner appear ordinary. It was a great success. Afterward, while talking in the kitchen, he inadvertently opened her pantry and discovered it bare except for a can of okra.

The single action of opening a pantry can reveal a lot about a character. She was not domestically inclined. She cared more about this man than she was letting on, and this meal was her only one at home besides Chinese takeout!

Narrative Creates Mood

Effective narrative can set the mood, the tone, and the texture of a script. It not only roots the audience in place but it gives them a sense of what the story is about.

"If the Shoe Fits," a Movie for Television that I scripted with Pamela Wallace, was optioned in 1988 by Earl Wallace under his banner Wallace Communications. In the opening of the script we needed to convey the feeling of magic. The readers needed to feel that they were stepping into a realm where all things were possible.

As producer, Earl stepped in and created the first page, which set the mood for the entire film. Read it. What does the narrative tell us?

FADE IN:

EXT. 5TH AVENUE—WORKDAY MORNING

In the Kingdom of Manhattan on this frosty new day of the winter holiday season, a sea of peasantry heaves and surges amid the chaos and clamor of the traffic-choked boulevard, far below the gleaming towers and burly parapets of the mighty rulers of the realm.

CAMERA FINDS AND GOES WITH one such work-bound toiler, an honest lass by the name of KELLY GARRETT, as she's carried along by the tide of folk . . .

Bright and sprightly in a small-town girl sort of way, she carries a shoe bag. Her attention is occasionally caught by:

SHOES

All sorts of them . . . on the feet of the young and the old, newsboys and stockbrokers, sales girls and shopkeepers, cops and cowboys, panhandlers and pretzel-benders . . . And all of them, in some way large or small, reflecting the personality of their wearers.

Shoes . . . striding and sliding and gliding, scuffing and shuffling and bustling, plodding and jogging and tripping along . . . vivid testimony to the enduring truth that, whatever our station in life, we are all as one where the sole meets the sidewalk.

BACK TO KELLY

But the wildest, most outrageous of all these shoes are on the feet of our heroine . . . red taffeta boots—sequined, beaded, jeweled and feathered—a fantasy realized. They're a vivid contrast to the rest of Kelly—her face, her hair, her clothes—which are frankly nondescript. At first glance she appears plain. But her shoes suggest there's more to her than meets the eye.

There is something very special about New York this time of year and Earl conveyed it. When the camera moves in on Kelly, we realize she is just one of the many peasants of Manhattan. Her attention is on shoes. Her dream is to design them, but a moment later we learn she is just a gopher in a New York fashion house.

Kelly is plain. Everything about her smacks of mediocrity—until we notice her red taffeta boots. They are a fantasy realized, and suggest there is more to her than meets the eye.

"If the Shoe Fits" is a contemporary fairy tale. In it, Kelly will be yanked off the street and pulled into a salon and made over by an outrageous beautician named Wanda. Kelly emerges drop-dead, head-turning gorgeous—every woman's fantasy—but she discovers this glamour comes with its own price. In the end, it all turns out happily. Kelly even gets her prince.

Earl's masterful narrative set up the theme of this film on the first page. Style of narrative writing varies greatly among writers. Read teleplays and screenplays and find a narrative style that really clicks for you, one with which you feel comfortable. Play with it; adapt it to yourself. Before long, you will discover that you are developing a narrative style that is all your own.

Dialogue

Television can entertain without words, but it can't exist without pictures. Therefore, visuals must take precedence over dialogue. However, the power of dialogue should not be diminished. It is crucial and a necessary element in all good scripts.

Dialogue reveals character and advances the plot.
It conveys conflict.
It communicates facts.
It foreshadows impending events.
It connects the scenes and ties the pictures together.

Good Dialogue Is Rewritten Dialogue

Wherever I go students ask me, "How can you teach us to write good dialogue? How does it happen? Where does it come from?" My answer is pat but honest: Good dialogue is rewritten dialogue. It is precise, economic, and mercilessly cut.

Rewriting is where good dialogue happens. As far as I'm concerned, first-draft dialogue exists to be rewritten. It's like letting the garbage out so you can sift through it, hone it, trim it, and find something valuable in it.

The late Paddy Chayefsky, one of our greatest television and motion picture writers, and Academy Award winner for the motion picture *Network,* said about dialogue, "My own rules are very simple. First, cut out all the wisdom. Then cut out all the adjectives. I've cut some of my favorite stuff. I have no compassion when it comes to cutting. No pity, or sympathy." Remember, if all good writers were doctors they'd be surgeons.

Good Dialogue Is Lean Dialogue

Good dialogue is a dance of two- and three-liners, a ball that keeps us riveted as it bounces between its characters. It is the moment a week later when you suddenly jump up in bed and think to yourself, "That's what I should have said. It would have been perfect. Why didn't I think of it then?"

If we went to a restaurant, recorded the conversation in the next booth, then placed the dialogue in a script, it would ramble, be wordy, would probably be riddled with "uhs" and "ahs," and most likely it would not be very interesting. Good dialogue is not real. It *sounds* real. It implies instead of explains. It is not redundant.

A character should say something once and never repeat it unless it's in character to do so. Writers must learn to trust their audiences. Otherwise, their words become overly explicit. While writing dialogue, ask yourself, "Does this need to be said at all? Can it be shown instead of talked about? What are my characters saying? Why are they saying it?" In teleplay writing every line counts. If dialogue does not advance the plot, if it does not reveal some new aspect of the character, then it does not belong in the script. It is excess.

Dialogue and Subtext

In my early days of writing episodic television, producers and story editors would sometimes make a notation on the script, "too on the nose," or "fix it." I soon learned that the phrase "on the nose" meant the dialogue was too literal, too obvious.

Good dialogue happens on two levels: what is being said and what is actually meant, or the subtext. As humans, we talk around things, we don't hit them on the head.

If, let's say, we've decided to end a relationship, it's highly unlikely that we will bust into the person's house and say, "Hey, let's break up." We'd use a little more finesse than that. At first we might hint or talk around the subject. Maybe we'd tell the person we need more space, or that we feel it's time in our relationship to start seeing other people. What is really going on? At the core, at a level beneath this exchange, is the fact that we want out.

In the Movie for Television I scripted, "Belly Up," my protagonist, Alex Holman, is a successful entrepreneur. He has it all. And then one day he has nothing. A model in his most ambitious project, a housing development built on the state's largest landfill, explodes from a gas migration. With buyers panicked and pulling out of their escrows, his company maxed, and his partner blown up in the model while lighting a joint with his secretary, Holman is left the sole debtor and lands in bankruptcy court. Adding to this disaster, the entrepreneur's spoiled wife splits, and his creditors hire an insolvency accountant to audit him.

Read the following scene. Here, we meet character Lindsay Rhinehart. (*Note:* Her name is capitalized because it is the first time she appears in the script.) What is being said in this scene? What is being implied? What is happening beneath the dialogue?

Notice how the narrative in the scene serves to punctuate the dialogue. Alex's use of the hose is a statement. It helps define the subtext of what is really taking place. He is outwardly cool, but underneath he is angry and afraid. The conflict and tension between the two characters moves the action of this scene forward.

EXT. HOLMAN HILLS ESTATES, MODELS—DAY

The entire development is ghostlike. Two of the three models remain on the block. The third is a mountain of debris where Haberman had his last joint.

MODEL AT END OF BLOCK

The only sign of life is Alex, in cutoffs and a tee shirt, washing his 380 SL in the driveway.

After a moment, a VW Rabbit, top down, comes into view. The driver, 28-year-old LINDSAY RHINEHART, slows, spots Alex washing his car, parks in front of the model. She is attractive, cerebral, all business. She gets out, walks over with her attaché case.

                    LINDSAY
Are you Alex Holman?

He continues washing the car.

                    ALEX
Yeah.

                    LINDSAY
According to my records, your
residence is 1250 Briarcliff . . .

ALEX
That's right.

LINDSAY
This is 1900 Piper Terrace.

ALEX
My wife took the furniture. I
moved into the model.

LINDSAY
The law states you are to contact
your creditors in the event of a
move.

He stops momentarily, assesses her.

ALEX
Who are you?

LINDSAY
My name is Lindsay Rhinehart. I've
been trying to reach you, but your
phone's been disconnected.

She hands Alex her card.

LINDSAY (continuing)
I've been retained by your
creditors.

Alex glances at the card, slips it into his wet pocket and turns his
attention back to the car.

ALEX
Contact my attorney.

LINDSAY
I've contacted Mr. Lemorio, that's
how I found you.

ALEX
Just what do you want?

LINDSAY
I've been hired to appraise your
financial condition, and to audit
your business.

He places his thumb over the nozzle, some of the spray hits her.

ALEX
You're going to be disappointed.
I'm honest.

> LINDSAY
> I hope so Mr. Holman, because when
> creditors are asked to forgive a
> portion of their claims, they have
> a right to know what happened to
> their money.
>
> He drops the hose, picks up a rag; Lindsay has to step out of the water.
>
> LINDSAY (continuing)
> That's a very nice car.
>
> ALEX
> I like it . . .
>
> LINDSAY
> Unfortunately, your creditors are
> not driving in such luxury.
>
> ALEX
> Are you finished, or would you like
> to help me dry?
>
> LINDSAY
> You'll be hearing from me, Mr. Holman.
> If you inhibit my investigation, I
> can cite you for contempt and prevent
> the dismissal of your debts. I hope
> I've made myself clear.
>
> As she walks away, Alex picks up the hose and squirts the car. This time
> she gets a healthy dose of the spray. She turns, knowing it was deliber-
> ate.
>
> ALEX (shrugging)
> I missed a spot.
>
> ON ALEX
>
> He meticulously dries his car, glances at the VW Rabbit as it pulls away.
>
> ON LINDSAY'S REAR BUMPER
>
> A sticker reads: "SAVE THE WHALES."

In the above scene we've supplied pertinent story information to
advance the plot:

Alex has been forced to move into the model home of his now
   defunct housing development.
An insolvency accountant has been retained by his creditors to
   investigate him.

Lindsay is suspicious of Alex and is out to prove he has ripped off her clients.

During my training as an actress, we had many exercises in subtext with teachers Lee Strasberg and Jeff Corey. I use these same exercises in my writers workshops today. Working with subtext is a wonderful device for writers. It creates a shift in consciousness from the spoken word to the truth of the moment. All dialogue has subtext. As people, we work on many different levels. Therefore, as writers we must do the same with our words.

Listen to yourself talk. Observe what you are saying as though you were watching yourself on television. Hear the dialogue and then go deeper and identify the subtext. What is really going on? This exercise is wonderful. Not only will it improve your dialogue skills but it will sharpen your self-awareness and save you untold costs in therapy sessions.

Dialogue as Metaphor

Some years ago, I returned from Portland, Oregon, where I was the keynote speaker at the Willamette Writers Conference. I had a wonderful two-day stay and my talk was a big success. I arrived at the airport at 11:00 P.M., still dressed from a party I had attended. The man I was dating had come to the airport to pick me up. He was grubby, unshaven, and had been packing all day. He was facing relocation and a job change, and though neither one of us had admitted it, our relationship was pretty much coming to an end.

On the ride home from the airport, I ecstatically relayed everything that had happened on my trip. Mid-sentence, he cut me off and said, "Look for a Seven-Eleven. I've got to find trash bags." What he *really* was saying was, "I don't want to hear about it." The trash bags were the metaphor for "Don't tell me any more." He didn't say, "I'm forty-three years old. I'm going through a midlife crisis. I'm under an incredible amount of stress and I've been packing all day." Why? Because in the context of our relationship I already knew that. Just as in the context of a script we would already know that. The metaphor was the trash bags, yet the idea behind it was completely discernible.

The use of metaphor and subtext in dialogue goes somewhat hand-in-hand. Throughout "Belly Up," Lindsay, the suspicious accountant, has been out to get Alex. She is certain that he has ripped off his creditors. Likewise, his dislike of her has been growing, but so has their attraction, which has been a gnawing source of aggravation to both of them.

Toward the end of the film they find themselves sharing adjoining rooms and a common bathroom at a mountain retreat. They have unknowingly arrived there on the suggestion of their mutual shrink. Now they have spied on each other naked at the salt baths and both are having trouble sleeping. The following scenes, which are examples of metaphoric dialogue, take place in Act VII of the television movie. The notation (o.s.) indicates we hear the character speak but do not see them—they are "off screen."

INT. LINDSAY'S BUNGALOW

Lindsay, in a robe, on top of the covers, gives up on her novel.

INT. ALEX'S BUNGALOW

Alex lies on the bed, staring at the ceiling.

INT. LINDSAY'S BUNGALOW

Lindsay lies on the bed staring at the ceiling. After a long moment, there is a KNOCK on the BATHROOM DOOR. She walks over.

> LINDSAY (to door)
> What is it?

> ALEX (O.S.)
> I need to talk to you.

> LINDSAY
> About what?

INT. BATHROOM

He thinks a minute.

> ALEX
> I have a confession to make . . .

He waits for a response; none . . .

> ALEX (continuing)
> . . . about the missing computers.

After a moment she unlatches the lock. He sees her standing there in her robe.

> LINDSAY
> What about them?

ALEX

What?

LINDSAY

. . . The computers.

ALEX

. . . Right.

LINDSAY

I'm listening.

He moves in closer.

ALEX

. . . It's like this. I had to call
a meeting and tell my employees
there was no money for paychecks.
I really cared about those people . . .

She moves in closer.

LINDSAY

That must have been very hard on
you.

ALEX

Yeah . . . very hard . . . I didn't want
them to leave empty-handed . . . you
know what I mean?

LINDSAY

Absolutely . . . You wanted to give
them something . . .

She brushes up against him; they are standing extremely close.

ALEX

We were stacked . . . (correcting himself) stocked, stocked
with supplies,
so I said . . .

LINDSAY (seductively)

. . . Help yourself . . .

ALEX

. . . They were very appreciative . . .

He begins kissing her shoulders and moving down toward her breasts.

LINDSAY

I'm sure that made them feel . . .
wonderful . . .

> ALEX
> . . . There was one problem . . .
>
> LINDSAY
> . . . I can't imagine what . . .
>
> ALEX
> . . . I thought they'd take the
> Liquid Paper, not the $10,000
> Comp-U-Pros.
>
> LINDSAY (very turned on)
> I'm going to have to report this.
>
> ALEX
> How do you think the creditors will
> take it?
>
> LINDSAY
> Any way they can . . .
>
> They collapse in a frenzy and roll around on the bathroom floor.

It has been said that writers either have an ear for dialogue or they don't. I believe this "ear" can be developed. Try to hear the dialogue as you write it. Visualize actors delivering the lines.

Once the dialogue is written, read it aloud to yourself or to a partner. An amazing thing happens in the process. You will naturally edit excess or awkward wording. You will also become conscious of pacing and tempo. Turn on the television set and *listen* to shows rather than watch them. With your visual sense turned off, your ear becomes much more in tune with the cadence and rhythm of the spoken word. We will study dialogue further in later chapters.

Some Camera Angles

Directors don't like to be told how to shoot their pictures. The misuse of camera angles is a dead tip-off that you are an amateur. Even if the camera angles are correct, too many of them make for a staccato read—they cut into the flow and momentum of the script. When can you legitimately use a camera angle? When you need the camera angle to tell your story.

Let's say, in a story you are scripting, a killer inadvertently drops a book of matches as he leaves the scene of the crime. Later the matches will incriminate him. At this point you can choose a camera angle "CLOSE ON" his foot as he steps over the matches. In this case you, the writer, are not telling the director how to direct; rather, you are foreshadowing your story.

Let's suppose in another script your hero walks into the kitchen and you "PULL BACK TO REVEAL" the killer waiting there for him with a knife. In this case, you are creating jeopardy and suspense with that camera angle. You are using it to progress your storyline forward. If the camera angle does not progress the storyline forward, leave it out. Don't tell directors how to direct!

We have now reviewed the tools of the telescripter: locales, narrative, dialogue, and some camera angles. Together, these tools combine and create the scene—they are the major building blocks of the script.

The Scene

The teleplay is built on the scene. It is the unit of action that moves the story forward. Imagine a set of children's building blocks. As the blocks come together they form the complete creation. In the teleplay, the scenes, or blocks of action, build together one upon the other to tell the complete story.

The technical definition of a scene is that it roots *place* and *time.* First, it establishes where the camera is set, either Interior (INT.) or Exterior (EXT.), and the locale. Next, it establishes if it is DAY or NIGHT.

At this moment, I am in my living room working on my word processor. It is daytime. If I were to set up the scene it would look like this:

INT. LIVING ROOM—DAY

Look around you. Where are you? In your office? At home? Perhaps you are reading this book in the park, or while you're on an airplane. Is it day or night? How would you set up the scene?

Now that you've established where the camera is located, including whether it is day or night, the next step is to describe what's there. In other words, add some narrative. What is taking place in the locale? What is inside the picture you have created?

I write in my living room because of the view. My window overlooks Lover's Point Beach on the Monterey Peninsula. How can I take you there? By constructing the scene.

EXT. LOVER'S POINT BEACH—DAY

It's Sunday. The cove is packed with tourists. Kids squeal as the locals protect their "spots." A class of scuba divers trucks its way into the water, praying for certification.

If, at this point, I choose to take you to the parking lot, it would constitute another scene. Why? Because the camera would have to be physically moved.

EXT. PARKING LOT—DAY

A group of teenagers is standing around. A few of them smoke; maybe cigarettes. Music BLASTS from a hopped-up van.

If you return to the beach, it would be considered a third scene.

Since the beach has already been established, additional narrative may or may not be necessary. Scenes do not require narrative, nor do they require dialogue. If, however, you focus on a particular portion of the beach, let's say two lovers embracing, additional description would be required since the couple was not established in the prior scene.

The Purpose of the Scene

Every scene must move the storyline forward and advance the plot. If a scene does not reveal new and relevant story information, it does not belong in the script regardless of how well it may be written. The scene must help the material as a whole. It is an integral part of the story's continuity.

To help us better understand the power of the scene, let's return to the building blocks we used earlier. Imagine that your creation is now complete. The blocks have been placed in a particular order to give the entire picture. Now let's suppose you remove one of the blocks. What happens to the picture? It doesn't work. Since each scene must reveal at least one new element to advance the plot, if you remove it your story will have a hole. It shouldn't work.

Types of Scenes

Scenes vary in length. They can run anywhere from a single shot to two-and-a-half or three pages long (taped shows are the exception since they use a different format; see page 178). It is important to note that anything that runs more than three pages should be a rare exception. Five- and six-page scenes are deadly. They kill the momentum and pacing of the script, and are a tip-off that the writer has not yet grasped the medium—that is, of *moving pictures.*

Scenes also vary in type. The storyline determines what kind of a scene you will need to convey a particular story point.

The Establishing Scene or Shot. Its purpose is to establish where we are. An example can be found on page 14. Here, we establish Alex's place of work, Century City. Since there are no camera angles, but rather one shot that encompasses the "whole" picture, this scene is in the *master scene* format.

On page 27, we have another example of an establishing scene. Here, we are placing the camera on the beach at Pacific Grove. It is also shot in the Master Scene format.

The Dialogue Scene. Its purpose is to convey information and to reveal character, conflict, and feelings. An example can be found on page 19. Since this scene uses *camera angles,* it is not in the master scene format. The angles do, however, serve the story; therefore, the writer is not directing. The angle on Alex at the end of the scene establishes that he knows he's in big trouble. The angle on Lindsay's rear bumper reveals more about her character.

The Scene Sequence. This series of scenes is tied together by a single idea. The seduction sequence on page 23 serves as an example of this technique. It consists of four scenes:

INT. LINDSAY'S BUNGALOW: Where we establish she's unable to concentrate
INT. ALEX'S BUNGALOW: Where we establish he cannot concentrate
INT. LINDSAY'S BUNGALOW: Where she hears Alex knock on her door and she decides to open it
INT. BATHROOM: Where they come together and in the end seduce one another

Establishing sequences, dialogue sequences, and action sequences are explored fully in chapter 7. Sequences essentially use the same components and serve the same purpose as the scene. Become aware of sequences as you watch television. They are a wonderful device for the scriptwriter. They allow you to cut between locales, maintain continuity, and keep the pictures moving.

The Crisis, Climax, and Resolution in the Scene and Scene Sequence

The scene and the scene sequence are essentially miniunits of the bigger whole. They contain within themselves the same components of the script, just as a cell contains within it the same components of the universe.

All scenes (except for establishing shots), and all sequences have a crisis, a climax, and a resolution.

> The crisis is the build. At this point the action could go either way, but an outcome is inevitable.
> The climax is the height of the dramatic action.
> The resolution is the result of the dramatic action.

Let's suppose that we are constructing a scene in which the dramatic action is a car winding its way along an icy road. Suddenly, another car coming from the opposite direction spins out of control and careens over the center divider. This event is the *crisis*. At this point the action could go either way. The cars collide. This event is the *climax*. It is the high point of the scene. The *resolution* is the result of the accident. What happens to the people inside the car? Do they live or die?

The luxury of writing for television or film is that the scriptwriter can cut into or out of a scene or sequence any time. In fact, it is rare that a scene or sequence is shown in its entirety. Why? Because of the time factor. The scripter gives pieces or fragments that give the illusion of completeness.

If we were to use the above example, perhaps your choice would be to cut away from the scene at the crisis and leave the climax to the audience's imagination. Or perhaps you would choose to cut directly into the climax at the point of sudden impact to jolt the audience. You could also come into the scene at the conclusion, or in the resolution, and only show the aftermath of the accident.

The scriptwriter is constantly making decisions. The medium allows for many choices. Each gives a different effect, a different feel. The best choices make the best scripts. Always ask yourself when constructing a scene or a sequence what choice will have the most impact and best convey what you want to say.

Cutting Between Scenes

Here is where contrast, mood, tone, and texture happen. A good writer can literally string an audience's emotions with one simple cut.

Paddy Chayefsky had a long and illustrious screenwriting career that began in television and eventually lead to motion picture Oscars. Among his works are *Marty, The Hospital,* and *Network,* which provided a satirical look at television networks and the people and power behind the rating wars.

In the famous "mad-as-hell" sequence in *Network,* Howard Beal, the television anchorman gone mad, tells his viewers on prime-time television that they should go to their windows and scream "I'm mad as hell and I'm not going to take it anymore!" It is magnificent writing by one of our greatest craftsmen. The sequence ends with incredible power: people screaming out in teaming, thunderous rain with a furor that in Chayefsky's own words "sounds like a Nuremberg rally." He then cuts away at the climax of the scene and in the next shot there is a plane descending on a runway. With that simple cut, we the viewing audience are being jolted from an emotional high. We are essentially, through that airplane, being made to touch down again. His choice of cutting between these pictures is emotionally moving.

Watch one-hour and two-hour television shows. Become conscious of the power of the scene. See if you can identify not only their structure but where they begin and end and how the writer chooses to cut between them.

Study the best. Watch quality television and analyze it. Study from the pros, from the writers who are selling. They will teach you a lot.

3

Restrictions of the Medium and How You Can Make Them Work for You

The rule of writing for television is that you play by the rules until you're big enough to call the shots. For the television free-lancer trying to break in, the rules have already been set.

Let's suppose that you decided to write a script for a weekly television show. In this particular series, the hero is a district attorney. You like the show, but feel it's unrealistic that he wins every case that hits the docks. In your story, you've decided to let him lose. The quality of the show is slipping and as far as you're concerned it's time a writer came in with a fresh approach. If the producers of the show will read your script, you are certain they will not only admire the writing but will commend your good judgment. Right? Wrong! If the show's existing format is that the D.A. always wins, there is only one thing you can be sure of—your script won't sell!

Any experimentation in television happens "in house," meaning by the developers, the producers, and the staff writers for that particular show. The television free-lancer does not forge new trails, but rather must take the path already set. Herein lies the challenge: to write an excellent script within these highly restrictive parameters and to give the show's creators and the "power people"—the producers and the network—what they want.

How can you do this? Since you can't change the beast, you must study it by repeatedly watching and analyzing the show. A thorough study of the show will tell you everything you need to know: structure, characters, the age the show is geared toward, locales, network practices assigned to the show, and even the storylines you can develop.

If you were studying "Family Ties," and in an episode Alex gets hooked on uppers during final exams, what does that tell you? Here is a comedy that relies heavily on realism for its humor. If you choose to write for this show, your job then would be to find a storyline that not only provided humor but was topical and timely, and that beared no derivative resemblance to any previous episodes. Therefore, you must watch the show!

I never missed a "Kojak." And this viewing was in the days before home VCRs, when writers had to remain glued to the TV. I knew every character in the Manhattan South precinct and just about every storyline that aired. I could even guess when the bald-headed lieutenant would pull out a lollypop! When Gene Kearney, the story editor for the series, read my script, "Death Is Driving You Home," he commented on how well I knew the show. It is a turn-on to producers and staff people when free-lancers thoroughly know and understand their show. It is like someone thoroughly knowing and understanding your own child. When you arrive at a parent–teacher conference, you expect it. After all, isn't that the teacher's job? Know the show before you ever attempt to write for it. Watch it, study it, tape the episodes, and watch them over and over.

Time Limitation

Television deals with highly restrictive time limitations. Just as the marathon runner could be equated to the novelist, the scriptwriter could be equated to the aerobicist. And of course the teleplay writer has the leanest and meanest workout of all.

A teleplay is the bare necessities, the bones, the skeleton. It is a blueprint of visuals or fragments that give the *illusion* of a complete story. Television writing is so economic that absolutely every word in the script *matters* and moves the story forward. There is no room for excess fat: Everything nonfunctional in the script goes! A novelist can say the book ran fifty pages longer than anticipated, but the story still works. This is not so for the teleplay writer.

Whether dealing with a half-hour sitcom, an hour episode, or a two-hour M.O.W. (Movie of the Week), the telescripter must come in on the number of pages allotted to the show's time frame. For example, the hour episode runs approximately one minute per page, meaning the telescripter must set up, develop, and resolve the story in about fifty-five pages. I call this "coming in on the dime." If the story can't be told in the time allotted, it won't work. Submitting a seventy-page "Beauty and the Beast" or "Midnight Caller" will get you absolutely nowhere except tipping yourself off as an amateur.

Since episodic shows vary in page lengths according to their repartee and style, it is very advisable to get your hands on television scripts for the particular show you want to write for. I've included a list of various script services in appendix A.

The Characters Are Set

When I began in episodic television, I had a hobby. Throughout the year I would make elaborate bread dough ornaments, which at Christmastime I'd give as gifts. I would carefully shop for very special ornaments, take them home, copy them, mold them, and paint them. Sometimes, because I took such pains, the copies turned out better than the originals. This effort is exactly what television writers do when studying a show's characters. They do not create from scratch, but rather create from what already exists. In episodic television it is the scriptwriter's job to know the characters.

When writing the spec script, the free-lancer not only needs to know the characters but must use *all* the characters that appear on the show each week. Let's not forget that these actors are under contract. More important, the basis of all programming decisions is the viewing audience. Week after week these characters come into their living rooms. For this reason, television is a much more personal medium than the feature film. Television audiences have a vested interest in recurring characters, especially in their favorite show.

At the time I was scripting a "Hart to Hart," an episode aired that caused great controversy. The Harts, in an attempt to set up the bad guy, separated and announced to outsiders that their marriage was over. The result was a flood of angry mail from the viewers who didn't want to see their favorite couple break up even if it was just a scam.

Why such a reaction? We must first look at what this show sold: a very beautiful, very wealthy, happily married couple who just happen to stumble over a murder each week. For the average audience, seeing the Harts separate is not what they wanted to watch. Know the characters and know what the show sells.

The Locales Are Set

Half-Hour Sitcoms
Half-hour sitcoms, which are filmed live, are highly restrictive in locales, which usually consist of three ongoing sets. Let's identify the existing sets of some popular half-hour series.

On "Alf," the majority of the action takes place in the Tanner house, which consists of the living room, the kitchen, and Kate and Willie's bedroom. On the "Cosby Show," we are primarily limited to the same sets: the living room, the kitchen, and the Huxtable's bedroom. On "The Golden Girls," the center of action takes place in Blanche's house, which consists of the living room, patio, kitchen, and a bedroom. On "Cheers," a show that centers around the work arena, almost the entire action takes place in the bar with occasional retreats to the back room.

The sets on each of these shows are established and run week after week. If another set is needed in the development of the story, it is called a swing—that is, an existing set that is swung around and reset. Changing sets is expensive and takes time. Since these shows are taped live, in terms of both cost and time it is more efficient to keep the number of sets to a bare minimum.

One-Hour and Two-Hour Shows

The one-hour episode and the two-hour Movie for Television open a much wider range of visuals and locales from which to choose. These shows are filmed and use one camera that relies heavily on location shooting over and above the already existing sets. The writer can now take the story anywhere in the city in which the show takes place.

If you were scripting an episode of "Beauty and the Beast," you'd have all of New York to choose from for your locales; in "L.A. Law," you'd have all of Los Angeles, and in "Midnight Caller," you'd have the breathtaking backdrop of San Francisco as your palette. *Never* relocate the show or transplant the characters out of their established area. Successful shows can jaunt to another location perhaps once a season. But watch the credits—I guarantee you that either the producer or the story editors wrote the show. Why? Because only they know how much money is in the till. To relocate the cast and crew is a highly expensive proposition. When it happens, it's the biggest show of the season, which guarantees that it won't be written by a free-lancer.

Be content to keep your characters at home, and research the places in which they live. There are rich and unique locales in every city.

Budget Limitations

Yet another aspect the free-lancer must contend with is the budget, which does not entail a detailed cost breakdown of the show, but rather common sense. If you are writing an action sequence, and you have the choice of a car falling off a cliff or coming to a screeching halt and teetering on the edge, which will you choose? Practically speaking, the latter. Again, the show will dictate everything you need to know.

If it is an action show that relies on extravagant stunts like "The Fall Guy" did, then certainly you should incorporate this type of action into the script. It would be a big mistake not to. Still, writers should always be conscious of budget. It would be a crime to write a good script only to discover that the cost of shooting it has priced you right out of the ballpark.

I had an idea for an episode of "Hart to Hart" in which Jonathan was a pilot. Certainly aerobatics was a glamorous and very expensive sport. It was a perfect type of recreation for the Harts, so I created what I thought was a wonderful crime around Jonathan and Jennifer at an air show. When I pitched the idea to the story editor he was horrified. "Are you kidding?" he said. "We can't afford that!" At the time, the cost of shooting a "Hart to Hart" was running $400,000 per episode and there was no excess in the budget for expensive stunt pilots. Obviously, I didn't get the job.

The problem then became how to give the show what it sells— wealth and glamour—yet keep it reasonably within budget? This problem always existed for the writers of that show. Watch the reruns and you'll find their solutions: What about the Harts on a picnic? Of course, not just any picnic—the fabulous duo is seated atop a Gucci blanket, sipping a two-hundred-dollar bottle of wine and nibbling expensive Russian caviar. Their Rolls Royce is parked in the background.

Further Considerations Regarding Budget

Stay away from special effects. If they do not exist within the format of the show they should be avoided.

Leave children out of the script. Unless they are regulars on the show don't include them. I'm sorry if you're raising child actors, but I've learned over the last fourteen years that stories involving children are a bad risk. Children, and rightly so, are protected by law, and are not allowed to work more than a set amount of hours. Also, they must have a guardian and school on the set, which can lead to shooting shutdowns and many other cost complications. In this industry, time is money. Once in a while a show will break down and, out of desperation for something fresh, develop a story around a child. Beware, however—it's a bad risk on a spec script.

Keep your exterior night locations to a minimum. Hollywood is literally locked in by the restraints of various unions and guilds. Night shooting means overtime, which can run into exorbitant costs. You do not have to exclude all exterior night shots from your script. You should try to be economical, using only those shots that are crucial in telling your story. If the scene can be just as effective shot by day, definitely place it there.

My first and only attempt at a horror story was on an episode of "Fantasy Island," entitled "Night of the Tormented Soul." The story was about a brother and sister returning to an old plantation house where they were raised years before. Their fantasy was to learn the truth about a murder that took place while they were there—a murder so harrowing that they had blocked the circumstances from their minds. They arrived at the haunted mansion at night in the teeming rain. Lightning was ripping and blasting away at the clinging vines that grew over the entrance. A child's swing thrashed in the wind; falling trees blocked their way. It was quite an effective entrance. As it turned out, the scene was shot in broad daylight. There was no teeming rain, no lightning, and no falling trees. What was left in was the swing.

In this particular script the effects I included helped the mood and feel of the story and therefore helped the read and the sale! Sometimes you must leave effects in even with a knowledge of budget. It is wise to be cost conscious, but on the other hand, don't be so extreme that you diminish the impact of your material. Why would anybody want to write a horror story in broad daylight? Again, the writer must discriminate.

Leave out canines and critters of all kinds. Unless they are running characters on the show don't use them. Here, not only are you adding the cost of animal trainers and liabilities to the cast and crew but there's the problem of defecation and more union people to clean it up. You'll also have animal rights and Doris Day to contend with.

In my episode of "Hart to Hart" entitled, "With These Harts I Thee Wed," Jennifer's auntie arrives on the doorstep with her pet Persian cat. Of course, the Hart's dog, Freeway, despised the furry creature throughout the show, until by the end of Act IV, the dog and cat became inseparable. When I turned in the script, the story editor deleted the entire bit, and one trainer and one Persian were looking for work. If you insist on putting a critter into your script, make it a fly. I used one on a "Starsky and Hutch," and the story editor kept it in. Flies don't come with animal trainers—they come with sound effects!

4

The Hooks That Sell

Once your television script sells you are required to join the Writers Guild of America, east or west, depending on where you live. (I will cover the benefits of the Guild in later chapters.)

At this point, it is very likely that you will have an agent representing you. If you don't, it's time to find one. The agent's job is to know what shows are buying, that is, which ones are open for scripts. The agent then sets up meetings with the various story editors and producers so that you can verbally tell them your ideas; this is called "pitching."

The reason for pitching is twofold: First, you no longer have to write entire scripts before you learn whether or not the show may be interested in your idea (if pitching were not used, a writer could have ten "L.A. Law" scripts stacked in his or her garage and still no sale). Second, a story meeting helps the story editor target the writers on what the show wants. The writer may have a good idea but the show may be a derivative of a previous plot, or the story editor may like certain elements but make suggestions that might enhance the story for a particular show.

My first pitch session was a horror story. It was for the "Streets of San Francisco." I racked my brain for what I believed was a good crime story and then rehearsed it over and over again in front of the mirror. When the day finally came, I was a wreck, but at least I was prepared. I knew the story inside out.

The story editor only nodded as I nervously talked. When I finished, he looked at me for a long moment and said, "You don't know our show, do you?" I turned bright red and choked. "Streets," he said, "sells character, not crime." Had I been an astute television viewer, I would have recognized that this series revolved around fascinating subsidiary characters, not regular members of the cast. What had I done? I had come in with only a crime and no subsidiary characters.

Though the story editor was polite, he, in so many words, told me to come prepared next time or I shouldn't waste his time. This learning experience was an embarrassing yet invaluable one. In television, humiliation is a wonderful teacher.

The next time I went in to pitch it was for a segment of "McCloud." This time I was really prepared. Not only did I have a good crime but I had wonderful subsidiary characters. But again, it wasn't enough. This time the story editor wanted an act breakdown. "Where's the cliff-hanger?" he asked. "What do you see for the one-, two-, three-, and four-act ends?" I sat there trying to figure it out. I had no idea! I hadn't really considered it before. Again, I didn't get the job. With each pitch meeting I'd come in prepared with what I had learned during the previous pitch meeting. Somehow it was never enough.

For "Barnaby Jones," I had a good crime, good subsidiary characters, and strong act ends, but the story editor felt there were not enough twists and turns in the plot. He said it was "too predictable." On "Canon," they wanted more jeopardy and a better cliff-hanger. I nodded like I knew what a cliff-hanger was. After the meeting, I went and found out.

On "The Jeffersons," I was told my idea did not have enough at stake for the characters. I needed more personal involvement for the stars. On "Maude," my idea was nixed because they didn't feel it was in keeping with her character. Therefore, it was not credible. "All in the Family" liked my idea but felt the setup was too long and they wanted a better runner. "A runner?" I thought. "What in the hell is a runner?"

In the end, these pitching meetings saved me a lot of time. All that would have resulted from turning these ideas into scripts would have been less room in my garage and no sales.

Unfortunately for a scriptwriter just starting out, a pitch session is highly unlikely. First you must write a completed script to serve as a sample of your writing. Producers and story editors are not going to be interested in your ideas unless you can prove you can execute them. Also, you must find representation; it is the agent who sets up the pitch meetings.

The lurid details of my early pitching experience should teach you what producers and story editors are looking for. As diverse as these shows were, they were all very similar in their needs. Each of the story editors asked the same kinds of questions, had the same concerns, and wanted the same elements in their stories. I began to realize that television rested on certain "hooks." Once I was able to identify these hooks, I started building my stories around them. Then I began getting work. Why? Because I was giving the story editors and producers the kind of stories they wanted.

How can what I learned be helpful to the beginning scriptwriter? Once you can recognize these hooks, you can use this knowledge when creating your stories. Also, every time you turn on the television set your education becomes perennial because you know what to look for.

Hook 'em Fast

At the movies, where we pay five or six dollars, we are inundated with popcorn and a motion picture shot on 70-millimeter film with Dolby sound. Even if the movie is bad, it is highly unlikely that we will walk out. However, if we are dissatisfied when watching TV, we don't even have to stand up to flick the channel. We simply use the remote control.

The entire purpose of television is to grab the audience fast and to keep them. Therefore, it is a medium that relies on gimmicks or hooks. It is important for the free-lancer to recognize these hooks before attempting to develop a story.

The Quick Setup

The setup is exactly what it says it is. It establishes everything we need to know to get the story moving. In episodic television, it is absolutely crucial that the setup happens quickly. Why? The sooner you get into the story, the sooner you "hook" your audience. Also, we are working with such crucial time limitations that unless the setup happens almost immediately there is insufficient time to develop the story.

One of the first comedies I had the pleasure of working on was "The Tony Randall Show." If you'll recall, in that show Mr. Randall played a widowed, somewhat exemplary, judge living in Boston with his son and his British housekeeper. In the segment I wrote entitled, "Case: Franklin vs. Casanova," Judge Walter Franklin discovers his stoic secretary, Janet Reubner, is dating the courthouse casanova, Charley Finmore. The judge, certain of his vast knowledge of human nature—and women—feels it is his duty to warn Miss Reubner of the dangerous course on which she is embarking, and of course he interferes with the relationship.

The setup of this story happens in the first two scenes. Scene 1 opens on the judge's chambers as the judge enters with two lawyers, Charley Finmore and a woman named Estelle. Estelle is so smitten with Charley that she has been raising no objections during a felony trial. When asked if she has anything to say about Finmore's obvious pandering to the jury she tells the judge, "I think it's kind of cute." Exasperated, Walter buzzes Miss Reubner to bring in coffee for everyone. The moment she enters, Charlie immediately moves over to the other end of the couch away from Estelle. When Miss Reubner leaves, Charley moves back to Estelle's side and makes more moves.

What purpose does this scene serve? Before we can establish Charley's paramour with Reubner, we must first establish that he is a playboy and that Walter is completely on to him.

Scene 2 of the setup takes place in the judge's outer offices. Walter exits with Charley and finds Miss Reubner waiting. When she asks if that will be all for the day, the judge says, "Yes." At that moment, she puts her arm in Charley's and they leave together. Walter stands horrified. When Jack, the court reporter, comes in, Walter tells him what just happened. "You didn't know about that?" Jack asks. He goes on to tell the judge that Reubner and Finmore are a hot item around town.

What does this scene establish? The relationship between Reubner and Finmore, and of course Walter's disapproval. Is the setup now complete? Yes, because we now know what the story is about. We have also established Walter's dramatic need, that is, to intervene and somehow try to save his innocent secretary.

For the hour show, the setup takes longer. That is, it happens in the first three to four scenes. In a "Switch" episode I scripted for Universal, "Formula for Murder," Detective Peterson T. Ryan, played by Robert Wagner, and partner Detective Frank McBride, played by Eddie Albert, discover that their clients are two fiery French sisters who are accusing each other of ripping off a million-dollar wrinkle cream from a cosmetic company they have inherited.

Scene 1 of the setup opens at night as a foreign coupe pulls into the drive of a Beverly Hills mansion. The elegantly gloved hand of the passenger, whose face we don't see, reaches into the glove compartment, pulls out an electronic device, and hands it to an unidentified man next to her. The driver presses the button on the electronic device.

In Scene 2, a thin strip of fire suddenly ignites in the master bedroom of the mansion. It reaches up and ignites the drape. Within moments the room becomes a raging inferno . . . then, there is the terrifying sound of an explosion.

Scene 3 of the script takes us to a church where an elaborate funeral is taking place. The deceased is the famous Louis Marcel, head of a giant cosmetic conglomerate, the House of Marcel. We learn at the tail end of the eulogy that a tragic accident was responsible for Marcel's untimely death. Also mentioned are Marcel's daughters, Genevieve and Miki, who we see seated on opposite sides of the church, shooting daggered looks at each other. When the eulogy is over, Miki rises, calmly walks past the attendant, picks up a wreath from a floral display ("Rest in Peace"), and wraps it over her sister's head.

Scene 4 of the setup takes us to the Bouziki Bar, the establishment beneath our detectives' offices, where playboy Pete is nursing a hangover. Miki storms in, still in her mourning clothes, and insists that Pete take her on as a client.

Again, our setup is complete: Scene 1 establishes jeopardy and suspense. Though we did not see their faces, we know we have a male and a female antagonist. Scene 2 establishes what they are doing. That is, they ignite the fire by using an electronic device. Scene 3 establishes who was murdered: Louis Marcel. It also establishes who his two daughters are, Genevieve and Miki, and their contempt for one another. In Scene 4, Miki hires Peterson T. Ryan. We learn that a million-dollar wrinkle cream formula has been stolen and Miki wants Pete to prove the culprit was her sister.

We now know everything we need to know. That is, what the story is about and the circumstances surrounding it. The setup of "Switch" takes place in the first eight minutes of the show.

If you want to hook your audience, you must get into the story quickly. We will cover the setup in more detail in later chapters.

The Star Is Pivotal

Television is a star's medium. The star is the initiator, the reason, and the result. The star is pivotal in moving the action of your story forward. What do I mean by pivotal? Suppose you are writing a weekly detective series and in one episode your detective is apprehended and held for ransom. In your script, you decide the detective's friend, a police officer, comes to the rescue and gets your hero out of jail. Would this decision be an error in judgment? Absolutely! Why? Because an outside force rather than your star is responsible for the escape. Your star is not moving the action forward.

In the Tony Randall show, though the episode revolved around Janet Reubner, it was the judge who reacted and initiated all the action. It was actually *his* story. He took it upon himself to intervene in the relationship.

In a show, can more than one star be pivotal? Yes, if the show sells more than one star. For example, let's use the very successful "Three's Company," which ran for many years and continues to air in syndication. This show sold three stars. In a particular segment, if the story focused around Jack, then Janet and Chrissy (or whichever roommate the show had on at the time) were just as important to Jack's story as he was. His problem became their elaborate problem. In "Hart to Hart," Jennifer came up with the clues and Jonathan carried them forward. Always remember, the star comes first.

Personal Involvement for the Star

Bring the problem home! This is a wonderful way to hook your audience. Though personal involvement isn't a necessity in every storyline, I've found it's a wonderful device to grab a producer's attention and to clinch a sale. What do I mean by personal involvement? The star or main character of your story has something personally at stake in that story.

Let's suppose you are writing an episodic cop show, and in the setup you want a body to turn up in a motel room. Why make this just any body? Why not connect it personally to your hero? Perhaps it's his ex-wife or ex-lover. Now, suddenly, there is something personally at stake for your hero. When your hero or heroine have more at stake, so does your audience.

In the "With These Harts I Thee Wed" episode of "Hart to Hart," Jennifer's aunt comes to town to get married. Her wedding takes place in the Hart's backyard. At the end of Act I, the groom takes a bite of the wedding cake and collapses from poisoning. Now there is personal involvement for Jonathan and Jennifer. Again, this is not just any "body," but a set of circumstances that brings the death directly home to our stars.

1. Jennifer's close aunt is involved.
2. The wedding takes place in the Hart's home.
3. The groom (Jennifer's new uncle) is the victim.
4. Whoever poisoned the groom was on the premises.

The circumstances come to rest directly on the stars. This story could have possibly worked if Jennifer's aunt was not involved. The Harts could have witnessed a murder while attending someone else's wedding. But the story is much more effective when you involve the stars directly.

Twists and Turns in the Plot

Since television can be so predictable, the more twists in the plot, the better the hook. What do I mean by twists? Twists are unexpected turns in the story. They can occur anywhere in the script.

In the "Starsky and Hutch" script "The Heroes," the boys are told by their captain that when they go out on the streets they won't be alone. A reporter by the name of C. D. Phelps from *The Dispatch* will be riding with them. Our guys are adamantly opposed to this until C. D. arrives and they discover that she is a beautiful woman. Her arrival occurs on page five of the script. At midpoint, when the men are jousting for her attention and we are wondering who will get the first date, she suddenly blasts them with a smearing article. Up until this point, she has camouflaged her true intentions.

In the "Newhart" we will study in chapter 6, Bob is coerced into flying to New Orleans on a last-minute notice by his buddy, the Peeper. Emily bets Bob that he can't pull the trip off. He does, but after untold hell. In the last scene, Bob and Emily make it to the airport where the Peeper reaches them by phone. It turns out that this trip was just another one of his practical jokes. Aggravated, Bob tells the Peep that he and Emily are going to New Orleans anyway and that they are going to have a ball. Emily grabs the phone, insisting that she wants to give the Peeper a piece of her mind. Once Bob is out of earshot, she surprises us all by saying, "Thanks, Peep, it worked like a charm!" All along, it was she who had instigated the trip.

Good scripts rely on twists, turns, and the unexpected. In whodunits, such as "Murder She Wrote," they supply the needed jeopardy and suspense that place the audience in the discovery process. The unexpected twist in the plot hooks us into our daily soaps, and it is the reason for such long-running shows as "Dynasty" and "Dallas." And in comedy, twists and turns in the plot provide the necessary conflict and irony that provide us with humor. When developing your script, ask yourself, What is the audience expecting here, and what can I do to surprise them?

The Good Runner

After countless pitch sessions, I learned never to come to a meeting without a good runner. What is a runner? A device that "runs" or pops up throughout the story. Runners can be both comedic or dramatic and they often open a window into the character's personal life. We see runners all the time.

Imagine Cagney and Lacey on the path of a treacherous serial killer. Now let's suppose that at the precinct Lacey checks her calendar and realizes she's forgotten about a parent–teacher conference for her son, Michael. Already she has had a run-in with the teacher, who she now suspects will think she's a negligent parent. Suddenly, we are brought into Lacey's personal life. We are reminded that she is a wife and a mother, a woman who juggles a career and home. She's more than just a good cop—she's human—and now we, the audience, can identify with her.

A runner is strictly a bit that *offsets* the main story. It is not to be confused with a subplot, which *subordinates* the main story. It is the salt and pepper, not the meat and potatoes. It is important that you don't overplay this device. Remember, it is just there to add to your story, certainly not to take it over. Although not a hard-and-fast rule, I like to play out a runner three times. A producer once told me three is a magical number.

While writing the "Starsky and Hutch," I was in the process of buying my first home. I thought this idea might be an amusing runner for our boys. What if Starsky is trying to convince Hutch to invest in a little fixer-upper? The show opens at the precinct where Starsky is giving his somewhat skeptical partner a sales pitch, "We get a little plaster, a little paint, buy a few shrubs . . . " He's certain the two of them can make a bundle. Midpoint in the show, Hutch hands over his money to Starsky to invest. At the show's end, Starsky takes Hutch to their little nest egg—it's a dump. "Wait a minute," he says. "You invested my three grand in that!" As he goes for his partner's neck he steps on the porch, his foot goes through it, and we freeze-frame and end the show.

Runners are just as effective in the half-hour comedy. I dare you to watch a half-hour sitcom without finding one.

Powerful Act Ends

Absolutely everything in television builds to the act end. *The more powerful the act ends, the bigger the hook.*

All one-hour scripts are broken into four acts. Each act averages fourteen to fifteen pages. Each act in the hour episode is a separate unit with a crisis and climax all its own. Why? The commercial breaks are placed between acts.

The most important act, and what the producers tag the "cliff-hanger," happens at the end of Act II because the break runs twice the length of the other commercials. The most teeth-clenching moment in the story takes place at this point. In character dramas and soaps, it is where the biggest crisis occurs. In action shows, car chases or big action sequences usually fill this spot.

In the end break of Act II of my "Hart to Hart," Jonathan and Jennifer return home after a shopping spree and discover their house has been ransacked. Max is found tied and gagged, and their dog, "Freeway," has been stashed in a trunk. Jonathan releases Max, then hears a noise in the kitchen and goes to investigate. As he enters, the camera pulls back to reveal the intruder standing behind the door holding a knife. There is an ensuing struggle where the intruder manages to escape. He jumps into his utility van and races down the driveway. Jonathan chases after him in his Mercedes. The van careens out of the driveway and onto a country road with Jonathan in pursuit. Just when it looks as though Jonathan may overtake his abductor, he looks ahead and sees a diesel truck headed straight for him.

In my draft of the script, Jonathan swerves to avoid the oncoming truck, narrowly escaping a collision. In the story editor's later draft, Jonathan swerves to avoid the oncoming truck, hits his brakes, and at the last possible moment the Mercedes comes to a screeching halt at the edge of a cliff. The car literally teeters with Jonathan hanging in the balance.

I like what the story editor did here. It may be somewhat of a literal translation of "cliff-hanger," but if it works, what the hell!

Powerful act ends are just as important in the half-hour comedy. This script is broken into two acts. The most important break is the Act I end. Here, a major complication in the plot takes place, which should leave the audience hanging.

Many new writers are overly concerned with television commercials. "How long do they run?" they'll ask, or "How can I account for them in my script?" The good news is you don't have to worry about them. How long the commercials run, or what they are about, is not your concern. Commercial decisions are up to the networks.

You only need to plot around your act ends. Structure them so they have power and impact. Remember your goal. It's to pull 'em back from the refrigerator.

Buttons

Just as act ends are important, in a smaller sense so are scene ends. A "button" refers to a punch or exclamation point that happens at the end of a scene. In a sense, it sort of puts the cap on it, or buttons it up, and thereby helps the cut.

In a scene from the "Newhart" script, "A Day in the Life," Bob gets overly frazzled with having to make so many last-minute decisions in his effort to leave town. At the end of the scene, Emily and Howard arrive at his office and ask where he'd like to go for lunch. "I don't care where we eat," he says. "I just don't want to have to make any more decisions." At that moment both elevator doors open at the same time. In this scene, the button came in the form of a visual joke.

Be conscious of buttons as you watch television. Observe the different ways in which writers punctuate their scenes.

The Teaser and the Tag

The teaser and the tag are hooks that are written into the format of a show. A teaser is a brief one-and-a-half- to three-page scene that starts the show. It is followed by a commercial break, so it literally does what it says—it teases the audience to stay tuned for more. "Cheers" uses a teaser. Each week the show opens on some inconsequential bit that has nothing to do with the story, but it reveals the characters at the bar and lets us glimpse the fun we are about to have. The teaser on "Hill Street Blues" week after week was roll call, and on "Fantasy Island" it was the seaplane arriving.

For "Fantasy Island," the first page and a half of the teaser used stock footage, which is a sequence of shots already "in the can" that is replayed each week. Once the seaplane landed, the writer would then introduce the character or characters arriving to live out their fantasies.

The teaser for my "Fantasy Island" episode follows:

FANTASY ISLAND

"Night of the Tormented Soul"

TEASER

FADE IN:

EXT. ISLAND—FULL SHOT—DAY (STOCK)

The lush island nestled in the sea.

EXT. MOUNTAINS—DAY (STOCK)

Soaring green peaks set against ocean and sky.

EXT. WATERFALL—DAY (STOCK)

Water cascades from the stone heights to the lovely tropical pool below.

SEAPLANE—DAY (STOCK)

Flies overhead.

EXT. THE HOUSE—DAY (STOCK)

CAMERA MOVES IN ON the window as it opens to reveal MR. ROARKE. He looks up at the seaplane O.S. and smiles.

INT. BELL TOWER—TATTOO—DAY (STOCK)

Climbing the stairs. He spots the plane, excitedly RINGS THE BELL, then moves downward and OUT OF SCENE.

EXT. MAIN HOUSE—PORCH—ROARKE—DAY (STOCK)

A bevy of happy native girls hurries around the porch and PAST CAMERA. Roarke emerges from the house, checks his watch, then reacts to:

TATTOO (STOCK)

Who now joins Roarke, addresses with a cheerful:

> TATTOO
> Good morning, boss.

> ROARKE
> Good morning, Tattoo.

They fall in step, move to the waiting Rover, and are driven off.

EXT. SEAPLANE DOCK—DAY (STOCK)

As the Rover arrives with Roarke and Tattoo, young male and female natives hurry to join the welcoming ceremony with flowers, leis, and exotic drinks.

> ROARKE
> Smiles . . . smiles everyone!

He turns and signals for the MUSICIANS to START PLAYING. As they do:

THEIR POV—PLANE DOCK—DAY

Attendants tie down the seaplane.

INTERCUT between incoming passengers and Roarke and Tattoo.

(DIRECTOR: Please give us individual shots of each passenger for identification purposes.)

Among the passengers is BETH MARTINIQUE, a very beautiful, ethereal, twenty-year-old. She is accompanied by her attractive brother, JASON, three years her senior.

(NOTE: Not only do these youngsters seem emotionally close, they are physical by nature. They joke, jab and tease with much affection, obviously delighted with each other's company.)

> TATTOO (studying them)
> Good-looking kids. They seem
> happy.

> ROARKE
> Mr. Jason Martinique, and his
> sister, Beth, have not seen each
> other in several years.

> TATTOO (slight recognition)
> Martinique . . . sounds familiar.

> ROARKE
> They are the shipwrecked children
> who were raised at Belle Mer on
> the north end of the island.

> TATTOO (his eyes widen)
> That farmer and his housekeeper
> who died such horrible deaths?

> ROARKE
> Yes, Tattoo. The farmer,
> Martinique, was their father,
> and the incident so traumatized
> their young minds that they
> blocked it from their memories.

> TATTOO
> Boss, what is their fantasy? And
> why would they want to come back?

Grave concern comes over Roarke's face.

> ROARKE
> Their fantasy is to find out what
> actually happened on that fateful
> night. They are older now, and
> they feel that they can accept
> the events, whatever they were,
> as they occurred. So that they
> can pursue their lives as adults,
> with the past laid to rest.
> Unfortunately, some events are
> best left to the unknown.

Tattoo reacts. A slave girl brings Roarke his usual drink and he raises it in a toast.

```
                      ROARKE (continuing)
            My dear guests, I am Mr. Roarke,
            your host . . . Welcome to Fantasy
            Island.

      As the guests return the toast, we:

                                                  FADE OUT:


                      END OF TEASER
```

In this episode, Beth and Jason will not only learn the truth about
the murders but will later be informed by the omniscient Roarke that
they are not actually brother and sister. I had a lot of trouble with this
idea when story editor, the late Larry Forrester, told me he wanted
it in the script. How could I play these two characters outwardly
attracted to each other without making it look incestuous? Larry, a
wonderful writer, helped me pull it off.

When Beth and Jason, as children, were washed ashore it was one
of the most treacherous winters on the island. Ships foundered up
and down the coast. Jason landed first; then Beth came ashore a few
nights later. "There were two shipwrecks," Roarke explains, and then
he shows their birth certificates. During our story meetings we decided that the man who raised the children, acting as their father, had
planned to tell them later. Meanwhile, he felt it would be less of a
problem if he raised them as brother and sister.

Beth and Jason have spent many years apart. They have come
to know each other as adults through their letters. Both are searching for someone who possesses the qualities they find in each
other. In the teaser, Beth and Jason arrive as brother and sister. In
the tag, they leave us with the feeling that one day they will be a
couple.

```
                            TAG


      FADE IN:


      EXT. SEAPLANE DOCK AREA—DAY

      Roarke and Tattoo are stationed for their good-byes. A rover arrives.
      Beth and Jason get out. They are obviously in love. Beth is bubbling;
      he lets her do all the talking, quietly enjoying her.
```

BETH

Mr. Roarke, we've been so much
trouble for you.

ROARKE

My dear young people . . . You cared
enough to unwind the threads of
your past, and by doing so, you
freed two couples last night.
You deserve a happy future. ·

JASON

Mr. Roarke . . . I accepted that job
in Europe.

TATTOO

Great. Send me some bread from
France.

BETH

I'm going with him to finish school.

ROARKE

I am very happy for you both.

Beth smiles. As they start up the ramp, Jason takes her hand.

TATTOO

What will become of Belle Mer,
boss?

ROARKE

Interesting that you should ask.
You know, it is not such a bad
house.

TATTOO

My idea exactly. A few cans of
paint, some new shingles. It could
make a nice Fantasy Island hideaway.
And I could manage it.

ROARKE

Oh? Are the ghosts gone?

TATTOO

They're not?

Roarke starts off.

ROARKE

Of course. However, one can
never tell about ghosts.

Tattoo hesitates and then hurries off after Roarke.

```
                    TATTOO
        Boss . . . Wait . . . Let me tell
        you about my other idea.


                                        FADE OUT:


                    THE END
```

As in the above example, the tag consists of one-and-a-half to three pages that are at the end of the script. The tag serves to wrap up, lighten up, or clarify what we have already seen. Some shows only use teasers whereas others only use tags. Some shows incorporate both, as in the example I just gave you. Many shows don't use either.

Have I made my point? You must order scripts of the show you choose to write for. If they use teasers and/or tags, you must incorporate them into your own script.

5

So You Think You've Got a Hot Idea

Your idea, the story you choose to develop for a particular show, is absolutely tantamount in making a sale. Too often, in my past years as a script consultant, I've come across good writing only to find it wasted on mediocre ideas. There are literally thousands of competent professionals floating around this industry. These writers are already on the inside; they are members of the WGA; they are represented by agents who, if they carry any weight at all, are sending them on interviews. Why then should story editors and producers take your idea above these proven professionals? They won't.

It is not enough for "outside" writers to write well. They must have something unique, an idea that doesn't smack of any derivative plots, one in which the producers and staffers on the show haven't even thought of yet. Ideas such as these are not easy to come by. It is important to remember that television relies much more heavily on "hot" ideas than do feature films.

I often tell new writers to spend as much time carefully thinking up their ideas as they do on the actual writing of the script. Why, they'll ask, when they see unoriginal, redundant plots week after week on the air. You must remember: These scripts are written by writers already on the inside, not by new writers trying to break in. Don't settle for something only partially good because you're judging yourself by the worst—compare yourself with the best. Don't be so eager to write that you settle for an idea that is less than wonderful. You must know in your gut that it's hot, that it feels right. It is something you absolutely have to work on.

When my former partner, Kathy Donnell, and I decided to write our first script (a "Kojak"), we stumbled across an idea that completely grabbed us. The seed of the idea took form one night when

Kathy returned from a party and told me about a strange incident that had occurred there. Morticians had come to the door and informed the hostess that they were there to pick up her husband's body. The hostess, of course, was completely upset by whoever could play such a terrible prank. She informed the men in black that her husband was fine, and sent them home. While Kathy was telling me this, something hit me: What if after sending these men away the woman went into the study and discovered her husband with his throat slit? The result was a script entitled "Death Is Driving You Home." In it, the killer's mode of operation (M.O.) was that he would call the mortuary and request that they pick up a body before his victims were dead.

At that time, "Kojak" was in its sixth season. The longer the series runs, the harder its search for new ideas. Up until that time, Kojak hadn't aired an episode that even smacked of a derivative plot. The script was by no means flawless, but the idea was fresh, the writing was good, and it was evident that we had a thorough understanding of the show. Gene Kearney, the story editor of "Kojak," gave us the deal, brought us in, and helped us develop the script further.

Another time I got that intuitive feeling that said "Yes!" was for the "Starsky and Hutch." At the time the show was considered one of the most violent of its kind on the air. Psychologists were predicting the effects that these types of shows would have on our youth. The press was so bad that some sponsors were pulling out. One day in the paper I came across a quote by Joe Naar, the producer of "Starsky and Hutch," in response to all the criticism. His responsibility, he stated, was for authenticity. For undercover cops on the L.A. streets there was and always will be brutality. Therefore, how much violence was too much violence, and where, exactly, does one draw the line between realism and responsibility?

Something struck me. If I could develop a story that defended Mr. Naar's point of view, I'd certainly have a shot at getting the job. May I add here that my goal was to get work, not to take issue or sides. I am against violence on television. I have a nine-year-old daughter. I take parental responsibility, as all parents should, and monitor the programs she watches. However, this does not mean that I won't write for these shows. For many years my daughter was fed and clothed off action-adventure, car chases, and shoot 'em-ups.

Defending the producer's point of view was only a "seed" of an idea. It had not yet flushed into a story, but I knew intuitively that I was correct. The problem then became how do I make this notion work? To begin, in order for somebody to perceive detectives Starsky and Hutch as too violent, there must be an outsider in the story who witnesses their tactics on the streets.

For those of you who remember, this show sold two hotdog cops in a hotdog car. Their red Torino was actually the third character in the show. Therefore, for someone to watch our cops, the best vantage point would be from inside the car. This posed a problem. People tuned in each week to see two sexy, single heros and their sexy car. A stranger would be an intrusion. Unless—and this is when I knew I had something—this stranger was a woman. Why would a woman work and not a man? Because a woman implied fun. Our boys would be competing for her attention.

Now, with this problem solved I faced yet another obstacle. Exactly what was she doing there? The first thought that came to me was that she had witnessed a crime. This idea was weak. It would mean that she was taking Starsky and Hutch from point A to B to C in order to progress the story. If she were leading our cops, she then was pivotal to the story, not our stars. I had to find some way for her to serve the story in a passive capacity.

After running past many ideas, I made her a reporter. She was doing an article on what she called "Counter-Culture Cops—The New Breed." Next I had to determine what kind of assignment our boys were on. They had to rough people up and use hard street tactics that she could misinterpret. Even more important, how could they look bad in her eyes and yet not in the audience's eyes?

I decided on a simple drug story. A dealer is out on the streets passing strychnine in heroin capsules. Drug stories are usually a bad risk. They are not unique enough and only so many of these shows can be done in a season, unless the show deals exclusively with drugs as did "Miami Vice." In this case drugs worked, however, since it was not the main story, but a subplot. Essentially, it only served to get the boys on the streets. It also allowed them to rough up dealers and other despicable low-lives who were passing to children. This way, Starsky and Hutch's actions would be less despicable.

To justify them even more, they are told not to take any in-progress calls. They are to concern themselves only with this one case. When they ignore the in-progress calls, the reporter perceives this as neglect, when in fact they've been ordered to do so by the captain.

By asking myself the necessary questions, I was forcing myself to come up with the answers. I still faced more problems ahead. How and when do the boys learn the reporter's true motives? After deliberating, I decided the reporter must come out with her smear article condemning our cops by the end of Act II, thereby allowing time (two remaining acts) for Starsky and Hutch to prove her wrong. But what was it that would create this major turnaround? I still faced the most critical part of the story. How could I show that Starsky and Hutch knew how much was too much violence? What incident could I create that would convey this to the audience? The answer came in subplot.

Starsky and Hutch, at the end of Act IV, track down the dealer in an abandoned apartment building. They tell the reporter to stay in the car as they race up the stairs. She gets out, follows them, and interferes in the stakeout. The pusher holds a gun to her head and cocks the trigger. Panicked, she screams, "Shoot him!" Instead, they very slowly and calmly drop their weapons, talk to the pusher, and convince him to hand over his revolver, thereby saving the reporter's life.

The reporter, of course, publicly apologizes to our heroes, and in the end prints a retraction. After further observation, she's found this "new breed" of cop to be educated, caring, and rational.

Finding the right idea and then developing that idea takes time, some pain, and a lot of effort, but it pays off. I got the job! So where do you find hot ideas? The universe is constantly providing them. You must learn to think like a writer so you'll recognize them when they present themselves.

I remember sitting at my word processor one day, stumped on how to end a scene in "Belly Up." In it, Alex is yelling and screaming on the telephone in a desperate attempt to realign his credit. I knew what the scene needed but I wanted a punch for the end—a button to cap it like an exclamation point. At that moment there was a knock at my front door. I answered to find two very solemn-looking men, dressed in black, holding Bibles. They had come, they said, to discuss their feelings on the end of the world. I told them I really didn't have time, bought their publication, and sent them on their way. The following is the result of that surprise interruption. The button for the scene was handed to me at my own front door.

INT. HOLMAN HILLS MODEL—LIVING ROOM—DAY

The room is in disarray; glasses, dishes, paperwork, are strewn about. On the coffee table is an open copy of "Why Bad Things Happen to Good People." Alex is pacing with the phone.

ALEX (into the phone)
I've been on hold for ten minutes.
How many people are ahead of me?

He continues to pace while waiting.

                    ALEX (continuing) (into phone)

>   . . . Yes, I'm still here. (the phone
>   beeps) Hold on, I have another call. (he
>   presses call waiting) Credit Office?
>   Good . . . I've been having some
>   difficulties. I need to rearrange my
>   payment schedule . . . account number?
>   Hold on, I'll get it for you. (back to the
>   first party) Are you still there? Swear to
>   me you won't hang up.

He sets the receiver down, quickly shuffles through a mass of paperwork on his desk.

                    ALEX (continuing) (to himself)

>   What the hell did I do with it! (rifling through)
>   American Express, Master Charge, Macy's . . .
>   (he comes across a melted chocolate chip
>   cookie) Mrs. Field's . . .

The chocolate is now all over him; he continues rifling through the
mess.

                    ALEX (continuing) (to himself)

>   God, I need some kind of filing
>   system. I need a secretary. I
>   need order. How can I get back
>   on top when I'm stuck with
>   piddly-ass things!?

He picks up the receiver, gets chocolate all over it.

                    ALEX (continuing) (into phone)

>   Be patient. (presses to other party) Are you
>   still there? . . . Yeah, well you too, lady!

Alex reacts to the slammed receiver.

                    ALEX (continuing) (into phone)

>   Hello? . . . Hello!? . . .

The DOORBELL RINGS. He sets down the phone, the chocolate is all
over one side of his face.

> ALEX (continuing) (to himself)
>
> Calm down. You're an entrepreneur.
> Get a handle on yourself.
>
> He takes a deep breath, walks to the door.
>
> ALEX (continuing) (to himself)
>
> Bankruptcy is not the end of the
> world.
>
> He opens the door to reveal TWO PALE-FACED MEN in black business suits, holding Bibles.
>
> ONE OF THE MEN
>
> We were in the neighborhood and
> wondered if we could share our
> thoughts on the end of the world.

Ideas are everywhere. All you need to do is observe. Read every publication you can get your hands on: the newspaper, tabloids, magazine articles. Watch "Geraldo," "Oprah," "Donahue," and "60 Minutes" to find out what's happening with people. Instead of listening to music on your car radio keep a mini-tape recorder by your side. Incredible ideas occur to me while I'm driving. It can be a tremendously creative time for any writer since there are no interruptions. Listen to your friends' stories and recall your own. *Find an idea you feel passionate about.*

6

Writing the Half-Hour Sitcom

The word *sitcom* is short for the half-hour situation comedy. These shows run a half-hour in length and rely on continuing characters and their *situations* to provide the humor and move the storyline forward. The majority of these shows are taped "live" in front of a studio audience. For this reason, the casts and sets are kept to a bare minimum.

"In-house" stories are ideal for sitcoms—that is, stories that use only the ongoing cast members. Since this type of story is difficult to create, and outside characters are often needed, it is wise to keep the additional cast to no more than one or two. An exception would be if the show used an array of outside characters each week, as did "Barney Miller."

The obvious reason for keeping the cast down is budget. There are also time constraints to be considered. Besides, why clutter your story with too many characters? The focus should always be on the stars of the show.

Writers of the spec sitcom script should also keep their stories limited to the sets they see week after week on the show. New sets cost money. As I mentioned in chapter 3, additional sets are called "swings." If a swing is absolutely essential in telling your story, use no more than one or two.

You may see episodes that break this rule. Recently I saw a rerun of "Family Ties," where Alex went east to interview for entrance into an Ivy League college. Except for the setup, which took place in the Keaton household, all of the show was done on swings.

There's a chance that next week you'll tune in to "Rosanne," and she and husband Dan will have decided to take off on a romantic second honeymoon, or "The Golden Girls" will end up at a nudist camp—who knows, maybe they'll find the Huxtables there.

Rules are broken, but staff writers break them. These episodes happen in-house. When you write on spec you should not take chances. You're gambling already, so why gamble more by limiting yourself? Don't give producers and story editors an easy out. You don't want to hear, "We really like the writing, but the show is going to be too difficult and/or costly to shoot."

Since sitcoms are limited by costs and sets, they rely much more heavily on dialogue and character than do other forms of television writing. I'm often asked by aspiring playwrights if the principles of writing for the theater lend themselves to television. Actually, the style of the half-hour comedy is very similar to a one-act play. Whereas episodes and Movies for Television rely on visuals, the sitcom cannot. It must rely on its characters, relationships, and the situation to develop the storyline and create the humor.

Writing Funny: Can It Be Taught?

Some professionals say yes, and others believe it is an inner sense that cannot be passed on. Comedy has a certain tempo and rhythm just like a piece of music. I believe that all writers can develop a better comedic ear through practice. But there are those fortunate few, like the Neil Simons of the world, who are born with perfect pitch.

When Ann Jillian was first beginning her career in Hollywood, she was teamed up with a friend of mine and very talented singer, Deborah Shulman. Jillian and Shulman made a wonderful singing duo but they needed comedy routines to complement their act. They came to me and asked for material since at that time I had some produced half-hour sitcoms to my credit.

I tried, but failed to come up with anything. I was stymied. I no longer had a situation or running characters to work with, but rather two very attractive, talented women who I was supposed to make funny.

Stand-up comedy or gag writing is a special talent. It's wonderful if you have the ability, but it's not a prerequisite for writing the situation comedy. Nor is being an unusually funny person. All good sitcom writers share one thing in common: their perception, their perspective—the way they interpret everyday circumstances.

Comedy and drama are essentially the flip side of a coin. The only difference is in their approach or point of view (P.O.V.). The comedy writer sees things as funny, whereas the dramatic writer sees them as serious. Yet the situation they are writing about could be identical.

"Belly Up" deals with bankruptcy. Is Alex's terrible dilemma a particularly funny one? Bankruptcy is a very serious business, but I chose the comedic P.O.V. His predicament allowed for great comedic possibilities. He was a winner in a losing situation. Sadistic? Perhaps, but all humor has a bit of cynicism. It bites and makes fun of human imperfection. Situation comedy thrives on it.

Look at Lucy's antics, or Archie Bunker having to come face to face with his own ethics. There was Sam and Diane's turbulent romance on "Cheers," and Alex Keaton, whose conservatism was constantly teaching him a hard lesson.

The comedic P.O.V. magnifies character flaws and we, the audience, laugh. We identify with these shortcomings. Why? Because we have them ourselves. If we don't, we know somebody who does.

Structure: The Most Essential Element

Almost all half-hour scripts are in two acts, with each act consisting of approximately four to six scenes. I say approximately because scripts can vary according to the particular show, which is why it is imperative that you read scripts from the sitcom you choose to write for (see appendix A for script-ordering services).

The situation comedy format is different from the screenplay and one-hour teleplay format, where the rule is one page equals one minute of film. Since half-hour scripts are typed double-spaced (see chapter 13 on teleplay form), each page equals about thirty seconds of tape or film. Consequently, these scripts run forty-five to fifty pages.

The scenes in a half-hour sitcom can average anywhere from three to seven pages long. It is important to note here that if you have a one-page scene or an eight-page scene, you don't necessarily have to scrap it. You are running under or over, and you'll need to compensate somewhere else. I simply use the averaging technique to keep myself on track. It is not a hard-and-fast rule. Rather, it is a device, or gauge, that I have found very useful in helping me to achieve the right page number, or as I tag it, "coming in on the dime."

As I mentioned in chapter 2, the technical definition of a scene is that it establishes a *place* and a *time,* which leads to another problem. What if the particular sitcom you are writing for uses only one set, perhaps two, as did the "Barney Miller" show? How then can you gauge yourself pagewise?

In "Cheers," almost all of the action takes place in the bar. If you watch reruns of "Three's Company," sometimes an entire act may take place in the trio's living room. But, watch these shows very carefully. You will discover that every one-and-a-half to three-and-a-half minutes (three to seven pages), a new element is introduced into the story. Although these story elements, or "beats," as I call them, may not technically constitute a scene, for your own benefit you can still count them as a scene to help you keep on track.

If we were to diagram the half-hour structure it would look like figure 1.

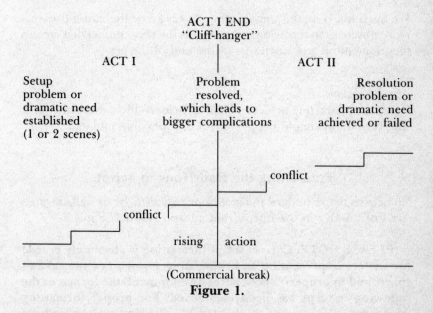

Figure 1.

The Setup

The setup tells us everything we need to get the ball rolling. It is the who, what, and why of the story. It establishes the dramatic need for our character or characters. With time restriction so great, the setup must be complete by the first or second scene.

Character + Dramatic Need + Obstacles = Conflict = Laughter

Once the dramatic need is established, every scene thereafter presents an obstacle to that need, thus creating the conflict that moves the storyline forward. *The stronger the dramatic need of your character and the bigger the obstacles, the more powerful and funny the script.*

The Major Complication

By the end of Act I, a problem is usually resolved, but this problem leads to a bigger complication. At the end of Act I, the audience should be left hanging.

Act II

We open Act II on the complication. Every scene thereafter presents more obstacles to resolving it. Again, it is the very conflict that creates the momentum and carries us to the end of the act.

The Resolution

Here, the characters achieve or fail to achieve their dramatic need. The resolution should happen at the last possible moment.

Translating the Half-Hour to Script

To help us better understand half-hour structure, let us walk through Act I of "A Day in the Life," from a "Bob Newhart Show."

(PLEASE NOTE: Correct script formatting is absolutely crucial for writers in presenting and submitting scripts. For the sake of space, and to properly show script development, the format of the following excerpt has been condensed. For proper formatting guidelines, please refer to chapter 13. The first two pages have been typeset to show correct formatting.)

Scene 1

Notice our setup is complete. Bob's dramatic need is established—that is, he must leave town on a last-minute notice. Since the Newhart character lacks any semblance of spontaneity, this hook is good. He is being forced to act on the spur of the moment, thus suggesting conflict.

Notice how we plant (foreshadow) the fact that Emily is on vacation. This is very important to the plot later.

When Emily bounces into the room, her presence provides a slight twist; we are expecting her to sleep in.

The runner is planted here also, which is Emily's wager with Bob.

THE BOB NEWHART SHOW

"A Day in the Life"

ACT I

FADE IN:

INT. BOB AND EMILY'S APARTMENT

HOWARD IS ASLEEP ON THE SOFA WITH THE TELEVISION ON. BOB EXITS FROM THE BEDROOM DRESSED FOR WORK. HE SHUTS OFF THE TELEVISION AND SHAKES HOWARD.

BOB

Howard, wake up!

HOWARD

I think I just overshot

Pittsburgh! What are you

doing in my apartment?

BOB

Howard, this is my apartment.

You fell asleep in front of

the television again.

HOWARD

Oh no! I missed it!

BOB

The end of the movie?

HOWARD

Channel Nine's Thought for the

Day. Now I won't have one.

BOB

Well, life's full of little

disappointments.

HOWARD

No, that was last Friday's

Thought for the Day.

BOB

Ah. Well, I've got to eat some

breakfast and get to work.

HOWARD

Oh boy, breakfast! I'm so

hungry!

BOB

Howard, keep it down. This is

Emily's first day of vacation

and I want her to sleep. She's

really tired.

EMILY ENTERS FROM THE BEDROOM DRESSED IN TENNIS
WARM-UPS AND SWINGING A RACQUET.

EMILY

(FULL OF ENTHUSIASM) Boy, I

can't wait to get to my tennis

lesson. Gotta work on my

backhand, my forehand, and my

footwork.

SHE DOES A COUPLE OF BACKHAND STROKES.

BOB
It's amazing what a little extra
sleep will do for you.

EMILY
Howard, did you fall asleep in
front of the television again?

HOWARD
'Fraid so.

EMILY
You didn't miss the Thought for
the Day, did you?

HOWARD
Yeah, I did.

EMILY
Well . . . Tomorrow is another day.

HOWARD
That was two weeks ago Wednesday.
(GOES TO DOOR) Well, I'm going
to freshen up. Gee, this is my
lucky day. I don't have to make
my bed.

BOB
Why don't you make that your
thought for the day?

HOWARD
Thank you, Bob.

HE EXITS.

BOB
Want some breakfast?

EMILY
No, I'm just going to make myself
a health drink. Bananas, papayas,
pineapple, mangos . . .

THROUGHOUT THE FOLLOWING EMILY PREPARES A
HEALTH DRINK AND BOB STARTS PREPARING A BOWL OF
CEREAL.

BOB
It sounds like you're going to eat
Carmen Miranda's hat. I thought
you were going to get some rest.

EMILY
No, I've decided to devote this
week to getting myself in shape.

EMILY (continued)
And this drink is an important
part of it. Because you know,
Bob, you are what you eat.

BOB
You had to tell me that just when
I fixed a bowl of Fruit Flakes.
THE PHONE RINGS.

EMILY (WORKING THE BLENDER)
Get that will you, Bob?

BOB (ANSWERS IT: INTO PHONE)
Hello . . . (EXCITED) Peeper?
Hey, Peep! Hiya Peep! What
d'ya say, Peep? (TO EMILY)
Emily, guess who this is.

EMILY
Prince Philip.

BOB (INTO PHONE)
. . . When are you
coming out Peeper? . . . You're
not . . . We're meeting you
tonight . . . for a week . . . in New
Orleans. (TO EMILY) He says
we're meeting him tonight for
a week in New Orleans.

EMILY
Come on, Bob. It's another one
of his practical jokes.

BOB (INTO PHONE)
Peeper, when did
you start drinking this early in
the morning? . . . It's no joke? . . .
But that's crazy! I can't just
pack up and leave! Peep, I know
it's a beautiful city . . . Yes,
great food . . . The music, too . . .
Al Hirt says he won't play another
note until I come? . . . Peeper my
patients are booked. I'm not a
party pooper. I've been known
to be a wild man!

EMILY (LAUGHS)
Yeah, you're a real heck-raiser.

BOB
Peep, I can be very spontaneous
if you give me a week or two to

BOB (continued)
plan it out . . . I'm an old lady,
am I? Well, I resent that,
Peeper, and I'm going to tell
you so tonight in person . . .
Okay, we'll be there. See ya.

HE HANGS UP AND LOOKS AT EMILY FOR A BEAT.

BOB (CONT'D)
Emily, how would you like to beat
your feet on the Mississippi mud?

EMILY
You know you hate to travel.
Usually wild horses can't pull
you away . . . The Peep makes one
phone call and you're out that
door.

BOB
Emily, you've got to be more
spontaneous.

EMILY
Really? Well, mister wild man.
What about all the appointments
you've booked for next week?

BOB
I'll reschedule them. I'll make
all the arrangements. We'll be
on a plane for New Orleans tonight.

EMILY (SMILES)
I think I smell a bet.

BOB (SMUGLY)
You name it.

EMILY
Okay. Every year we have trouble
finding somebody to play the
Easter Bunny at the school egg hunt.

BOB
What do I get if I win?

EMILY
If you win, you get to spend
a week in New Orleans with a
beautiful, sensuous woman.

BOB
Do I get to pick her? (OFF
HER LOOK) Fair enough, Emily.

BOB (continued)
Now . . . (rubs his hands together)
what do I need to do first?

EMILY
First we have to have you measured
for your bunny outfit. Then you'll
need to get airplane reservations
on incredibly short notice.

HOWARD ENTERS.

HOWARD
Hi, Bob. Hi, Emily. Breakfast ready?

BOB
Howard, can you get plane
reservations?

HOWARD
I don't need reservations, I sit
in the cockpit.

■ ■ ■

Scene 2

Obstacles are presented for Bob's dramatic need. From the moment he steps off the elevator he will experience one conflict
after another.
Notice how the narrative in half-hour comedy is strictly *functional*.
It serves only to tell us what the characters are doing.

INT. RECEPTION AREA
CAROL IS AT HER DESK. THE ELEVATOR PINGS AND BOB
GETS OFF.

BOB
Carol, I'm on my way to New
Orleans.

CAROL
You took the wrong elevator.

BOB
Emily and I are going to spend
a week's vacation down there.

CAROL
A week's vacation? Now see here.
We're trying to run a business,

CAROL (continued)
my friend, not a Holiday Inn.
We can't have people coming and
going at the drop of a hat, now
can we? What do you have to say
for yourself Hartley?

BOB
You're fired.

CAROL
You need a vacation.

BOB
Welcome back. (THEN) Now look,
I've got this all worked out.
(HE PULLS A PIECE OF PAPER OUT
OF HIS POCKET.) I'm going to
transfer some of my patients
to Dr. Walburn. The others we
have to double up the week after
next. Thusly . . . (READING)
Move Mr. Marsh to 2:00 . . .

CAROL
He works afternoons.

BOB
Scratch that. (HE TEARS OFF
THE TOP STRIP OF PAPER.) Put
Mr. Voltz at 3:00 . . .

CAROL
Bob, you know Mr. Voltz is
terrified of the number three.

BOB
Oh, that's right. (HE TEARS
OFF ANOTHER STRIP OF PAPER.)
Shift Mrs. Slater to Thursday . . .

CAROL
She lifts weights on Thursdays.

BOB
Of course. (TEARS OFF MORE PAPER)
Put Mr. Harris on Friday . . .

CAROL
Uh, Bob . . . Mr. Harris on
Friday?

BOB
(GETTING HER POINT) Oh, right.
(RIPS OFF ANOTHER STRIP) And
put Petersen in the morning . . .

> CAROL
> That's okay.
>
> BOB
> Fine. (HANDS HER ONE TINY BIT
> OF PAPER) You fill in the gaps.
>
> CAROL
> Right, Bob. (THEN) Mr. Carlin
> is in your office.
>
> BOB
> Already?
>
> CAROL
> He's been waiting an hour.
>
> BOB
> Sometimes I don't know whether
> to charge him fees or rent.
> (HE OPENS HIS OFFICE DOOR)
> Carol, get me Dr. Walburn on
> the phone.
>
> AND AS HE EXITS INTO HIS OFFICE, WE: RESET TO:

■　■　■

Scene 3

Here, Mr. Carlin presents Bob with yet more obstacles.

At the time I was writing this script, I was reading a book on positive thinking that prescribed to its readers to spend a day listing negative thoughts. This little exercise worked wonderfully for this scene.

Monologue and/or long telephone conversations are usually deadly for the television writer. They work in this case, however, because it is what Newhart is noted for.

> INT. BOB'S OFFICE
> BOB ENTERS. CARLIN IS ON THE COUCH.
>
> CARLIN
> What do you want with Walburn?
>
> BOB
> Hello, Mr. Carlin. I'm going
> to be leaving for a week, and
> I'm going to refer some of my
> patients to him.

                   CARLIN
Not this patient—Walburn's
a turkey.

                   BOB
Walburn is a very reputable
doctor.

                   CARLIN
He hates me.

                   BOB
Dr. Walburn doesn't hate you.
You two just got off on the
wrong foot.

                   CARLIN
It wasn't my fault about the
hamster. How was I to know it
was his pet. Besides, all I
did was feed it.

                   BOB
Putting a little bit of cheese
in a mouse trap is not feeding.

                   CARLIN
Well, he went for it.
THERE'S A BUZZ ON THE INTERCOM.

                   BOB (PRESSES BUTTON)
Yes?

                   CAROL
Excuse me, Bob, Dr. Walburn's
on the phone.

                   BOB
Thanks, Carol. (THEN) One
moment, Mr. Carlin.
HE PICKS UP THE PHONE.

                   BOB (CONT'D) (INTO PHONE)
Hello, Frank . . .
How are you? . . . Good. I'm calling
because I'm going away. Can
you cover for me next week?
The regulars and the group . . .
Yeah, Mr. Carlin will be there
too . . . You'd rather be staked
to an anthill? . . . Listen, Frank,
if you'll remember, I took care
of your patients last fall, and
as I recall, I had a lot of trouble
with that hockey player . . . I don't
care if she is nice off the ice . . .

BOB (continued)
You still think Carlin's worse?
You'll gladly take the rest of
them? Well, good. I really
appreciate it, Frank . . . Good-bye.

HE HANGS UP

CARLIN
He's still sore about the rat.

BOB
I have a suggestion, Mr. Carlin.

CARLIN
Nothing doing, Hartley. I
can't go a whole week without
a session.

BOB
Well, I could call you up and
we could have sessions over
the phone.

CARLIN
Not a chance. How would I know
you weren't making faces at me?

BOB (HEAVES A BIG SIGH)
Well, if that's the way you feel . . .
I guess I'll call off the trip.

CARLIN
I'll tell you what. If you're
gone for a week then you'll
owe me five sessions, right?

BOB
That's right.

CARLIN
You can give them all to me today.

BOB
Five sessions or an Easter Bunny.

CARLIN
Take it or leave it.

BOB
Then I guess we'd better get
started. Where did we leave
off last time?

CARLIN
You told me to get a notebook
and keep a list of all my
negative thoughts.

CARLIN OPENS UP HIS NOTEBOOK.

CARLIN
Where do you want me to start?

BOB
Let's take it from the top.

CARLIN (READING)
"Number One, a dollar-
ninety-five for this stupid
notebook . . .

ON BOB'S REACTION, WE:

DISSOLVE TO:

■ ■ ■

Scene 4

A scene establishes place and time. Here, we are at the same locale,
Bob's office, but it is an hour later. The transitional camera
technique most commonly used to denote time change is called
a "dissolve" (see chapter 13 for further explanation).
Notice how the dialogue serves to connect the scenes and helps the
time lapse.

INT. BOB'S OFFICE—ONE HOUR LATER
BOB AND CARLIN ARE SEATED. CARLIN IS STILL READING
FROM THE NOTEBOOK.

CARLIN (READING)
687, my pajamas
itch . . . 688, Ed McMahon will
laugh at anything . . .

BOB
Has this list taught you anything
about yourself?

CARLIN
Yes. I'm not a happy man . . . but
I'm very observant.

BOB
Don't you feel you're a little
too negative about everything?

CARLIN
No.

> BOB
> Why don't we pick it up next
> time, okay?
>
> CARLIN
> So what I should remember is
> not to take all these things
> so seriously.
>
> BOB
> Exactly. Like my going away.
>
> CARLIN OPENS HIS NOTEPAD, BEGINS WRITING.
>
> CARLIN
> Number 689, Hartley abandons
> patient.
>
> THEY EXIT.
> RESET TO:

■ ■ ■

Scene 5

Here, a new element is introduced into the story: the Swerdlow
family.

The Swerdlows were written in at the last minute, long after my
partner and I had turned in our script. They are not our creation, but
that of the staff writers who were working on the show at the time.
The producers originally wanted a scuba diver to step off the elevator
in full gear for a session with Bob. He was a twin, and was having an
identity crisis with his brother. When we arrived for the taping of the
show, we were told that they had found something that worked better
in rehearsals.

> OUTER OFFICE:
> BOB & CARLIN COME OUT
>
> CARLIN
> Who's the next group?
>
> BOB
> It's a family. The Swerdlows.
>
> CARLIN
> You're treating a whole family?

> BOB
> Well, when they came to me six
> months ago, they had tremendous
> hostilities toward each other.
> They were arguing, fighting.

> CARLIN
> Makes me feel kinda homesick.

> BOB
> But lately they've really
> started making an effort to
> get close to each other.

THE ELEVATOR DOORS OPEN AND THE SWERDLOWS ARE
STANDING THERE, MAN AND WIFE AND TWO TEENAGE KIDS.
THEY'RE POSED JUST LIKE AN OLD-FASHIONED FAMILY POR-
TRAIT, STANDING VERY CLOSE TO EACH OTHER.

> SWERDLOWS (IN UNISON)
> Good morning, Dr.
> Hartley.

> BOB
> Good morning.

> FATHER (TO HIS WIFE)
> After you, honey.

> MOTHER
> No, no. The children must go
> first.

> TOM
> No, Mother, after you.

> BECKY
> Yes, we insist that our beloved
> parents . . .

THE ELEVATOR DOOR CLOSES.

> CARLIN
> It's a good thing they weren't
> on the *Titanic.*

THE DOORS OPEN AGAIN.

> MOTHER
> Silly us.

> FATHER
> Okay. Everybody move out at the
> same time.

THEY ALL PUT THEIR ARMS AROUND EACH OTHER AND STEP
OFF THE ELEVATOR IN UNISON.

> BECKY
> Wasn't that a pleasant elevator ride?

> TOM
> I particularly enjoyed the sixth
> floor.
>
> MOTHER
> The important thing is that we
> all rode together.
>
> BOB
> Mr. and Mrs. Swerdlow, Tom, Becky,
> I'd like you to meet Mr. Carlin.
> CARLIN AND THE SWERDLOWS AD LIB HELLOS.
>
> BOB (CONT'D)
> Mr. Carlin, I'll be done in an
> hour. (TO THE FAMILY) Shall
> we go in the office?
>
> BECKY
> Oh, boy, another session!
>
> TOM
> We love Dr. Hartley's office.
>
> BECKY
> We love Dr. Hartley.
> THE SWERDLOWS GO INTO BOB'S OFFICE. BOB FOLLOWS
> THEM IN.
> RESET TO:

■ ■ ■

Scene 6

We are now building to our Act I end. It appears at this point that
Bob has solved his problem with Carlin. But, as we'll soon discover, this problem leads to a greater complication, on which we
end Act I.

> INT. BOB'S OFFICE
> THE SWERDLOWS ALL SIT ON THE COUCH. CARLIN COMES
> IN BEHIND BOB AND, UNSEEN BY BOB, SITS ON THE COUCH
> WITH THE FAMILY. BOB CLOSES THE DOOR, THEN TURNS
> AROUND AND SEES CARLIN.
>
> BOB
> Mr. Carlin, what do you think
> you're doing?

CARLIN

This'll be one of my sessions.
I wouldn't miss this for the
world.

BOB

Absolutely not. You can't stay.
This is not your session.

FATHER

Please, Dr. Hartley, if he'd like
to stay, I'd like him to stay. We
want nothing here but good feelings.

MOTHER

Since we've been coming to Dr.
Hartley, we've been trying to
like everyone.

BOB

Well, this will be your first
big test.

TOM

You're a beautiful person, Mom.

BECKY

Don't forget Dad, Tom.

TOM

He's beautiful, too.

CARLIN

Am I dreaming this?

BOB

If you're going to stay, Mr.
Carlin, please be quiet. (THEN,
TO THE FAMILY) Well, I want to
tell you how pleased I am that
you're no longer fighting and
that you're working so hard to
get along . . .

MOTHER

We're doing our best.

BECKY

We couldn't do it without Dad.
He's a gem.

FATHER

Well, I'd be lost without all
of you. You're the best family
a man's ever been blessed with.

MOTHER
Amen.

CARLIN
Hartley, somebody's trying to
put you on.

BOB
Mr. and Mrs. Swerdlow, Tom and
Becky, it's good for a family
to cooperate, but it's also
important not to hide our feelings.
Imitating a happy family is not
the same as being one.

FATHER
But we love each other, Dr.
Hartley. You've shown us that
love is better than hostility.

MOTHER
God bless you, Dr. Hartley.

TOM
God bless us every one.

CARLIN
These people have taken a cab.

BOB
Mr. Carlin, if you don't be
quiet, you're going to have to
leave. (THEN TO THE SWERDLOWS)
Some patients overreact to
therapy . . . In trying to correct
their behavior they go too far
the other way.

TOM
Could I say something, Dr.
Hartley?

BOB
Of course, Tom.

CARLIN
This is going to be good.

TOM
I made a decision today. I'm
going to sell my motorcycle,
give up the guitar, and go
into business with you, Dad.

FATHER
Oh, son! (HE HUGS TOM HAPPILY)

BOB
Mr. Swerdlow . . . you're a mailman.

FATHER
Yes, Dr. Hartley . . . you're right.
But Tom can take one side of the
street and I'll take the other.

TOM
You can take the sunny side.

FATHER
Any side you're on is the sunny
side.

CARLIN
(TO BOB) These people could win
the Pillsbury Bore-Off. (TO
SWERDLOWS) You can't kid me.
No family's this happy.

BECKY
That's not true. We're as happy
as we can be.

CARLIN
I think you're out of your tree.

BOB
All right, Mr. Carlin, that's
it. You have to leave.

CARLIN
Okay, I'll go. (RISES AND
GOES TO THE DOOR) But tell
me, Dr. Hartley . . . Have you
broken your news to the Waltons
here?

MOTHER
What news, Dr. Hartley?

FATHER
I'm sure if it's Dr. Hartley's
news, it'll be delightful.

BECKY
He's finally going to come to
dinner!
THEY ALL CHEER.

TOM
What'll we have?

MOTHER
I'll fix him my special fried
chicken.

> BECKY
> And apple pie!

> TOM
> I'll say grace.

> FATHER
> And plenty of good, fresh milk.

> CARLIN
> Hartley's leaving town next
> week and leaving you in
> the lurch.

A DEADLY SILENCE FALLS OVER THE ROOM.

> TOM
> He wouldn't do that to us.
> Not Dr. Hartley.

> BOB
> Well, I'm not doing it to
> anyone, I just . . .

> MOTHER (IN HORROR)
> You mean it's true?

> CARLIN
> He's flying to New Orleans
> tonight.

> BOB
> I'm leaving you in very capable
> hands . . .

> MOTHER
> You're going . . . out of the state?

> FATHER (TO MOTHER)
> Of course it's out of the state. Where do
> you think New Orleans is, stupid?

> MOTHER
> Who do you think you're calling
> stupid, Liver Lips?

> TOM
> Dad, you can't let him do this.
> We can't get along without
> these sessions.

> MOTHER
> I'll tell you what we can get
> along without. Your big mouth!

> BECKY
> Oh shut up.

FATHER
Don't sass your mother.

BECKY
I'd rather sass you anyway,
Liver Lips.
THE FAMILY DISSOLVES INTO A BROUHAHA. BOB LOOKS AT
CARLIN.

CARLIN
Now this is what I call a
family.
HE EXITS AND WE:

FADE OUT:

END OF ACT ONE

∎ ∎ ∎

The situation in "A Day in the Life" allows for the humor. Yes, many of the lines are very funny, and many of these lines aren't mine. There were some jokes that my partner and I wrote that I was very proud of but even these have been embellished and improved by staffers on the show. What *was* important to the producers was that the script supplied the hooks that television rested on:

1. The *idea* was fresh and not a derivative of something that had been on the air previously.
2. The *setup* happened fast. We knew what the story was about in the first scene.
3. The *structure* worked. The story could be told on limited and existing sets (this particular episode required two swing sets), and was developed and resolved adequately in the half-hour time frame.
4. There was personal involvement for the star. The story was happening directly to Bob. It was Bob's conflict that progressed the action forward.
5. There are twists and turns in the plot.

Bob, of course, faces more difficulties in Act II. He is besieged with yet more obstacles to his dramatic need. Just when it appears that he's a sure candidate for the bunny suit, in a last-ditch effort he manages to go on the trip.

INT. AIRPORT WAITING AREA—GATE 5—DAY
BOB AND EMILY ARE WAITING AT THE GATE WITH
THEIR LUGGAGE. THEY MOVE UP IN LINE.

> BOB
>
> Emily, I must admit there were
> times today I didn't think I'd
> make it.

> EMILY
>
> I'm proud of you, Bob. You know,
> you really are a wild man. (GIVES
> HIM A LITTLE HUG)

THEY START TO HAND THEIR TICKETS TO THE STEWARD.
THE PHONE AT THE DESK RINGS; THE STEWARD PICKS IT UP.

> STEWARD (INTO PHONE)
>
> Gate five . . . One
> moment. (INTO LOUDSPEAKER
> microphone) Phone call for
> Dr. Robert Hartley.

> BOB
>
> I'm Dr. Hartley.

> STEWARD (INTO MICROPHONE)
>
> Very well, there's a call for . . . Oh. (STEPS AWAY FROM
> THE MICROPHONE)

BOB TAKES THE PHONE.

> BOB
>
> (into phone) Hello? Hey,
> Peeper, we're on our way.
> Jazz on Bourbon Street, Creole
> food . . . What's that, Peep? . . .
> It's one on us . . . because you're
> not going? . . . It's a gag . . .
> That's real funny, Peep. (TO
> EMILY) Do you believe that?
> He's not going. (INTO PHONE)
> Do you know what I went through
> to get here? The rescheduling!
> The aggravation! The Swerdlows!
> . . . Well, listen—we're going
> anyway! You hear that, Peep?
> . . . and it's going to be a
> million laughs . . . (TO EMILY)
> Right, Emily?

> EMILY
>
> That's telling him, Bob. Why
> don't you put our things on

BOB (continued)
the plane. Let me give him a
piece of my mind!
SHE TAKES THE PHONE.

BOB
Go easy with him, Emily.
BOB HANDS HIS TICKET TO THE STEWARD, PICKS UP THE
LUGGAGE AND WALKS THROUGH THE GATE.

EMILY
(waits until he's gone; then
into phone) Thanks, Peep . . .
It worked like a charm . . . I owe
you one.
SHE GRINS, HANGS UP AND HANDS HER TICKET TO THE
STEWARD. AS SHE WALKS THROUGH THE GATE, WE:

FADE OUT:

END OF ACT TWO

■ ■ ■

I was once told by a very successful comedy team that when writing
the half-hour comedy, the writer should never try to be funny. These
two men were very successful and very funny. Their scripts had kept
us laughing for years. And yet, what were they saying? When writers
work at being funny, they write for the joke or the punchline, and this
is deadly. Instead, they told me, the sitcom writer should create a
story with so much conflict and with so many obstacles that the
situation itself is funny. This input was invaluable, because it freed
me of a terrible burden. I hope it does the same for you.

7

Writing the Hour Episode

Hour scripts consist of four acts and use the same format rule as the two-hour M.O.W. (Movie of the Week) and feature films. That is, one page equals one minute of film (see chapter 14). Therefore, the running time of these scripts is about fifty-five to sixty pages.

There are exceptions to this rule. "Moonlighting" scripts ran anywhere from eighty to ninety-five pages. The reason is evident if you watched the show: David and Maddy's biting banter resembled the speed of a Ping-Pong game. Again, I must reinforce that you should buy and study scripts for the show for which you write.

Scripting the hour episode in many ways is less restrictive than the half-hour comedy. We are no longer limited to three sets on a sound stage with canned laughter. We now have a myriad locales and visual possibilities. There is all of New York, all of Los Angeles, or all of wherever the show takes place to use as our locations.

The power of the half-hour comedy rested with character and dialogue. The power of the one-hour episode and the two-hour M.O.W. is in the picture. Regardless of the plot lines, these shows use quick-paced visuals to keep their audiences riveted. Just watch a prime-time hour episode and count how often the locales change.

Since we have now expanded into the sixty-minute time frame, our stories become more complex and our costs are greater. Unlike the half-hour comedy, where the action rarely leaves the stars, in the one-hour episode we must cut away from the main characters to reveal the needed layers of more intricate plotting. In the action episode, which sells jeopardy and suspense, the writer must cut away to the antagonist (the villains), and their M.O. (modus operandi).

The Action Hour

Creating Jeopardy and Suspense

Action shows *sell action*. I don't mean action in one act, but rather action sustained throughout all four acts. I learned the hard way with my "Hart to Hart."

I considered the episode I wrote, "With These Harts I Thee Wed," to be about one of the worst that ever aired—other than one written by the producers themselves! I am safe in saying this because over the show's long run there were many who filled this seat. Some of the problems with the script were my fault; a lot of them weren't.

The story editors told me what they wanted. Jennifer's Auntie Mame was coming into town for her fifth wedding, which as I've mentioned was to be held at the Hart mansion. At the Act I end, the groom was to take a bite of the wedding cake and drop dead. That was the extent of what I was told, other than they wanted to use one of the Gabor sisters.

Like a good writer, I went to work figuring out who did it, why they were doing it, and how they were going about it.

Next, I researched the poison. After all, I wanted to be accurate. I called a local poison control center and asked the man on duty, "What kind of poison could be injected into a cake and kill immediately after it was ingested?" There was silence on the other end, after which he asked for my name and where I could be located! Realizing how this must have sounded, I quickly clicked down the receiver, which probably scared him further. To this day, the poor soul has probably never set foot inside another bakery!

In Act I, it was important that I reveal some necessary backstory. I needed to establish Jennifer's relationship with her aunt, and also that she was a wealthy and extravagant lady, so that when she arrives at their front door we are as surprised as Jonathan and Jennifer that Auntie has given up her very worldly possessions and tastes and has joined a religious sect. Donned in a robe with her groom-to-be at her side, she introduces the Harts to her future husband, a brother in the Fellowship of the Tent and Robe. I also needed to establish the red herring (the person we will suspect as the killer). He was one of Auntie's ex-hubbies, who comes to the wedding and disrupts the ceremony. Later, of course, it turns out the only reason the poor chump was there was because he loved her.

My fatal flaw while constructing this act was that I was so busy establishing the above elements that there was virtually no action or suspense until the end of Act I. What the story editor did to combat this problem, and what I feel serves as a wonderful lesson, is he inserted a scene at the top of the act: It is night and we are on the exterior of a bakery. Inside, a shadowy figure of a man pulls out a hypodermic needle. He begins injecting a cake. The camera pulls down to reveal the card in front of it that reads HOLD FOR JEN-NIFER HART. There you have it: action, jeopardy, and suspense—don't leave an act without them!

The Superior and Inferior Position of the Audience

There are different ways of creating jeopardy and suspense. One technique is by placing your audience in the superior position—that is, letting them know beforehand what could happen to your hero or heroes. By letting the audience know that the cake was reserved for the Harts, we knew that the Harts were in danger. We care about the Harts, so we stay tuned.

Let's create a scenario. A couple is going camping. We the writers establish beforehand that a brutal beast is stalking the area in which they are headed. They reach their destination, pitch their tent, and then cosily tuck in for the night. The beast approaches in the wee hours. He ravages their campsite, rips them apart, and has them for dinner (who said I didn't have any gore in my guts).

Where have we placed the audience? In the inferior or superior position? The *superior*, because *they know* before the campers what is about to happen. By inserting the bakery scene in the "Hart to Hart," this is precisely what the story editor was doing. He was letting us know up front that the cake was poisoned.

Let's return to our campers. Imagine now that we place our audience inside the tent. They hear a noise—something is lurking outside. After an eerie silence, the noise comes again. It approaches the tent. Suddenly, and without warning, a hideous presence bursts forth. Here, we have placed the audience in the *inferior* position. They are *discovering* the beast along *with* the campers.

In the "Columbo" series, the audience always saw the crime beforehand. They knew who did it, and even to a certain extent how the villains went about the crime. This superior position of the audience existed within the format of the show.

In "Murder She Wrote," the audience is always placed in the inferior position. We discover along with Jessica and watch as she unravels the clues. Shows such as "Columbo" and "Murder She Wrote" are unique. In most one-hour action episodes the writer bounces between both points of view. Again, writing is making choices. Consider both the superior and the inferior positions. Imagine yourself in the audience: Which, for you, would deliver the greatest impact?

Character + Dramatic Need + Obstacles = Conflict = Action

The bigger the obstacles, the stronger the conflict, and the more powerful the action. All too often in my script consulting, I've come across stories that are contrived and too convenient on the part of the writer. If you are scripting a story in which an undercover agent has to penetrate a high-security installation, do yourself a favor and don't let him conveniently slip through an open window. Such contrivances not only demean and diminish the power of your hero but they also destroy the credibility of your script. It is better to make it hard on yourself than easy on your hero. The trade-off is worth it. Push your characters to the limits. If you want to grab your audience, create a dilemma that pushes them against a wall; increase their jeopardy so they must climb up the wall; begin throwing rocks at them to raise the stakes until it appears there is no way out. Not until the last moment does your character, using cunning and ingenuity, manage to escape.

The Strong Antagonist and the Bold M.O.
You've probably guessed by now that in my writing I like to pull from personal experience. I suppose that is why, in the beginning, I had some problems with crime stories. Fortunately, I never had any run-ins with the law other than a few speeding tickets. Since I didn't have a criminal mind, and since my sole source of income was cop shows (at least for the first three years), I'd peruse newspapers and periodicals desperately searching for a crime or M.O. that grabbed me and that I could fictionalize. Actually, this method worked rather well. Producers love anything timely. If it's on the front page, they consider it a hot item.

Next, I'd go to work fully developing the crime: beginning, middle, and end. I'd jot down all the necessary story beats that needed to be revealed, then weave them into each act. The audience is continually fed bits of information. But, always in crafting suspense, you must keep them guessing.

It is crucial in creating all drama, whether action or character, that you give your main characters worthy opponents. The stronger the antagonist is, the stronger the protagonist must be. Who could be more ruthless than Alexis Carrington or J. R. Ewing? It is the opposing forces of good and evil, the battle of wills, that creates the conflict that moves the story forward. (We will cover character development in a later chapter.)

Structuring the One-Hour Episode

The hour show consists of four acts. These scripts are about fifty-five to sixty pages, or about one minute per page. On the average, each act runs about fourteen pages. I must stress again that this averaging technique is only a gauge to help the writer stay on track, pagewise, to "come in on the dime." If an act runs twenty pages you don't have to scrap it; you simply need to compensate somewhere else.

In the hour structure, I find it too confusing to average the number of scenes per act. The reason is that you may have many establishing shots. Technically, these constitute a scene (see the example on the following pages). What is important is that your scenes do not exceed two-and-a-half to three pages each.

A friend, and very successful television writer, once told me that he gets very nervous when his scenes run long. Why? Because the writer then is relying too heavily on dialogue and exposition rather than on visuals to pace and progress the story forward. A diagram of the four-act structure appears on page 89.

Act I is the setup act. As we have covered in earlier chapters, it establishes what the story is about and the dramatic need of the character or characters. Because of time limitation, the writer must get into the story quickly and hook the audience fast. The setup must be complete by the third or fourth scene.

Acts II and III are the confrontation acts. It is here that your characters meet the majority of their obstacles. Each obstacle creates conflict that builds the necessary tension. Act IV is the resolution act. Here, the plot builds to a climax and is resolved.

The Act Breaks

Each act in the hour episode is a separate unit with a crisis and a climax all its own. Acts are separated by commercial breaks.

The most important act end, what producers tag the cliff-hanger, happens at the end of Act II, because the break here runs twice the length of the other commercials. This point is where the biggest crisis, the most teeth-clenching moment in your story, should take place.

The second most powerful act end, or high point, is at the end of Act I. Here, audience interest must be peaked so they will return to the show after the break. Next comes the Act III end, and finally Act IV. At the end of each act there's a commercial. The running time of

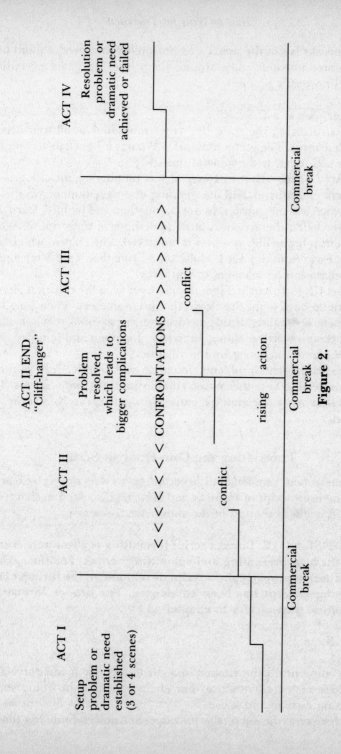

Figure 2.

these breaks is not the writer's responsibility; however, a good tele-play writer not only plots around them but also gears everything toward powerful act ends.

Each Act Serves a Purpose

While structuring the show the writer must look at all four acts as complete units. The writer must ask, "What is it I need to accomplish in this act? What is the general thrust?"

In Act I of the "Hart to Hart," it was Jennifer's aunt, the groom, an angry ex-husband, and the wedding that were building to the act end, which was the murder. In Act II, Jonathan and Jennifer learn that whoever killed the groom is after something in their house. When they return home they discover it ransacked. The culprit, who is still inside, escapes in the Act II cliff-hanger. Jonathan goes after him in a car chase but he manages to slip away.

In Act III, Jonathan and Jennifer discover what the culprit is after—an antique book—but they learn that it is valueless. Then Jonathan rips open the binding. Inside, he discovers a passbook to a Bahamian bank account worth millions. In Act IV, Jonathan and Jennifer, with Auntie Mame's help, set up the villains.

Each act presents problems. Jonathan and Jennifer resolve them, but they lead to yet other unsolved questions or complications. The conflict carries us through the entire show and is resolved at the Act IV end.

Translating the One-Hour to Script

To help us better understand structure, let us walk through excerpts of a one-hour script of "Starsky and Hutch," discussed in chapter 5. We will begin at the top of the show, Act I, Scene 1.

(PLEASE NOTE: Correct script formatting is absolutely crucial for writers in presenting and submitting scripts. For the sake of space, and to properly show script development, the format of the following excerpt has been condensed. For proper formatting guidelines, please refer to chapter 13.)

Act I, Scene 1

We come in on the runner, though this is not mandatory. This device is excellent since your characters must be doing some-thing in time and space.

In this scene the subplot is introduced. Another body has turned up from strychnine poisoning. Dobey announces there is something else that Starsky and Hutch need to know, and asks the boys to come into his office.

The scene was running two-and-a-half pages here—time to change locales and keep the pictures moving.

STARSKY AND HUTCH

"The Heroes"

ACT I

FADE IN:

INT. SQUAD ROOM—DAY

STARSKY and HUTCH enter and head for the coffee.

>   STARSKY
> I'm telling ya, it's the only way
> to go nowadays . . . (pouring coffee)
> Look, the way property's going up,
> you can almost double your money!

>   HUTCH
> What are you going to invest with?

>   STARSKY
> We'll take out a loan.

>   HUTCH
> Oh, *we* will?!

>   STARSKY
> Yeah! You know Yost in homicide?
> He did it, bought a little place,
> sat on it, then turned it over . . .
> Made a bundle on the deal. We
> could do the same thing!

>   HUTCH
> Starsky, are you asking me to live
> with you?

>   STARSKY
> We're not going to live there;
> it's an investment. (a beat) We'll get ourselves
> a little fixer-upper.

> HUTCH
>
> Who's going to do the fixing?

> STARSKY
>
> Us!

> HUTCH
>
> Starsky, you can't even drive a
> nail straight!

> STARSKY
>
> No, listen, a little paint . . . a
> little plaster . . . a few shrubs . . .

> HUTCH
>
> A roof . . . Maybe some plumbing . . .

> STARSKY (enthusiastic)
>
> Yeah, yeah!

> HUTCH
>
> How much you figure this little
> venture's going to cost?

> STARSKY
>
> Let's see . . . With a loan, I'd say
> we can make the down for about
> three grand.

> HUTCH
>
> Each?

> STARSKY
>
> No, together . . . pooled.

> HUTCH
>
> Where do you plan to find this
> house?

> STARSKY
>
> There're places.

> HUTCH (a beat)
>
> Three grand, huh? You can't even
> pick up a camper for that.

DOBEY comes out of his office; walks over.

> DOBEY (holding file)
>
> I got the Coroner's report on Wells.

> HUTCH
>
> Strychnine?

> DOBEY (nods yes)
>
> Gelatin capsules again.

> STARSKY
>
> That's the second one this week.

> **HUTCH**
> We better get word out; looks like
> somebody's passing bad stuff.
>
> **DOBEY**
> Run it through RI . . . Check for
> similar MOs. We may have some
> nut out there making a sport of
> killing junkies. (handing file)
> Here, Wells used to work at the
> Temple Street Market. (a beat)
> There's one more thing . . . We might
> as well get this over with . . . Want
> to come in the office?
>
> Starsky and Hutch exchange a glance. As they move for Dobey's office:
>
> **HUTCH**
> Captain, what's this about?

■   ■   ■

Act I, Scene 2

Notice how conflict creates the dialogue and the necessary exposition to move the story forward.

Pointing an arrow—This technique is wonderful for plugging holes in a story. A question arose while scripting: Why, out of all the cops in Los Angeles, does this columnist want Starsky and Hutch? By pointing an arrow through dialogue, Dobey answers the question.

The reporter enters and introduces the main story. She also provides a fun twist.

> **INT. DOBEY'S OFFICE**
>
> Dobey at his desk; Starsky and Hutch across from him.
>
> **DOBEY**
> Well . . . You see . . . (not relishing this)
> You're not going alone . . .
> You're going to have company.
>
> **STARSKY**
> What?!
>
> **DOBEY**
> C. D. Phelps, a syndicated
> columnist for the Tribune, is
> going with you.

STARSKY
What's he doing with us?!

DOBEY
Writing a two-part article on what
he calls "Counter Culture Cops—
The New Breed."

HUTCH
Look, Captain, we've got two
possible homicides . . . We could be
into something heavy . . . Assign him
to somebody else!

DOBEY
He likes your track record; you're
the ones he wants.

STARSKY
This is the street we're talking
about; we might have to arm
wrestle, you know?!

DOBEY
The Department needs to build
public relations; I'm in agreement.
Look, it's only for four days.

STARSKY
I don't care what the Department
needs; stick Walter Cronkite in
somebody else's backseat!
(There's a KNOCK at the door.)

DOBEY
Yeah?

A woman sticks her head in.

CHRISTINE
Captain Dobey?

DOBEY
What can I do for you?

She walks over and extends her hand. Dobey stands.

CHRISTINE
C. D. Phelps.

She is not what Starsky and Hutch expected. Cerebral, yes . . . enough
to make any guy think all sorts of thoughts. She's got a sexy, intellectual
look, full mouth and warm eyes underneath a pair of very stylish glasses
. . . and under that loose-fitting silk blouse and tailored skirt . . . a body

that's incitement to riot. Starsky and Hutch exchange a glance; get a load of that!

> DOBEY (shaking hands;
> awkwardly)
> Miss . . . Ms. Phelps, it's a pleasure.

> CHRISTINE
> Call me Chris.

> DOBEY
> All right . . . Well, I suppose there
> should be some introduction. (gesturing)
> Chris . . . this is Det. Sgt. Hutchinson . . .

> HUTCH (a big smile)
> Ken.

> CHRISTINE (extending her hand)
> Hello, Ken.

> DOBEY
> And Det. Sgt. Starsky.

> STARSKY (totally taken)
> Hi . . .

> CHRISTINE (shaking his hand)
> Hello.

> STARSKY
> My name's Dave.

She smiles; takes a beat.

> CHRISTINE
> I'm looking forward to working
> with the two of you.

> DOBEY
> There may be some change . . .

> STARSKY (interrupting)
> Captain, can we have a word with
> you?

■ ■ ■

Act I, Scene 3

By the scene end, our setup is complete. We know what the story is about. The boys have decided to take Christine on the streets with them.

Dobey tells Starsky and Hutch not to take any in-progress calls.
Later, this action will be interpreted by Christine to be neglect.
We are foreshadowing.

INT. SQUAD ROOM
Starsky, Hutch and Dobey stand outside the office.

> DOBEY
> What is it, Starsky?

> STARSKY
> Well, Capt'n, if it's just for a
> few days . . . I think we can manage
> . . . Don't you think so, Hutch?

> HUTCH
> Oh, yeah . . . I don't see any . . . ah
> . . . reason why we can't handle it.

> DOBEY
> You're all heart! (a beat) Okay, I'm pulling
> you off every thing except the dope. Don't
> answer calls . . . Don't concern yourselves
> with anything other than the one case. She's
> very important to us . . . Give the Department
> a good image, huh? Show her the good side.

> HUTCH
> You got it, Captain.

Dobey walks back in the office; as Hutch starts to follow, Starsky taps
him on the shoulder.

> STARSKY
> Hey, you got some of that breath
> spray?

> HUTCH
> Don't you know; aerosols destroy
> the ozone!

He pulls out a Binaca bottle, puts a few drops on his hand, licks
it.

> STARSKY
> Gimme that.

Starsky takes the bottle, puts it directly on his tongue.

> HUTCH
> Do *you* mind?! You just got your
> germs all over my breath freshener.

> STARSKY (handing it back)
> Here.
>
> HUTCH
> Keep it.
>
> They enter Dobey's office.

· · ·

Act I, Scenes 4 and 5

We are moving with the Torino. This opportunity is Christine's first to question Starsky and Hutch. It is an excellent time to get out needed exposition.

On page 9, another arrow is pointed: Strychnine is almost impossible to come by. The hole is plugged when Christine asks her question.

> EXT. TORINO—ESTABLISHING—DAY
>
> INT. TORINO—STARSKY, HUTCH AND CHRISTINE
>
> CHRISTINE
> I'm not out to do a hatchet job;
> I'm here to do a story . . . Are
> either of you familiar with my
> column?
>
> HUTCH
> We know of it, we read the Tribune.
>
> CHRISTINE
> Good. Then you know what I'm
> after . . . There's a new breed of
> cop out there . . .
>
> STARSKY
> And we're it, huh?
>
> CHRISTINE
> I want my readers to know about
> you . . . How you perceive crime . . .
> relate to each other . . . I have to
> experience it . . . It's the only
> way I can capture you.
>
> STARSKY (lightly)
> Anytime!
>
> She smiles; a beat then:

CHRISTINE
So, you want to fill me in? What
are you working on?

HUTCH
Two junkies, both dead from
strychnine. We're trying to find
the supplier . . . Get word out.

STARSKY
Right now, the only thing we've
got to go on; he's using
conventional bags . . . He's passing
it out in capsules.

CHRISTINE
Isn't strychnine hard to come by?

STARSKY
Not in rat poison.

CHRISTINE
But it was banned.

HUTCH
Only over the counter . . . There's
old store rooms . . . people's
garages . . .

The radio sounds.

RADIO VOICE
All units, all units in the
vicinity, robbery in progress,
liquor store, Fifth and Mason.

CHRISTINE
A couple of blocks from here . . .

Starsky and Hutch exchange a glance.

CHRISTINE (continuing)
Aren't you going to answer that?

STARSKY
Somebody else will get it.

Hutch slings his arm over the seat.

HUTCH (big smile)
So, Chris . . . Tell me about yourself.
How long have you been writing?

■ ■ ■

Act I, Scene 6

Notice how the choice of locales created the dialogue for this scene. The narrative is visual and keeps the audience occupied while more exposition is revealed.

INT. TEMPLE STREET MARKET—DAY

A small open-end market, à la the Hollywood Ranch. The place is loaded with activity. Starsky, Hutch and Christine walk past the fruit and vegetable stands to the meat section.

INT. BACK ROOM—MEAT SECTION

TONY, a grubby, unshaven man, late forties, quarters a slab of beef. A cigarette dangles from his mouth. On the counter lie various cuts of stacked meat, uncovered; haven for an occasional fly. A sticky transistor nearby PLAYS LOUDLY. Starsky, Hutch and Christine enter.

> STARSKY (fighting the
> music)
> You Tony?! Hey, you Tony?!

> TONY (turning down
> the radio)
> Yeah, what about it?

> STARSKY (flashing badge)
> Police.

Tony takes a long drag from his cigarette, places it on the counter and grabs for another piece of meat. He continues cutting.

> TONY
> What do you want?

> HUTCH
> Information. Remember a guy named
> Wells? He used to work here.

> TONY
> Never heard of him.

He turns the radio back up. Hutch grabs it and turns it off.

> HUTCH
> You're just loaded with personality!

> TONY
> Can't you see I'm busy here?!

> STARSKY
> Hey, Hutch, would you look at the
> size of that!

HUTCH
What, the filet?

STARSKY
The fly. (hitting his arm) There's another one!

HUTCH
The place is crawling with them!
I wonder what the Board of Health'll
say about that!

TONY
All right . . . So Wells worked here
a short time.

STARSKY
Our galloping gourmet has a tongue! (a beat)
What do you know about him?

TONY
He was a hype . . . strung out . . . I
let him go.

STARSKY
When?

TONY
Two, three months back.

HUTCH
Any idea where he bought his
stuff?

TONY
No way I get messed up in that.

STARSKY
What about friends, did he hang
out anywhere?

TONY
Yeah, there was some place, I
think it was called Al's. He used
to play pool down there. Enough,
huh? I got work to do.

HUTCH
Thanks, you've been a real help.

STARSKY
Prime cut.

■ ■ ■

Starsky and Hutch chase down and interrogate these leads, all the while playfully coming on to Christine. At Al's (a pool and bar joint referred to in the earlier scene), they talk to Sweet Alice, a hooker and user who rents a room upstairs. She remembers the dead man, Wells, who hung out downstairs, but has no idea where he got his stuff. As they leave, Alice desperately calls Hutch aside and tells him business has been really bad lately. He slips her a bill while Christine watches in the background.

As the act builds to an end, Starsky, Hutch, and Christine are seated at an outdoor cafe having lunch. Starsky glances to the street and notices something. This scene is the last in the act (Scene 11). The act runs twenty pages.

Act I, Scene 11

Notice how the device of the fall guy provides a needed punch for the act end. He serves to substantiate Christine's already negative feelings toward the cops and also provides us with more action.

It is here that Christine tips her hand, thereby placing the audience in the superior position. We, the audience, now know that she is out to get Starsky and Hutch.

The camera angle (P.O.V.) is necessary in order to establish what Starsky is watching. When the camera returns to the original picture it is called a *resume* shot.

Each camera angle in this sequence helps to further tell our story.

STARSKY, HUTCH AND CHRISTINE

Sitting at a table, halfway through lunch. A portable tape recorder is running.

> CHRISTINE
> What about this "Sweet Alice?"

> STARSKY
> What about her?

> CHRISTINE
> She's a hooker . . . You said she
> uses, may even push . . . Why do
> you let her operate?

> STARSKY
> Same reason we let a lot of
> people operate. They're
> informers, we need them.

CHRISTINE
In other words, it's okay to break
the law if you're useful.

HUTCH
No; it's just that, without them,
we've got no link to the street . . . (a beat)
Look, today they're informants,
tomorrow suspects and arrestees.
Right now they serve more purpose
where they are.

ON STARSKY

His attention is somewhere else. He's spotted something across the street.

HIS P.O.V.—A MAN

Mid-thirties, walks slowly along the curb. He spots a Cadillac Seville rounding the corner; waits a beat; then does his number; an incredibly good and terrifying flop in front of the wheels. The car screeches to a halt. The driver, a rich-looking elderly woman, gets out, hysterical.

DRIVER
Oh my God!

She looks down at the moaning victim; practically wedged beneath the wheels.

VICTIM
My back . . . I can't move . . .

RESUME STARSKY, HUTCH AND CHRISTINE

Starsky takes another bite of his burrito.

STARSKY
There's always something to screw
up your lunch.

HUTCH
No kidding.

They get up; casually walk over. Starsky takes his Coke with him.

ANGLE ON THE MOANING VICTIM

The Driver kneels beside him; trying to help. Starsky and Hutch walk into SHOT.

DRIVER (frantic)
What should I do?! Tell me what
to do!

With a reassuring look, like it's going to be okay; Hutch extends his hand to her; helps her up.

> HUTCH
> It's going to be all right.

Starsky takes a long look at the victim.

> STARSKY
> Well . . . Well . . . Well . . .

While the victim continues moaning, Starsky, still holding his Coke, tips the cup, pouring the remains on the victim's head.

> DRIVER (hysterically)
> Are you out of your mind?! The
> man is in pain!

ON CHRISTINE

At table, watching incredulously.

RESUME STARSKY, VICTIM

He's stopped moaning; wipes the Coke out of his eyes.

> VICTIM (yelling)
> Hey, what do you think you're
> doing?!

He looks up and sees Starsky.

> STARSKY
> Depositing my Coke.

> DRIVER
> How can you do such a thing?!

> HUTCH (to Driver)
> He's not hurt . . . You didn't hit
> him. This is his specialty;
> insurance scams.

> STARSKY
> Larry "the fall guy." He takes
> a better dive than "The Flying
> Berninis." (to the Victim) Get up.

> VICTIM
> Okay, okay, I'm up.

> STARSKY
> Next time you take a tumble, make
> it the freeway. Now get outta here!

The Victim heeds Starsky's advice; hightails it out of there, with all the agility and quickness of a very well man.

> HUTCH (to Driver)
> Are you all right?

> DRIVER (still watching Victim)
> I don't believe it.

STARSKY, HUTCH

They walk back toward Christine, cocky as hell.

> STARSKY
> She's checking me out.

> HUTCH
> She's looking at me.

> STARSKY
> Think so, huh? Wanna up that
> little wager?

> HUTCH
> You're on, hotshot.

ON CHRISTINE

Talking into tape recorder.

> CHRISTINE
> These two think they're a couple
> of real "heroes."

> FADE OUT.

> END OF ACT I

■　■　■

Act II

At the top of Act II, Paul Rizzo is introduced—the man Starsky and Hutch's investigation will lead them to. (*Note:* This point is extremely late in the story to plant the antagonist. It works only because the Rizzo theme is the subplot, not the main story. The true antagonist is Christine and she was introduced on page 5 of the script. It is also important to note that one act should never be closed or another one opened without the star being in one or both scenes. Since Starsky and Hutch were in the last scene of Act I, we could open Act II without them.)

We first see Rizzo watching inconspicuously from a corner table as Sweet Alice pleads with dealer Karl Reagan. Alice needs a fix but the unsympathetic Reagan tells her she has come up short too many times.

Starsky, Hutch, and Christine are in the car when the call comes over the radio: Another body has turned up from a possible overdose. The Torino races through the streets and arrives on the heels of the coroner's wagon. The location is Al's. Upstairs, Alice lies on the floor, a tourniquet and syringe beside her. The medical examiner identifies the cause of death as strychnine poisoning.

Christine is sickened by what she sees and tells Starsky and Hutch that this death might not have happened had they pulled Alice in when they were supposed to. Downstairs at Al's, Starsky and Hutch harass the regulars in the bar for needed information.

The action in Act II continues to build until the act end, or Cliff-hanger.

The Cliff-hanger (Act II End)

Here Starsky and Hutch discover Christine's true motives and the major crisis in the story takes place. (*Note:* In episodes and Movies of the Week, all acts end with FADE OUT and begin with FADE IN.)

INT. SQUAD ROOM—MORNING

Starsky enters. Hutch is seated at his desk reading the newspaper.

>   STARSKY
> Good morning.

>   HUTCH
> You think so?

He throws the paper to Starsky, who catches it.

>   STARSKY
> The Tribune?

>   HUTCH
> The bet's off, she's all yours.

CLOSE ON THE OPINION SECTION

In bold print: "The Heroes," by C. D. Phelps.

>   HUTCH (continuing)
> Read it, it's lovely.

Starsky skims the article while Hutch gives a verbal synopsis.

HUTCH (continuing)
"Long hair . . . hot dog car . . . Popeye
tactics" . . . The nicest thing she
called us was belligerent!

STARSKY
I don't believe it!

HUTCH
Believe it! You want the prize
quotes? I've committed them to
memory. "Does bravado and
belligerence hide behind the
badge?" . . .

STARSKY (finding the spot; reading)
"For two days now, I've witnessed
leisurely police work; calls
being ignored and literally seen
harassment of the innocent! This
is the New Breed? A case in point . . . "

HUTCH (from memory)
"Two undercover police officers
that for the time being we'll
call . . . "

STARSKY (looking up)
Mutt and Jeff?!

FADE OUT

END OF ACT II

. . .

Act III

We open Act III with Starsky and Hutch in Dobey's office. The ser-
geant is on the phone, getting heavy flack from Internal Affairs. What
began as an attempt at good PR has turned into a terrible embarrass-
ment for the department. Starsky and Hutch want Christine out of
their car, but Dobey insists getting rid of her would be playing right
into her hands. There is nothing they can do; she's in until her next
column is out. The brief scene that follows consists of four short
speeches. It is all that is needed.

INT. SQUAD ROOM—DAY

Christine is waiting by Starsky and Hutch's desks when they exit
Dobey's office. They look at her a moment.

> HUTCH
> Thanks for the hurrah.

> STARSKY
> You are really something, Lady!

> CHRISTINE
> I call them as I see them.

> STARSKY
> What you *saw* was censored, now
> you're going to see the real
> thing.

■ ■ ■

(Notice how the last line in the prior scene makes for a powerful
cut.) What follows is a short action sequence with Starsky and Hutch
pursuing the lead they got on Karl Reagan during their investigation
in Act II. The sequence consists of five camera angles.

Angle 1: Torino
Angle 2: Various angles (this suggests many shots, but the writer
   is essentially saying to the director, they are up to you)
Angle 3: Mustang
Angle 4: Torino
Angle 5: Karl Reagan

TORINO

As it fishtails around a corner; in hot pursuit of a vintage Mustang.

VARIOUS ANGLES

As the chase continues through the city streets.

MUSTANG

takes a sharp turn . . . too sharp, goes into a spin then crashes into the
curb.

TORINO

screeches to a halt. Starsky and Hutch jump out; rush over.

               STARSKY
        Get out!

ANGLE ON KARL REAGAN

Behind the wheel. He gets out.

               REAGAN (assuming the position)
        Look, that stuff Alice got. It
        wasn't mine!

Hutch begins frisking.

               REAGAN (continuing)
        Don't get excited, I got nothin'
        on me!

               HUTCH (pulls out a wad of bills)
        Oh, look at this, Starsky, big ones.
        Good day huh, Reagan?

               REAGAN (turning around; angered)
        You got no right to do this!
        I'm not holding!

               STARSKY
        Oh, you're just full of your
        rights, aren't you. What'd you
        do, swallow it? We can find
        that out real fast.

Starsky clenches his fist.

               REAGAN (reacting)
        No!

ON CHRISTINE

Standing near the car, watching.

RESUME—STARSKY, HUTCH AND REAGAN

               REAGAN
        I swear I didn't give Alice
        nothin'! She called, said she
        had some buyers, when I got
        there she didn't have the
        price. Ask Al, he knows, he
        saw us there.

The stories jibe; they've got nothing to hold him on.

> STARSKY
> Word has it you've started
> passing down to high schools
> . . . Bend your ear, Reagan,
> cause if I catch you within
> five miles of one I'm going
> to smear you across the
> street. Understood?!
>
> Hutch stuffs the wad back in Reagan's shirt.

■ ■ ■

The easiest and most effective device for revealing character exposition is through conflict. In this scene that directly follows, Starsky, Hutch, and Christine lay their cards on the table.

> STARSKY AND HUTCH
>
> They walk back to the Torino.
>
> STARSKY (to Christine)
> You gonna stand there, or are
> you going to get in?!
>
> CHRISTINE
> Like to give everybody a rough
> time, don't you.
>
> HUTCH
> That's good coming from you.
>
> CHRISTINE
> Look, maybe we better get this
> out in the open.
>
> STARSKY
> All right, shoot.
>
> CHRISTINE
> I write a commentary on the times,
> the police department not excluded
> . . . No names were mentioned . . . no
> lies were printed . . . It was all
> subjective to my point of view.
>
> HUTCH
> You make Rex Reed look mellow!

        CHRISTINE
Why are you so defensive? I made
a social statement, not a personal
attack.

        HUTCH
Where do you get off writing a
commentary on something you know
nothing about?!

        CHRISTINE
Look, I can defend my actions,
can you? I was there, I saw you
ignore those calls, there was no
reason for it!

Starsky and Hutch exchange a glance, she's the reason.

        CHRISTINE (continuing)
First you play games then you
play cop . . . Where do you get
off using mindless, needless
violence, harassing people you
don't have enough evidence to
pull in!

        STARSKY (throwing up his arms)
Oh! . . . Now she screams brutality!

        HUTCH
Look, you can't possibly understand
what's coming down . . .

        STARSKY
Maybe you're not too clear on what
we're doing here. Some nut's out
there playing with strychnine . . .
just waiting for another victim
. . . he's probably making a deal
right now! I'm too violent?!
Fine. Tell me how much violence
is just enough to stop him!

Christine doesn't have an answer.

■ ■ ■

    In the remainder of the act, Rizzo kills another victim, and Starsky
and Hutch still have no leads. En route to the precinct with Christine,
they respond to an attempted rape call. The car screeches to a halt
in front of an abandoned laundry where a woman's screams can be
heard coming from inside. Starsky and Hutch burst through the door,

guns leveled, and corner the attacker like an animal. It appears this act may turn Christine around, but instead it creates even bigger problems.

Again, it is the conflict that carries the scene and builds us to our Act III end. Notice where the scene opens—at the tail end. Often, while scripting, it helps to cut into the scene as late as possible, thus cutting out unnecessary explaining and getting right to the guts of the matter.

INT. SQUAD ROOM—DAY

Starsky, Hutch and Christine.

> CHRISTINE
> You mean you've got to let
> him go?!

> STARSKY
> We're not going to let him do
> anything . . . She refuses to sign
> the crime report!

> CHRISTINE
> You mean a rapist is just going
> to walk out of here?!

> STARSKY
> Look, she insists he didn't
> harm her.

> HUTCH
> Without the victim's cooperation,
> odds are the DA won't even file.
> It wouldn't hold up in court.

> CHRISTINE
> But I was a witness, so were you!

> STARSKY (losing patience)
> That's not the way it works, Chris!

> CHRISTINE
> The way it works! That's exactly
> what I'm talking about! You throw
> a pool player around for information
> and you handle a rapist with kid
> gloves! What's with you guys?!

> STARSKY
> All you people do is talk! We're
> the ones that have to work with
> these laws . . . I'm sick of you
> trying to lay a guilt trip on me!

> STARSKY (continued)
> What do you think, we enjoy it?!
> If the girl won't press charges,
> there's nothing we can do about it.
>
> CHRISTINE
> She's scared . . . Let me talk to her.
>
> HUTCH
> Chris, she spoke with a woman; we
> have a trained staff for that.
>
> STARSKY
> What do you want from us?!
>
> CHRISTINE (a beat)
> Maybe a little more sensitivity.
>
> STARSKY
> You could use some of that in
> your article!

She storms out.

> HUTCH
> Cool down, Starsk.
>
> STARSKY
> She's something else! . . . What is
> her problem?!
>
> HUTCH
> Look, don't let her get to you.
> She's only got one more day.
> Right now we've got more
> important things to worry about.

■ ■ ■

The last scene of Act III is visual, and implies there will be yet another victim.

EXT. STREET—DAY

Rizzo stands near a cheap food concession; making a deal with a young pusher. We watch the transaction. Rizzo hands him some packets in exchange for a bill.

FADE OUT

END OF ACT III

■ ■ ■

Act IV

In the Act IV resolution, Starsky and Hutch track Paul Rizzo to Woodview Psychiatric Hospital where they learn he was a voluntary patient who has recently been released. Rizzo had arrived there distraught after his sister's death; he had raised her. With this information, Starsky and Hutch have what they need. The bulk of Act IV, the entire thrust, is locating Rizzo.

They track him down in an abandoned apartment building. The *action sequence* follows, which takes us to the end of Act IV.

In this act, the main story and the subplot come together, or dovetail, and of course Starsky and Hutch's actions are justified. (Christine, later in the tag, which follows the commercial, will make a public apology and print a retraction in her article.)

Notice the fast-paced cuts between INT. and EXT. shots, and the various locations used to add jeopardy, suspense, and needed action.

EXT. RIZZO APARTMENT BUILDING—DAY

The Torino pulls up and stops. Starsky and Hutch climb out.

> STARSKY (to Christine)
> Stay in the car.

> CHRISTINE
> I signed a waiver, you're not
> responsible.

> STARSKY
> Have it your way, just don't
> get in ours.

Starsky and Hutch start toward the building.

INT. HALLWAY

Starsky and Hutch enter. The shabby entranceway is filled with garbage; the paint on the walls peeling off in great chunks. They walk down the narrow hallway and stop in front of a door.

> HUTCH (pounding)
> Open up Rizzo, police!

No answer.

CUT INSIDE TO:

INT. RIZZO APARTMENT

Rizzo stands frozen, pressed against the wall. After a moment he reaches for a gun.

> STARSKY (V.O.)
> Come on, Rizzo, we know you're
> in there!

Rizzo makes a move toward the window.

INT. HALLWAY

Starsky and Hutch take opposite ends of the door; guns at their sides. Hutch signals; ready. With great force, Starsky kicks open the door. They burst in, guns leveled.

INT. RIZZO'S APARTMENT

The room is empty. Starsky and Hutch head for the open window leading to the fire escape.

EXT. FIRE ESCAPE

They appear on the landing. We notice now that Rizzo is waiting on the landing above.

ANGLE ON CHRISTINE

as she enters the building.

STARSKY AND HUTCH

They slowly ascend the fire escape. Hutch leads. Rizzo pointing a .38.

Hutch moves into sight. He spots Rizzo; ducks. A bullet ricochets off a rung; just missing him.

Rizzo moves for the roof.

Starsky and Hutch follow. They have him in perfect gun sight now.

> HUTCH
> Hold it, Rizzo!

Rizzo continues for the roof; manages to climb on.

EXT. ROOF—DAY

Rizzo races across the roof.

Starsky and Hutch emerge just as Christine appears at the doorway leading to the roof.

Rizzo grabs her and pulls them both to cover behind an electrical unit. He fires.

                    STARSKY (to Hutch)
          I'll take the other side.

There is an exchange of fire as Starsky dashes across the roof; makes
it.

                    HUTCH
          Rizzo . . .

                    RIZZO
          Leave me alone!

                    HUTCH
          We don't want to hurt you.

                    RIZZO (frightened, shaking)
          Stay away! . . . You're just like
          the others.

                    HUTCH
          What others, Rizzo?

Starsky appears behind Rizzo and very carefully begins moving in.

                    RIZZO (yelling)
          The ones that hurt my sister . . .
          They paid for it . . . I'm glad
          they're dead!

                    HUTCH
          We know why you did it, Rizzo.
          We want to help you.

                    RIZZO (voice cracking)
          They got her on that stuff, then
          they killed her with it!

ANGLE ON CHRISTINE

panicked; watching.

RESUME RIZZO

Starsky is almost upon him. Rizzo hears something, turns, sees Starsky
with a gun.

                    CHRISTINE (yelling to Starsky)
          Shoot him!

Rizzo's gun is pointed at Starsky; he's a quivering wreck of a man.

Starsky takes his gun by the barrel and very carefully places it on the
electrical unit.

                    STARSKY
          You see?! (a beat) I don't want to hurt you . . .
          Why do you want to hurt me?

                    RIZZO
          I have to. Those people . . .
          Somebody has to stop them . . .
          They deserve to die.

                    STARSKY
          Lori wouldn't have wanted that.

Rizzo begins to cry.

                    RIZZO
          They killed her . . . those pushers
          . . . they killed my little sister . . .

Starsky gently takes the gun from Rizzo's hand.

                    STARSKY
          I know.

CAMERA WIDENS to include Christine and Hutch who have joined
Starsky.

                    CHRISTINE (to Starsky)
          He could have killed you . . . Why
          didn't you shoot him?

Starsky looks down at the sobbing Rizzo.

                    HUTCH
          It wasn't necessary.

                                        FADE OUT

                    END OF ACT IV

                    ▪ ▪ ▪

Action shows work on the conflict of life and death. In creating
these shows, place your characters in a great amount of danger and
then play it out until the end of Act IV. Jeopardy and suspense are
killed unless you wait until the very last moment.

Hour Dramas and the Soaps

Hour dramas and the soaps rely on larger casts, simultaneous storylines, subplots, runners, and a fast pace, cutting between these elements to grab their audiences. Examples of these types of shows

include "L.A. Law," "thirtysomething," "China Beach," and the highly unique and romantic "Beauty and the Beast."

Among the favorite nighttime soaps are the long-running "Dallas," "Dynasty," "Falcon Crest," and "Knots Landing." Many of these shows incorporate jeopardy and suspense into their scripts, but these elements are not what they sell. Rather, they sell characters and conflict. The storylines of these shows are more personal and revolve around such human emotions as love, fear, loss, anxiety, jealousy, ambition—essentially all of the conflicts we experience in our everyday lives.

"L.A. Law" is not about lawyers but about people who happen to be lawyers. It is not about the McKenzie Brackman law offices but rather the people who work inside.

"Beauty and the Beast" is not about a career woman, or the secret underground passageways of the city. It is about the very special relationship between Katherine and Vincent.

"China Beach" is not about Vietnam. It's about people, their relationships, and the hardships and sacrifices of living through war. Vietnam is only the arena or backdrop that the show is set against—it could be any war.

Character + Dramatic Need + Obstacles = Conflict = Drama

Like the half-hour comedy, hour dramas and the soaps play off the conflicts of the human condition. They focus on human weaknesses, imperfections, and difficult predicaments. Instead of laughing we, the audience, are looking from the flip side of the coin, the dramatic viewpoint. We identify with these characters because we have the same shortcomings and problems.

How, you may wonder, do you identify with J. R. Ewing? You've never been to Texas, and the only thing you know about oil is that it comes with vinegar on your salad. And what about the Carringtons on "Dynasty"? Ten years ago the networks did not want shows dealing with wealth. They felt middle America couldn't identify with them.

One day my former partner and I got a call from producer Leonard Katzman, who we had worked with earlier on "Petrocelli." He gave us a pilot script to read that was being developed by David Jacobs, entitled "Dallas." I read the script and knew it would be a hit. It was television's version of one of the all-time classics, *Giant*. David Jacobs' characters were sensational and so was his writing.

Needless to say, the show has been incredibly successful, with viewers across all socioeconomic lines. Why? Because it doesn't matter how rich these characters are; we identify with their conflicts. Their problems are as bad as ours. There's anger, contempt, backstabbing, and revenge seeking. This show sells problems and conflicts in the family arena.

Structuring
The format for one-hour dramas and the soaps is identical to that of action episodes. The structuring is a bit more complicated, however.

For an example, let's use an episode of "L.A. Law." The script was cut between four storylines:

1. *The main story:* Abby Perkins takes on a high-paying drug dealer client. She gets him paroled and he skips bail.
2. *The alternate main story:* Anne Kelsey and her husband, tax attorney Stuart Markowitz, learn that the mother of their adopted child is taking legal action to get her baby back.
3. *The subplot:* Roxanne's very nice but boring husband wins the businessman of the year award.
4. *The alternate subplot:* Jonathan, the junior member of the firm, hires and becomes very smitten with his beautiful new law clerk. He discovers she is married.

In addition, riddled throughout the show were multiple runners that used the entire cast. When scripting this type of show, the writer must develop each story separately, with a strong beginning, middle, and end, and then decide how to cut and weave between the stories to achieve good pacing and to create the strongest effect. Following is an exercise that can help you. Order a script from the show you choose to write for and make a photocopy. Using this copy, identify the main stories and subplots. Cut and paste each story so you can read it separately in its entirety. Then read the shooting draft again. Study how the writer chose to cut between the various storylines to give the script momentum, tempo, and impact.

When developing your own script proceed the same way. First, identify each story separately, by beginning, middle, and end. Then step out of the script, focusing on how you can most effectively cut between the stories.

Writing for these types of shows is fun and more challenging than writing for linear shows. The device of cutting away from the dramatic action of one story and into another can be very powerful.

A Word About Dramadies

Dramadies, or drama-comedies, run a half-hour in length and are filmed. These shows use both the dramatic and the comedic viewpoints, and therefore incorporate elements of both the drama and the situation comedy. They use the same format as the hour and two-hour Movies for Television (see chapter 13): One page equals one minute of film. Therefore, the scripts are about twenty-eight to thirty-one pages.

Since these shows are not limited in their set structure or by casts, they can be scripted in the same fashion as a one-hour episode. Examples of dramadies are "The Days and Nights of Molly Dodd" and "Hooperman." "The Wonder Years" is also filmed and uses this same format.

8

Developing the Teleplay from the Seed of the Idea to the Finished Draft

We have learned the tools of television writing, the hooks of the medium, and the structure of the half-hour and one-hour shows. Now let's get down to the nuts and bolts. How can we apply what we've learned? Where does a script begin? What are the necessary steps the writer needs to take in developing a story?

Rather than theorizing, it is better that you actually see the development process. For this purpose, I will walk you through each step I took in developing one of my own scripts for "Three's Company." I've chosen a half-hour show simply because the structure is smaller and faster to step through. Most of us are familiar with this show or have at some time caught the reruns. It is important to note that the process we will use is the same for the half-hour show, the one-hour show, and the two-hour M.O.W.

Step 1: The Seed of the Idea

Television is a mass media. When trying to come up with an idea, the telescripter must always ask, Will this appeal to at least seven or eight million people? This question can be highly intimidating! How can we possibly know what will appeal to such vast numbers? We can't, unless we realize that *we* are that audience; *we* are the gauge. If an idea appeals to us, if we can relate to it, then there's a good chance the audience will identify with it also. If it will keep us from flicking the channel, it's likely that the same will hold true for the majority of the viewing masses.

When I first got the call that I was to pitch for "Three's Company," I asked myself what all episodic writers must ask: What does this show sell? "Three's Company" sold T and A (tits and ass), cohabitation, and youth. I then asked myself: What was I doing in my late teens and early twenties? What difficult situations did I find myself in? Who was I dating? What problems was I experiencing? What were *my* conflicts? I always turn to myself first because it is a shortcut. If nothing clicks, then I look outside. In this case, something clicked. I recalled an incident that had the possibilities for a story.

Like all starving actors, I often took part-time jobs so I could be free for auditions. This particular week my job was passing out perfume samples at a well-known department store on Wilshire Boulevard. One day a very attractive U.S.C. law student came in. We hit it off immediately and talked for quite a while. When he left, he didn't ask for my phone number. I figured that was it. To my surprise he turned up the next day and asked me out. Our date was wonderful! We never ran out of things to talk about. I sensed that this date was the beginning of something special.

So, I waited by the phone. Weeks passed, and with each one I became more obsessed, wondering why he didn't call. The mind can be a great friend or a tremendous enemy. In this case, it was the latter. What had happened? Maybe I did something wrong. Perhaps he was already involved with someone else. On and on the thoughts went. I was wasting my energy, consumed with not knowing.

A year later, when I had finally forgotten this man, he called. A *year* later! He apologized and explained that he had not passed the bar and had been bogged down studying. His excuse sounded legitimate, so I accepted another date. Again I waited by the phone. Again he didn't call. Again I became obsessed with not knowing what had happened to him. (Fortunately, times have changed. Today all women have to do is call and say, "Hey, so what's the deal!")

I finally managed to get over him a second time when about a year later I received another call. And yes, as embarrassed as I am to admit it, he gave more persuasive excuses, and I accepted another date. We went out on three dates in three years! Finally, after the last date, he disappeared, and to this day I don't know what became of him! For all I know, he could be your attorney right now. Given his ability to b.s., I keep waiting for him to turn up on some ballot!

After recalling this incident, I asked myself, Could my experience be identifiable to the masses? Was there something in it the viewers could relate to? Yes, because it deals with rejection. Regardless of who you are or what you look like, who has not at some time been rejected? When the seed of an idea sticks or feels right, it's time for the writer to move on to the next step.

Step 2: Broadstroking

At this point the writers begin asking themselves questions so that they can come up with the appropriate answers. Essentially, they plant the seed to see if it takes, or grows. Whose story must it be? Jack's, Janet's, or Chrissy's? Actually, this story could happen to any one of them. "Three's Company" sold three stars. Thus, if it's Jack's story, Janet and Chrissy must be pivotal. If it's Janet's story, Jack and Chrissy must be pivotal. Regardless of who the story was happening to, all three would have to be crucial to the outcome.

Let's suppose it's Jack's story. Who is the lady who pops in and out of his life? What should she do for a living? If she can come and go on a whim, maybe she could work for the airlines. Will we want to like her? If her pattern is to repeatedly come into Jack's life, turn it upside down, and then split, the answer would be no. It also follows that after being given the shaft so many times, Jack would not want to see her.

How should this story end? Think and weigh the possibilities, what works best for you. Writing is making choices, and the more interesting the choices, the better the script. Let's suppose the woman's name is Susan and that for the time being we make her a flight attendant. We don't want to like her, simply because she uses Jack. Since we care about Jack, we don't want to see him used again. Jack must be the one who wins in the end.

We now have the *spine* of the story. We can define it in one or two lines: An old paramour of Jack's returns, and makes him fall head over heels all over again. This time he finally gets wise and sends her on her way. I call this part the spine because everything hinges on it. Inherent within those two lines are:

Beginning, middle, and end
Character, conflict, and action

Before writers can go one step further in the development process, they must identify the spine of their story. If you can't define it, then you can't write it.

Since we are now clear on what the story is about, let us devise our runner next. (If we were working in the one-hour or two-hour structure, at this juncture we would identify our subplot and runner.) What could be happening that would nicely offset the main story? Since the main story is Jack's, let's devise a runner revolving around Janet and Chrissy: It's Jack's birthday and the girls are planning a surprise party for him. With our main story and runner in place, we now have everything we need to begin structuring the script.

Step 3: Stepping Out the Scenes

This step is the single most important element in developing the teleplay. It is where structure happens. A good idea is simply not enough. The writer must know the story can be set up, developed, and successfully resolved in the half-hour, one-hour, or two-hour time frame.

For the stepping-out process, I use index cards. Each card represents a scene. On each card I write the locale, who is in the scene, and what story point must be made. Remember, if a scene does not progress the plot, if it does not reveal pertinent story elements or character revelations, then it does not belong in the script. In the medium of television there is no time for excess fat!

We will begin by structuring Act I. Take a stack of index cards and write on each with me as we walk through the process together. Where does the story begin? In episodic television our setup must happen quickly. The setup establishes who and what the story is about. In the half-hour structure it must happen by the first or second scene. How do we introduce Susan into the story? In what way does she reappear in Jack's life? Where do we first meet her?

Perhaps Jack could accidently run into Susan at the airport. Or she could call. What if she showed up at the trio's apartment? Consider what would be the fastest, most immediate way to bring her into the story. The airport would require a swing set. We would also need to establish what Jack was doing there. Since Jack does not really want to see Susan, he could easily avoid her. Having Susan arrive at Jack's apartment is the best choice. Why? Because it quickly presents Jack with the biggest problem and provides the most conflict.

The relationship between Jack and Susan has a backstory—that is, a history or a past: Susan has repeatedly appeared in Jack's life. Each time he loses control and each time she leaves him. Once Susan arrives, how can we get this necessary exposition out? Would it be easier with Jack there, or with him gone? If Janet and Chrissy knew nothing about the relationship, it would be easier with Jack gone. We, the audience, can be fed the information as Susan talks to the girls.

Next we must determine what Janet and Chrissy are doing when the doorbell rings. They must be doing something in time and space. Let's suppose they are in the kitchen preparing for Jack's birthday party, an excellent place to establish our runner. Take your first index card and write the locale, who is in the scene, and what must be established. Your first card will look like figure 3.

```
┌─────────────────────────────────────────────┐
│                                        #1   │
│  INT. TRIO'S KITCHEN—DAY                     │
│  Janet and Chrissy                           │
│  Establish:   Jack's birthday party          │
│                                              │
│                                              │
│                                              │
└─────────────────────────────────────────────┘
```

Figure 3.

Never clutter your cards with dialogue or unnecessary words. We are not writing; we are *structuring*. If a wonderful line occurs to you, flip the card over, jot it down, and get back to the business at hand. Never commit yourself to writing unless you know that structurally the story works.

Now, ask yourself, What happens in Scene 2? Susan arrives. Take another index card and write it down (see figure 4). What absolutely must happen next in the scene? Jack must appear. Up until now, we have only heard Susan's side of the romance. His view will be entirely different. Will this step be easier with Susan there or with her gone? In order for Jack to relay his true feelings about her to Janet and Chrissy, it will be easier with Susan gone.

```
┌─────────────────────────────────────────────┐
│                                        #2   │
│  INT. TRIO'S LIVING ROOM—DAY                 │
│  Janet, Chrissy and Susan                    │
│  Establish:   Susan's relationship with Jack │
│                                              │
│                                              │
│                                              │
└─────────────────────────────────────────────┘
```

Figure 4.

How can we momentarily remove Susan from the scene, yet still keep her nearby for our purposes? Perhaps she discovers it's Jack's birthday and she goes to the bathroom to freshen up. Here we'd have to add a notation to card 2: Susan exits to the bathroom (see figure 5).

#2

INT. TRIO'S LIVING ROOM—DAY

Janet, Chrissy and Susan

Establish: Susan's relationship with Jack

Susan exits to the bathroom

Figure 5.

In the next beat, Jack returns home. His return does not technically constitute a new scene because it is the same locale, but since it adds a new element to the story we shall count it as one (refer to page 126).

How should Jack discover Susan is in the apartment? The girls can possibly tease him about a certain surprise visitor. What if he then hears Susan singing from the bathroom, recognizes her voice, and panics? Now he can explain to the girls that every time he sees Susan he loses it. Here is a perfect opportunity to provide more backstory. Now we can fill in the needed exposition from Jack's point of view. Susan has filed him away so many times he feels like a catalogue number! Jack wants to flee. He knows if he stays he's a goner.

The girls have to keep Jack in the apartment for the surprise party. What can they do to keep him there? The writers are constantly asking themselves questions. The process goes on and on.

Perhaps Janet and Chrissy tell Jack he must face up to Susan or he will never get over her; running away won't solve a thing. Since Jack wants to rid himself of this problem, he's convinced to confront it. Our next index card will look like figure 6.

What absolutely has to happen next? Susan must make her appearance. Again, this entrance does not technically constitute a new scene since we are still in the trio's living room, but it presents a new element into the story so for our purposes we shall count it as one.

```
                                                              #3
INT. TRIO'S LIVING ROOM—DAY

Janet and Chrissy—Jack arrives.
He discovers Susan singing in the
bathroom; panics.

Establish:   The relationship with Susan from Jack's POV.

Janet and Chrissy convince Jack to stay.
```

Figure 6.

What should Jack's reaction be when he first sees Susan? What if she's slipped out of her uniform and into something slinky? At first he could act cool. Then Susan starts coming on to him. His knees start to weaken. Soon Jack can no longer stand it. Suddenly, he grabs her and they both fall passionately to the floor together—while Janet and Chrissy watch. Here, we could end Act I. Janet and Chrissy have resolved their problem—that is, they have managed to keep Jack in the apartment. But in the process, they have created a bigger complication—he is out of control. They have created their own monster. They are now pivotal to the story. Jack's problem has become their problem. They have brought Jack and Susan together. In Act II they will have to devise some way to get them apart. Card 4 of our step process would look like figure 7.

```
                                                              #4
INT. TRIO'S LIVING ROOM—DAY

Janet, Chrissy, Jack and Susan

Susan exits bathroom

Establish:   Jack cool at first, then he loses control


                    END ACT ONE
```

Figure 7.

At this point it's a good idea to step back and look at the sweep of your cards. Ask yourself, Is there anything missing? At the time I was stepping out this show, I looked back and realized there was something important that I had left out.

If you can recall, "Three's Company" during these years had the "Ropers" (the apartment managers who lived downstairs) as secondary characters. As covered in chapter 3, scripts must use *all* of the ongoing cast members.

How, then, can we use the Ropers in Act I? Perhaps they could somehow be involved with Jack's birthday. Maybe the surprise can be in their apartment. Where could a scene with the Ropers be placed without breaking the continuity of the story? What if we decided to open Act I with them? They could be inside their apartment preparing for Jack's party.

The benefit of working with cards is that they can be shifted around very easily. Rearrange them. We are now making a new card for Scene 1 (see figure 8).

INT. ROPER'S LIVING ROOM—DAY   #1

Mr. and Mrs. Roper

Establish: Jack's surprise birthday party will be in their
             apartment

Figure 8.

Does Act I work? When you are certain it does, then renumber the cards. The original number 1 card now becomes card 2, 2 becomes 3, and so on. The final card becomes 5. Remember, Act I must work before you can begin structuring Act II.

In Act I we have made certain that:

Each scene progresses the story forward.
Each scene provides conflict.
We have established a runner.
A problem is presented and a problem is resolved, which, in turn, has led to a greater complication.
There is a strong act end.

For Act II, we repeat the process. Again we ask the questions. How should the act open? What is Chrissy and Janet's plan to lure Jack away from Susan? How do we resolve the story? Exactly when does Jack become "wise"?

Using the cards, we step out each scene until the Act II end. Does each scene advance the plot? Do the scenes build? Is the story successfully resolved? When you are finished, look at the cards for Act I and Act II together. Do both acts flow? Is there a good transition between the acts? Are you completely satisfied?

Remember, the stepping-out process takes time. You think about each scene as you're driving around in your car, while shaving, or in the morning when you're waiting for your coffee. Sometimes thoughts flow; other times you will reach an impasse. At difficult times, there's no point in beating your head against the wall. Pick the script up the next day and look at it with fresh eyes.

One of the advantages of writing on spec is that you don't have a deadline: Nobody is rushing you or screaming for pages. Speed is important in television writing, but you can worry about that once you break in. Right now, your only concern should be getting it right. Remember: You must be absolutely certain that your script works structurally before you are ready to move on to the next step.

Step 4: The Treatment

I was once told by a very successful story editor that no matter how many scripts you write or how successful you become, never write without a treatment. What is the treatment? It is the narrative description, or synopsis, of what is taking place in each scene.

We already know at this stage that the scene needs to be there to progress the story forward. Now we are ready to get down to the business of finding the inner components that make the scene work. The treatment is a highly creative step in the development process. Here, the writer is making the story come alive—giving it breath.

I am asked by many students why at this stage they can't just go directly to the first draft. Something very strange happens to writers when they rush into dialogue—they get off track! Their concern becomes words instead of the content behind them. Ideas are not yet thoroughly milked; or a wonderful thought may occur, but since the writer is as yet unable to execute it, it's cut out entirely.

Once you break in and become a bona fide member of the Writers Guild, treatment becomes a *required* step in the payment process. It is with rare exception that producers will give the go-ahead for the writer to go directly into first draft. They almost always want to see the treatment first. Why? Because it is easier to spot problems and correct them in a ten- to fourteen-page treatment than it is in the first draft.

The writer can work on a treatment just like an artist works on a drafting table. You can cut and paste, and make all the necessary corrections *before* you begin the actual writing. Once you are into writing the first draft, making major changes becomes a monumental task. It is like playing with a set of dominos. One change affects the entire script. The work becomes endless. Good writing comes after thorough thinking, which happens in treatment—don't bypass this step. A shortcut is not a shortcut in the long run.

Let's return to the index cards. In Act I, Scene 1, we open on the Ropers preparing for Jack's party. We already know who is in the scene, where the scene is taking place, and what must be established. Now let the stream of consciousness go and begin to free associate. Envision the scene. How do you see it happening? Where does the scene begin? How does it end? What exactly are the Ropers doing? What are they talking about? Let's read the treatment for Scene 1.

INT. ROPER LIVING ROOM—DAY

Mrs. Roper is in the living room, standing on a chair hanging crepe paper decorations and humming "Happy Birthday." Mr. Roper is blowing up balloons. He complains, "You need a lot of air for this." Helen figures she's picked the right man for the job. Where would Helen like him to put the balloons? She's tempted for a moment, then tells him to put them on the walls.

Stanley can't understand why they are going to so much trouble for Jack's party. Why is it that Helen has never gone to so much trouble for his birthday? She insists that isn't true! She had a wonderful present for him on his last birthday. She could never understand why he didn't want it. "I told you," Stanley retorts, "I had a headache."

Helen fondly recalls her 35th birthday. Does Stanley remember? That was the day she walked out on him. It was because of the bleached blonde in 307. Stanley was always going upstairs to inspect her pipes. Stanley insists he was just doing his job. He asks what made her decide to come back. "Well," says Helen, "I figured you spend a lot of time in our apartment too, and nothing ever happened here."

Stanley wants to know why the kids can't just throw the party upstairs. Helen tells him they want it to be a surprise. She wants Stanley to try and be nice to Jack. "Why?" he insists. "Because," she says, "they want Jack to be surprised."

• • •

The more detailed the treatment, the easier it is to write the first draft. The writer can literally pull dialogue and action off the pages and place them into the script.

Let's move on to Scene 2 (refer to figure 3). The scene takes place in the trio's kitchen with Janet and Chrissy. The card reads, "Establish Jack's birthday party." Ask yourself, What are the components that could make this scene work? We already know (Scene 1) that the party is a surprise and it will be at the Ropers. We don't know, however, what the girls' plans are. How do Janet and Chrissy intend to get Jack to the party? What is physically going on in the kitchen? What are the girls doing? Think—play with the scene. Try to see it in your head. No two writers will envision the same scene. Here is what I envisioned and placed in the treatment for Scene 2.

INT. TRIO'S KITCHEN—DAY

Chrissy, in an old sloppy shirt and jeans, her hair in curlers, is decorating Jack's birthday cake. Janet enters, also in grubbies, and asks Chrissy how Jack's cake is coming along. Chrissy proudly holds it up. It reads "Happy Birthda." Janet asks what happened to the "y." Chrissy tilts the cake and shows she iced it on the side. "And where's the Jack?" asks Janet. Chrissy doesn't think putting his name on the cake is necessary. Jack already knows it's his birthday. And he already knows his name is Jack. After all, they're not going to be singing "Happy Birthday Harry."

The girls discuss how they are going to get Jack downstairs to the Ropers unsuspectedly. Chrissy suggests a ridiculous convoluted plan that could only make sense to her. Janet is a bit more practical—why doesn't Chrissy simply take Jack for a walk on the beach and keep him there for half an hour. Chrissy thinks for a moment. "Yeah," she says, "that might work, too."

The girls decide the cake would look better with a border. Chrissy picks up the cake decorator and squeezes it. Nothing comes out. She looks in the nozzle and squeezes it again and gets a full face of frosting. THE DOORBELL RINGS.

■ ■ ■

Pick up the index card for Scene 3. Here, Susan arrives at the door. The girls meet her for the first time. The card reads, "Establish Susan's relationship with Jack." How can we do this? It is important that we don't like Susan. Otherwise, it would be unfair of the girls to try and get her away from Jack. How can we show her for what she really is? What are the components that will make this scene work? What follows is the treatment for Scene 3.

INT. LIVING ROOM—NIGHT

Janet opens the front door and reveals Susan Walters, an airline flight attendant, in uniform. She carries an overnighter. Susan thinks she's at the wrong apartment—she's looking for Jack Tripper. Janet explains she's at the right place but Jack is gone. They expect him back at any moment.

Susan says she'll wait, enters, and sits on the couch. "Are you the cleaning lady?" she asks. "I live here," Janet explains. Chrissy comes out of the kitchen and she introduces her roommate, Chrissy Snow. Susan tries to get it straight that they are all "roommates." The girls make it clear they're just friends. They don't want her to think there is anything more. Susan looks both of them over and asks why she should think anything like that.

Janet excuses the grubbies, explaining neither she nor Chrissy usually go around looking like this. Susan never judges by appearances. "After all," she says, "people can't help the way they look."

After some prying the girls learn that Susan and Jack are very "close," but that they have not seen each other lately because Susan has been doing so much flying. When they mention it's Jack's birthday and they're throwing a surprise party, Susan uses the bathroom to freshen up.

In the treatment stage don't concern yourself with dialogue. If lines occur to you then go ahead and write them in. How something is said is not as important as *what* is said and the *natural progression* of the scene itself. The dialogue will happen but first you must lay the necessary groundwork. This way you won't digress, your dialogue will stay on track, and it will remain focused.

Next, we move to card 4. In this "beat," Jack returns home. He discovers Susan singing in the bathroom and panics. The card reads, "Establish the relationship with Susan from Jack's P.O.V. Janet and Chrissy convince Jack to stay." Here, in the treatment, are the components I envisioned that could make the scene work.

MOMENTS LATER

Jack returns. The girls stare at him with silly grins on their faces and tell him a girl has come to see him. When he hears the singing coming from the bathroom he recognizes the voice as that of Susan Walters.

"How did you guess?" Chrissy asks. Jack says he'd recognize those lungs anywhere. He panics. Janet and Chrissy start asking questions about the relationship. It's a long story, Jack tells them, and in the end Susan left him. It was for the best. He had absolutely no control when it came to Susan, she was like a drug. Every time he saw her, every time he heard her name he'd go crazy. He's get stomach aches and headaches, he couldn't eat and sleep—he was absolutely miserable. Did she leave him more than once, Chrissy asks. She filed him away so many

> times, he tells the girls, that he thought he had a catalog number. He must get out of there—if he so much as says "Hello," it'll be good-bye.
>
> The girls, who must keep him there, tell Jack that he has to face up to Susan and that this is a perfect opportunity to prove to himself that he's over her. Jack agrees, maybe they're right. He'll be cool as an iceberg. Like Bogie in Casablanca, he will show no mercy.

You will discover as you write treatment that ideas and dialogue will come to you more freely than when you are writing script format, because you have removed your "inner critic." At this stage you're letting ideas out without the stress of having to execute them. Gems pop out—they are rough and need to be honed and polished, which happens later when you're writing the script.

Let's turn to card 5, the final card in Act I. Here, Susan exits the bathroom. The card reads, "Establish Jack, cool at first then he loses control." This beat is very important. Here, we provide the complication on which we end Act I. Ask yourself how you see it playing out. How can we milk it for its best effect? The harder we make it on Jack, the bigger the conflict and the more powerful the act end. Following is how I envisioned it playing out.

> INT. LIVING ROOM—NIGHT
>
> Susan exits from the bathroom, wearing a gorgeous, sexy dress. Jack works at being cool. She warmly asks how he's been. Jack acts like a rock, a cold one, but he's having a tough time of it. He eyes the girls for support. Their looks say he's doing fine.
>
> Susan begins to move in closer. Jack calmly asks her what brought her back to Los Angeles. "Don't you know?" she tells him. "I came in for your birthday." Janet and Chrissy exchange glances. Susan moves in even closer. Does Jack remember how they spent her birthday last year? Jack can no longer stand it. Suddenly and passionately he embraces Susan while Janet and Chrissy look on. He is out of control. He has completely lost it. And we end Act I.

■   ■   ■

Be certain the treatment for the entire script is complete *before* you type one word of the first draft. Read it in its entirety. Study it. Try to envision it on film. Does the story flow? Perhaps you have revealed too much too soon, or the information in one of your scenes is redundant. Maybe a hole needs to be plugged or a story point should be planted in an earlier scene.

Cut, paste, change, rewrite: It is in this step that you make all of your necessary revisions. Overlook nothing. You are in the business of making your story work. It has to, or else you cannot move to the next step. *Do not bypass this process and jump prematurely into first draft.*

Writers can get off track once they commit themselves to dialogue. The flow of ideas stops, because the focus is on the sound of the words. Gems can be overlooked, because you're trying to execute individual lines.

Preparing a treatment allows you to take chances. And the more depth the treatment has, the easier the first draft is. Pull out all the stops. Take risks. Be innovative.

Harlan Ellison, who has won the Writers Guild of America award for Most Outstanding Teleplay three times, says, *"Always* write the treatment, not the screenplay first; only fools and amateurs try to write and/or sell a screenplay without a treatment."

It is important to note that treatments should not be turned in to producers or story editors along with a speculation script. In the beginning, this step only serves to help the writer. Once you are in the Writers Guild and treatment becomes a requirement, the material should be presented polished and double-spaced.

Step 5: At Last, the First Draft

Finally, the preparation is done. The foundation has been laid. For the first time you're working in script format, telling your story with the only tools the television writer can use: dialogue, narrative, and locales. Now you face the blank page and that inevitable question pops up: Can I do it? Yes, but probably not without a struggle.

I absolutely hate my first drafts. Everything at first seems contrived, wooden, unnatural. Don't be too critical of yourself at this step. You'll defeat yourself before you're ever out of the gate.

When I first broke up with my writing partner, Kathy Donnell, I had a very rude awakening when it came to writing first drafts. We had a routine that we had followed for years: First we would sit across the table from each other and talk out the scenes. Then she would jot down in longhand what we came up with. Since she was the typist, she'd go home and place this "rough" as we called it into script format. The next day she'd bring over the material and I'd rewrite it.

I have always been exceedingly critical of my work. At times, it's gotten in my way, making things hard on myself and my partners. Unfortunately, it is said this trait comes with being a double Virgo. Considering my personality, I was very fortunate during those years that Kathy took home the legal pad with our rough material. This way, I never had to look at it or judge it until the following day when it was in script format and I had a clear head.

Imagine the shock I experienced later when I no longer had a partner who yanked the pages away from me. Now I was sitting alone in front of a word processor, and I had to look at what I was writing on a screen! I started to think I couldn't write anymore. What if I had lost it? After all, the evidence was right there on the screen. God, I thought, how could anyone call this writing! This was it. It was over for me. Maybe I had peaked early. Along with the garbage I *thought* I saw on the page, I was creating more garbage in my head.

Soon, I was so busy being critical that I was unable to write at all. I'd go to my office, stare out the window, and wonder about insignificant things like what would it be like to be in a relationship with Mel Gibson. On more productive days, I'd busy myself with alphabetizing junk mail or deciding I needed a new door stopper. Once, I bought fifty dollars worth of lotto tickets and spent the entire afternoon scraping them off. I realized I had hit rock bottom. Something had to be done, especially since I didn't have a winning ticket.

I've learned over the years that in order to get past this devilish and defeating inner critic, I have to play little games with myself. One of the games I've devised is that I simply will not look at, read, or judge anything that I've written that day. I wait until I've accumulated a nice little batch of material. Then I sit down with a cup of coffee very early in the morning and go to work rewriting with a fresh head. After I spend a couple of hours rewriting, I return to the arduous task of writing the first draft. Recently, I had my first root canal. Everyone warned me that it would be awful. I actually didn't find it difficult at all, probably because I've written so many first drafts.

When I'm working on the first draft, I'm aware of each and every minute. When I'm rewriting, I literally lose track of the time. By rewriting first, I get myself out of the gate every morning with a good start. Essentially, I am priming the pump. I'm not suggesting that you work this way. What I am saying is that you must find the little triggers that will get you going. The old addage "know thyself" is especially true for writers.

While writing the first draft, remember that you know the story already works structurally since you've done the groundwork. Concern yourself only with completing it, not with getting it perfect. You'll have plenty of time for perfection in the next step.

Step 6: Rewrites

Notice I use the plural! Many writers believe their scripts are ready to submit when in truth they have only begun rewriting. Rewrites are the last and most important part in the writing process. Here, corrections are made, points are clarified and defined, characters are intensified, and dialogue and narrative are tightened and sharpened.

Since there is so much to do at this point, I rewrite in stages, with each rewrite having a specific purpose. First, I read the material for an overall perspective. As thoughts occur to me, I jot them in the margins. I don't stop to correct at this point; I only make notes so that I can get the feel and general sweep of the material.

Next, I go back and fill in any hole or mistake in the material. It is crucial that you plug holes before you move on. If you have made the same story point in two different scenes, determine where it is more effective and take the extra one out. If a story point wasn't planted properly or clearly enough, or if there are any contradictions in the material, now is the time to carefully clean them up.

Once all the holes are plugged, I begin looking at dialogue. Do your lines really seem as though they are coming from your characters? Is there something else your characters could say that would be more effective? Always ask yourself, "How can I say it with fewer words?" *Light dialogue is good dialogue.* If your speeches are consistently running four and five lines, you are writing too long! Take four-line speeches and turn them into two-line speeches. Take two-line speeches and turn them into a single line. Clean up your narrative in this stage as well. Remember, there is no room for excess. Punch up, clean up, lean up, and make your words fly. Don't let your ego get in the way. Be merciless with your material.

The last and final rewrite I call the polish. At this point, the material is tightened and you've done absolutely everything that needs to be done. Now you are going through the material with a fine-tooth comb. You are attempting here to make it perfect. An excess article, the shifting of a word—everything makes a difference. This point is where your inner critic belongs. Make his day—let him go!

I am often asked, "How do you know when you are done rewriting?" When you are absolutely not capable of doing any better at this stage in your life! Harold Green, a very successful, veteran agent, once told me, "Never let the script go until it is absolutely the best you can do."

Writers will sometimes make excuses: "Well, a good director can bring that to the script," or, "If a good actor is cast, he can take care of that." Nobody will take care of anything unless you have good material first! Be meticulous; be a perfectionist. It can make the difference between a sale and no sale!

9

How to Create Riveting Characters

Structure holds the story in place, but it is character, scene by scene, line by line, that takes you through the script. In writing episodic television, it is our job to know the characters. In writing pilots and the Movies for Television, our job is to create them. Once you have determined the spine, time frame, and turning points of the story, the character, if fully developed, will tell you where to go. I can illustrate this point best with one of my past "horror" stories.

My partner and I had been successful in television for a number of years when a producer, the late Phil Mandelker, called us in to develop our first Movie of the Week. He gave us the spine of what was essentially to become a sultry, soapy, NBC version of *The Turning Point.* We bounced ideas around and were told to go home and develop the characters.

Having had experience only in episodic television, where characters for the most part are already established, my partner and I jotted down a few quick pages and brought them back to Phil. I will never forget sitting in his office, watching him read those pages. After a few moments, he looked at me and asked, "Do you call this writing?" At that point I wanted to jump off his balcony, but I was afraid anything that theatrical would go unnoticed on the Warner Bros. lot.

Instead of cutting us off (writers jargon for getting axed), he had us meet at his home, where for the next two weeks we developed our characters. I consider the time I spent with Phil one of the high points of my career. What he taught me I teach in my classes today. I have yet to find a character development process that works better.

The Back Life of the Character

We began with the characters' history, or back life—that is, everything of consequence that had taken place in their lives before the film. Who were their parents? How much money did they have? Where did they live? Did they compete with their brother or sister? Were they popular in school? When was their first sexual experience? How were they perceived by the opposite sex? Who were their friends in the neighborhood? What side of the tracks did they live on? What church did they go to? Phil was such a stickler for detail!

There were times when I felt that he went too far. I failed to see that knowing how much money my characters' parents had in the bank when they were born would have any effect on my two-hour movie, but I went along with Phil regardlessly. After all, he was the producer and we were the writers, and if nothing else came out of this, at least we were making a good contact.

It was odd, but after a few of these sessions I found myself getting totally caught up in them. I could hardly wait to arrive at Phil's. I found myself thinking about one particular character a lot. On my long commute from Westlake Village, I'd wonder how she would react and relate to other characters in the script. I even wondered how she would relate to people in my own life! It was as though she was beginning to exist on some invisible plane.

Our protagonist, Sharon, was a high-powered female executive. One day Phil asked me, "What does her office look like?" I said, "It's exquisite!" He bellowed, "What the hell is exquisite?" I jumped, completely intimidated. Suddenly, I was being made to think like a *filmmaker!* He was forcing me to think visually. The office no longer was exquisite. It became marble and muted pastels, Renoir sketches, a Louis XIV desk, and decor audacious enough to compete with the city skyline. It was eccentric and exceedingly feminine, like the president who occupied it.

To this day, Sharon, in "California Reunion," is one of my favorite characters. I came to know her like you would an intimate friend. I knew about:

Her abusive father and the alcoholic mother who had resigned herself to living with him.
The humiliation her parents had caused her in school.
Her early sexual permissiveness and the skeletons in her closet.
Her climb to the top of the corporate ladder.

When developing the character's backstory don't concern yourself with how it will translate to film. The rewards of such background work will come to you as you write.

It is amazing, but through investigating your main character, other characters will happen, locales will be created, and dialogue will come to life. It is as though these characters are helping you to develop your script.

I decided Alex Holman, in "Belly Up," did not come from money, yet things still seemed to come easily to him. He was attractive, bright, and never had to stretch too far. He went to Stanford on a student loan. While there he met Jerry Weiner, an idealistic pre-med student studying plastic surgery. Jerry's vision was to one day perform microsurgery, help burn victims, climb the Himalayas, and go into remote villages and work with lepers.

At the top of the script Jerry has instead become a very successful Beverly Hills plastic surgeon who drives a red Ferrari. His posh office looks like a war zone, filled with bandaged egomanic patients who will never be content. Up to his eyeballs in liposuctions and implants, he has a not-so-happy marriage with an outrageously beautiful model. Jerry manages to get to the Himalayas once a year, but it's to compensate for guilt. In truth, these treks along with a little bit of golf are his only form of R & R.

Act II of the movie opens at Harry's Bar and Grill. Alex has just gone bankrupt and Jerry's wife has left him. They're drinking martinis and commiserating as they line up the olives, reminiscing about the old days at Stanford, when they used to bronze their jock straps and send them to the sorority housemothers. This scene happened as a result of the back life of Alex.

While at Stanford, I decided that Alex met his wife, Felicia. She came from money—this is not why he married her, but it's very typical of the kind of woman he would be drawn to. Felicia is happily ensconced in Bay Area society when Alex decides to relocate the family to Los Angeles.

In bankruptcy court, the spoiled former debutante has a complete breakdown. She is having her first crisis. Her nails are breaking, her furs have been sold in a distress sale, and she can no longer afford manicures or even Jane Fonda's workout. In a tantrum, she throws herself on the courtroom floor. "You son-of-a-bitch!" she screams. "I never wanted to leave Palo Alto!" Where did this dialogue come from? It came from the back life of Alex's character.

I decided that when Alex relocated to Los Angeles, he went to work for two very conservative Jewish land developers named Haberman and Hern. Alex's "hot dog" enthusiasm and innovative ideas proved a shot in the arm for the company. Haberman and Hern made a fortune and in return they made the "goy" wonder a partner.

When the movie opens, Hern is dead: He has keeled over from a heart attack some three months earlier. A black wreath is still hanging on his door. Haberman has totally flipped out over Hern's death. He keeps a picture of his deceased partner on an empty conference room chair and confers with it in business meetings. He is also trying to have sex with every temp girl who comes through the office. Needless to say, his volatile condition has left investors nervous and Alex has the sole responsibility of the company.

In developing the back life of Alex, I now had three secondary characters for my movie: Jerry Weiner, the frustrated plastic surgeon; Felicia, the spoiled wife; and Sidney Haberman, the neurotic partner.

Alex took financial chances. His philosophy was that life is a gamble and he is a winner. It occurred to me that a man with this kind of attitude could make some pretty heavy wagers on the golf course. Early in the script he wins a thousand-dollar bet. Later he not only loses his five-thousand-dollar Rolex due to a missed putt but he must also run naked to the parking lot, where the cops are waiting to arrest him for indecent exposure. In flushing out my character's back life, I was not only creating locales—I was creating entire sequences in my movie! Where your characters go—the places they frequent, their friends, their homes, their offices—become the necessary elements of your script.

The Character's Present Life

With the back life complete, focus turns to the present life of the characters. The present includes everything of significance in their professional, personal, and private lives once the film begins.

Professional: How the characters relate and interact at work.
Personal: How the characters relate and interact with family and friends.
Private: What the characters do when no one is watching.

The Professional Life of the Character

A character's professional life is more than an office or a title. It is a series of moving pictures, a routine. It becomes an alarm clock. It is what the character eats for breakfast and the route he drives to work.

When your character arrives at the office, is there a space reserved for him in a subterranean parking lot? Is there a doorman who greets him? On what floor is his office? When he steps off the elevator, how wide is the hallway? When he reaches the office, what does the logo on the door say? Inside, how many secretaries are at work? How many phones are ringing? What do the pictures on the walls reveal?

I needed to establish that Alex was in land development. The challenge for the scriptwriter is always how to *show* something instead of talking about it. So I decided to have photographs in the outer office of the company's various developments: the three partners cutting a ribbon in front of a new supermarket, photographs of bulldozers clearing land, a photograph of a landfill with Alex in a hardhat. Each picture revealed more about the company.

Who is your character's secretary? What is their relationship? Is it business? Are they best of friends, or is it more intimate? Who are their partners and the people they work with? Remember, these people are the possible characters in your script.

The Personal Life of the Character

This aspect of the character's life is everything that is not professional or private. Just think of your own personal life. Who are the people in it? How do you interact socially? What are your hobbies?

Let's begin with the family. Is your character married? Who is he married to? What is the interaction between the couple? What do they talk about? Is their sex life spontaneous or do they only consider making love on the weekends?

We have all been to parties and in social situations where we have seen couples who are outwardly pleasant, caring, even loving, and yet there is an obvious unspoken tension between them. We have also seen couples who bat words back and forth, tease, and give each other a rough time, and yet there is a sense of underlying love beneath these behaviors. There is a group consciousness and there is a couple consciousness, a dialogue, a routine, a pattern of interaction that is as unique as the partners participating.

A great being was once asked by a follower, "Why is it in the old days people were tested? There were floods, fires, the seas would part and then swallow us up, and if you looked the wrong way you could turn into a pillar of salt. Why aren't we tested like this today?" The great being said, "Today you don't need those theatrics, you've got each other!" Isn't it true? Nowhere can we learn to push each others' buttons as we can in intimate relationships. Think about your character's "buttons." What are they?

How about children? Do your characters have any? What are they like? How do parent and child interact, and what roles do they play? Playmate? Friend? Advisor? Children find their own strategy, or dialogue, in dealing with parents, be it silence, honesty, deception, or forthrightness.

Alex's daughter, Brooke, is fourteen, teetering on punk, bright, and definitely her own person. We first meet her when she comes out of her room carrying a pressed blouse and asks Maria, the maid, to wrinkle it.

Brooke's obsession is with photography. She takes still photographs of inanimate objects, like composites of apples shot from nine different angles. Felicia considers this behavior antisocial and wishes her daughter were more urbane. When she discovers a hunk of hair strategically missing from Brooke's scalp, she demands to know what happened. "The scissors slipped," Brooke tells her. This answer is obviously not the truth but it's her way of dealing with her mother.

She is more straightforward with her father. Alex cares a great deal for her, but when he nods approvingly at her photos, it's while conducting business on the phone. When she asks him for money, he responds like an automatic bank teller. It's not until later, when Alex goes under and finds time on his hands, that he genuinely begins looking at his relationship with his daughter. He realizes that he has not really been listening to her.

Identify your characters' relationships and how these relationships change over the course of the story.

In my advanced workshop, I have an exercise where writers must create a sequence of visuals revealing who the character or characters are without having them in one single shot. Look around. What do the pictures tell us about you? Are there family photographs? Is the kitchen strictly functional or is it a focal point where everyone congregates? Is the living room lived in? Is the house a showplace? Where is the television situated? How big is it? I love to peruse people's bookshelves. It tells you a lot about them.

Into the personal life of the character come friends. Who are they? With whom has your character chosen to associate? In college, Alex Holman chose Jerry Weiner. Alex wanted the material. Jerry was esoteric and idealistic. What was their bond? It was youth, Stanford, and they complemented one another.

Most of my friends don't want what I want. I'm glad. It's our differences that have created the bond between us. Jerry and Alex will, later in life, flip-flop. Jerry has completely bought into the material and the stress that goes along with it. Alex, who has had his possessions ripped away, must now search for something more meaningful.

What do your characters like to do socially? What sports are they into? Golf? Bowling? Softball? These pictures will become your locales. When you develop your characters' personal lives, you are developing a large portion of your television pilot or movie.

The Private Life of the Character

Private moments are an open window into the soul of your character. What do they do when no one is looking? Unfortunately, in most spec scripts you rarely find the private moment.

Recently, I read the original teleplay of "The Days and Nights of Molly Dodd." It was wonderfully crafted by its creator, Jay Tarses. In it, Molly wakes up and, in Jay's words, "begins the difficult ritual of facing the day." She is clad in an old out-of-shape T-shirt that hangs over sweatpants. Cat Stevens music is playing on the clock radio. Freezing, she tiptoes to an old heating unit that does little to affect the New York morning chill.

In the bathroom, Molly makes grotesque faces at herself in the mirror while inspecting her chin for a possible zit. She contemplates shaving her legs, then decides against it. Trudging into her tiny kitchen with a ratty afghan over her shoulders, Molly puts on the kettle, opens and shuts the refrigerator, sees and destroys a roach, takes some megavitamins, sighs at her clothes in the closet, and disappears into the shower.

What Jay Tarses has given us in these private moments is a wonderful insight into the character of Molly. We have a sense of who she is before there is one word of dialogue!

One of my favorite screenplays is *Ordinary People,* adapted for the screen by Alvin Sargent. In it, Sargent gives us a "window" into Beth through a sequence of private moments. In this sequence, Beth comes through the front door and Sargent comments on her perfect body. She walks into her very neat, organized kitchen and she opens the refrigerator. There is a closeup of the interior, and we can tell by the description that it is a metaphor for Beth: cold, sparse, foods evenly distributed and perfectly covered with Saran Wrap. She closes the refrigerator door, then takes a stack of towels from the service porch and walks up a flight of stairs. She notices a plant stand. It is crooked, so she moves it just slightly to the right.

Next she goes into the bedroom and puts the towels away. Then, Sargent writes, "something occurs to Beth." She walks to her perfect desk, removes a perfect pencil, and jots down a note. There is a closeup on the note that reads, "Don't forget the Johnson's Xmas." This woman was so consumed with appearances that later in the script her husband comments that she asked what he would wear to their own son's funeral.

There were wonderful private moments in *Rocky I* where we, the audience, were let into the has-been boxer's compassionate soul. Early in the film, Rocky enters his run-down apartment where an old mattress serves as a makeshift punching bag. He takes his pet turtle and places its bowl next to the bowl of his pet fish, Moby Dick, so they can keep each other company. We sense his loneliness. It's as though these two creatures are his only intimate friends.

At the mirror he looks at his bruised and battered face. Nearby is a picture of himself as a child, innocent and untarnished. He looks at the picture and then back into the mirror. Resigned, he grabs ice from the fridge, places it on his bruises, and flops dejectedly on his bed. In this private moment our hearts go out to this man.

Think back to your own private moments. One day in a script you may use them. When I was under contract in series development, I was under a great deal of stress. A lot of it had to do with the studio executive, who was responsible for getting us our contract. I was grateful, yet it didn't change the fact that she was extremely difficult to work with. To block these days out of my mind, I'd leave the studio around 7:00 P.M., get in my red sports car, buy some wine and a pack of cigarettes, smoke and drink in rush hour traffic, listen to heavy metal, and flirt on the freeway all the way home to Westlake Village. I hated heavy metal, I didn't smoke, I was a moderate drinker, and I was faithful to my husband! But come 7:00 P.M., I was transformed into a wild woman. When I reached the off-ramp to Westlake Village, I'd stash the smokes, stash the wine, stash the Styrofoam cup, spray the inside of the car, drive to my suburban house, use the garage door opener, go inside, and make dinner.

I'm sharing this private and foolish time in my life not to shock you but to drive home a point, if you'll pardon a pun. Imagine opening a TV movie with this female road warrior in a red sports car. She is drinking, smoking, flirting, and blasting heavy metal on the freeway. Then, when she arrives home we discover she leads a very quiet, mundane life. Why, we wonder? As the film progresses, through exposition we begin to understand the reasons behind her actions. Meanwhile, the audience had to wait and guess and wonder. This process is a good hook in script writing. First you provide the picture and then you explain the "why."

Sometimes what we do out of character is just as revealing as what we do in character. Maybe you haven't been Mad Max on the freeway, but most likely you've done something just as bizarre or outrageous.

Pull from these experiences. Your audience will identify with such moments.

I pulled from the above incident for "Belly Up." It worked wonderfully for the neurotic Sidney Haberman, who was overreacting to his partner's death (see page 139). After reading the script people invariably ask, "How did you ever think of that!" How indeed!

The Compelling Characteristic

You now have anywhere from five to perhaps fifteen pages on your character. You know his back life and his present life, which you have broken down into professional, personal, and private categories. How can you take this information and translate it to film? For this purpose we turn to the compelling characteristic.

Think about your character. Ask yourself which characteristic is the most dominant or profound. What single trait drives him the most? At first, this process may seem highly simplistic. You may feel that in playing only one compelling characteristic your character may appear one-dimensional.

In chapter 8 we discussed the importance of identifying the spine of the story. This process is also simplistic. It is this very simplicity that enables the writer to stay on track! "A lost alien is befriended by a young boy who helps him find his way back home." This spine is from *E.T. The Extra-Terrestrial.* It is not all of *E.T.* The story is filled with twists, turns, surprises, jeopardy, suspense, and numerous subplots, but the spine is the cohesive thrust: Everything attaches to it. All of the story is inherent in those few words.

The same can be said about the compelling characteristic. Everything the character is inherently exists within one dominant force or what motivates the character the most. Playing the compelling characteristic keeps us, the audience, rooted in clarity; it defines and keeps the character on track.

Let's look more closely at some characters we have discussed earlier and try to identify their compelling characteristic. Molly Dodd is a thirty-three-year-old divorced woman. She doesn't have a particularly good job, nor does she happen to be in a particularly good relationship. She is like many people, not quite floundering but not really latched onto anything. Though there is nothing viable or solid in her life, Molly keeps hoping that something will materialize, even though she may not know what it is. Molly is a fighter. She will never give up. What is it that keeps her going? Optimism is her compelling characteristic.

For Beth Jarrett in *Ordinary People,* the compelling characteristic is her perfectionism. Her compulsion is constantly crafted throughout the screenplay by Alvin Sargent. Beth's body is perfect, and so is the way she runs her house. Everything is in order. Even the plant stand must be moved just slightly so it, too, is perfect. Beth shows little emotion: Emotion is messy and wouldn't live up to her standards.

Though Conrad, her son, is having severe emotional problems, Beth prefers that he not see a psychiatrist. She also refuses family counseling, which could expose her as a not-so-perfect mother. Conrad finally comes to terms with his guilt and grief over his brother's boating accident. So does his father. But growth can be unpleasant and painful, and so in the end Beth, who is incapable of change, must leave.

The unforgettable Rocky Balboa's compelling characteristic is his compassion. Writer Sylvester Stallone plays it out in almost every scene. Rocky pulls winos off the street, tells hookers to go home, and stops and talks to orphaned animals in pet shops. He strategically places his turtle and goldfish bowls together so the two can keep each other company. Employed as a strong arm for a numbers runner, Rocky gives the client another chance. He finds a very plain woman beautiful, and he doesn't even dislike his adversary, Apollo Creed. Who wouldn't be rooting for this character? We care so much for him that in the last ten minutes of the film we're inside the ring taking our licks with him!

I pondered Alex Holman's compelling characteristic for quite a while. The very thing that motivated Alex, that brought him success and was the source of his downfall, was his ambition. It stemmed from Alex's perception of himself and his world: Life is a gamble and I am a winner. I played with this attitude throughout the script—Alex the winner, but now he was in a losing situation. This situation created all the humor. Alex is inept with the small things. People paid his bills, they did his laundry, and they even lined up his appointments for him. All he had to do was what he did best: make money. Now he can't. He's stuck with the little details of life, like doing his own laundry. He's a big leaguer, but unfortunately he's now in Little League.

I am often asked by writers how much character work is necessary for secondary and minor cast members. Is this kind of detail needed for them? No. I only do such intense work on my main characters. The bio on Alex ran about thirteen pages. It was much less for the supporting cast of Felicia and Jerry Weiner, possibly a third of that. Come to know your main characters like you would a member of your family. As you do your work on them you will come to know your secondary characters. They will require much less work.

You can use the compelling characteristic even for a bit part or a walk-on. It is a wonderful device and gives the character a point of view and an attitude.

An underdeveloped protagonist results in a one-dimensional script, whereas intense character work not only opens the screenwriter visually but also develops other aspects of the script. The people in your characters' personal and professional lives become characters in your story. Their routines and the places they frequent become your locales. Their compelling characteristic becomes the force that moves the action forward.

10

Creating the Television Pilot

It is highly unlikely that an unknown writer without a track record can break into the industry with a pilot idea. This statement is not meant to squelch your dreams of someday becoming another Stephen Cannell or Steven Bochco. It's just to warn you that developing and writing a pilot is the riskiest, most difficult, and biggest crap shoot of all areas of television for the new writer to pursue. Why? There is more money to be made here than in any other aspect of the industry. For example, Gary David Goldberg received a check in the amount of thirty-two million dollars for the syndication of his show "Family Ties." With price tags going this high for successful series, the pilot field has attracted the biggest names in the industry. The cost of producing pilots is so exorbitant that the networks will always turn to writers with proven track records: creators/writers/producers with prior successful series, or A-list writers (writers whose produced credits have pulled in good numbers in the ratings).

I have no idea what it is you have in that writer's head of yours. You are the one who faces the blank page, and you are the one who must make your own decisions on how to proceed with your career. What if an instructor told you that writing historical scripts was a bad gamble because they don't sell? You then go home and decide to forget about scripting *Out of Africa,* or you decide that *Dangerous Liaisons* just won't work. Historical pieces are hard to sell, but there are exceptions. Only you know what you have.

When I first began teaching, I'd tell new writers not to use voice-overs, flashbacks, or to insert songs into their scripts, unless these devices were written into the format of the show. Flashbacks and voice-overs, with few exceptions, are viewed by producers and the networks as old and tired techniques. Since novice scripters tend to overuse and misuse them anyway, I felt safe telling writers to leave them out. A short time later, I found myself using flashbacks, voice-overs, and even a banjo sequence in my movie "Belly Up." I worked at staying away from these techniques, but no matter what I did the script was more effective with them. Needless to say, I had to take another look at what I had been telling people. Instructors can give you the basics—the dos and don'ts. First, you must learn the rules and then it is up to you whether or not you choose to break them.

For breaking into the pilot field, the traditional way is to write an episodic spec script. Keep writing until you get one sold. Sell more episodic scripts and then land a staff job on a show. Now you're in a place of power. You have a track record and the networks know you. Besides, the numerous credits you've collected helped make powerful contacts along the way. You're in a position where people can say "yes." If you choose to bypass the conventional route, then it is crucial as an unknown that you find a well-known producer or writer who will attach to your project. These people can wield the power for you. We will discuss marketing techniques in a later chapter.

The Pilot Concept

In 1978 and 1979, I was under contract with Paramount Studios along with my partner, Kathy Donnell, as a story consultant and series developer. Our sole purpose on the lot was to write and develop pilots exclusively for the studio. We did a lot of pitching that year at the three major networks: ABC, CBS, and NBC. At these meetings, the first thing the executives would ask was, "What is your concept?" By "concept," they meant the one or two lines of description that could best describe our show. To better understand, let's look at the concepts of some successful series, past and current.

What was the concept of "Starsky and Hutch"? Two single male undercover cops living in Los Angeles who drive a red Torino. Some years later came "Vega$": A single male private eye living in Las Vegas who drives a 1956 Thunderbird. Then came "Magnum, P.I.": A single male private eye who lives in Hawaii and drives a red Ferrari. "Cagney and Lacey": Two female undercover cops, one married and one single, living in New York City. "Lou Grant": The people of the press and the internal workings of the newspaper business. Later came "Hill Street Blues": Officers in uniform and the internal workings of a police precinct. And "St. Elsewhere": The men and women in white and the internal workings of a hospital. Today, there is "L.A. Law": The lives of civil servants and the internal workings of a law office.

Do I make my point? "Ben Casey" is "Julie Farr, M.D." is "Trapper

John" is "Heartbeat" is "Nightingales." This is not to comment on the high quality or the lack of quality of any of these shows. It is just to say that a concept is no great shakes.

Even what we consider innovative can be found in an obscure "B" film if we look hard enough. Just go to your nearby video store and tell the kid behind the counter your sensational, "fresh" idea and he'll spout off a list of movies with the same concept in different genres. What, then, makes a concept work? It is *characters.* Characters breathe life into the concept and provide the necessary conflict that gives the series its ongoing potential.

Why is it we so often see the most unlikely types thrown together— the ex-judge and the ex-con, the character who goes by the book and the character who can't, the crackpot and the straight man, the conservative and the liberal? There's Archie Bunker and Meathead, Alex and the Keatons, David and Maddie, Lucy and Desi, Magnum and Higgins. Be it the family arena, the work arena, or the battle between the sexes, good characters with big conflicts mean unlimited storylines: ongoing potential and the possibility of a long-running show, which is exactly what producers and the networks want.

Filling in the Concept

Some eight to ten years ago, it was in vogue not to have children. (Today, having babies is back in style.) At this same time, interest rates were going up so fast that many young couples were trying to grab condos for ten percent down, for fear if they didn't that they'd never own anything. I kept thinking to myself that somewhere in this national predicament there was a timely concept for a television series. Besides God and apple pie, what is more a part of the American dream than credit cards and owning your own home?

The pilot that resulted was entitled "Common Ground." It was the story of three working, childless couples in their geriatric twenties who were chasing the good life even if it killed them. These three couples were far from recent acquaintances. They went to college together. Two of the wives were best friends growing up. One had even dated the other's husband for a while. The concept for the show was simply three childless, young couples who share "common ground" (condominium walls). It was cute, it was timely, but it certainly, as yet, was not a well-developed idea that could sell.

The entire concept of the pilot rested on who was inside those condominiums. Who were the couples? Who shared those walls? There are two ways to develop characters: One is from scratch, which we covered in the last chapter. The other is from a composite of the people we already know. Sometimes the human imagination cannot manufacture anything better than the real thing!

I asked myself who I could place in the first condo. Who did I know, out of many friends, acquaintances, and family who had dominant, fun characteristics I could work with to exaggerate and intensify? My brother came to mind. At eight, he had decided he wanted to become a millionaire. He subscribed to the *Wall Street Journal* when most kids were reading *Popeye* comic books. He used to borrow my parents' car, take it to the car wash, and get excited when tipping the attendants. His first bottle of wine was Château Lafite-Rothschild. My father almost choked when he discovered how much it cost.

One of my brother's first jobs was as a caddie at a southern California country club, where later he became the youngest member and got his golfing buddies to invest in his first project. A few years ago after his first child was born, he went to Gucci's and bought her a rattle. In all fairness to my brother, there are many more positive aspects to his personality than this very one-sided view I have just given you.

The goal of the writer here is not to copy a person. It is rather to find a trait or particular traits that can be exaggerated in creating another person. Using my brother as the prototype, my partner and I created a character named Tony Berman.

Tony Berman

Tony is a real estate agent who looks, feels, thinks, and acts successful. He's got everything but the money to back him up—a fancy car, a country club membership, etc. He feels these "toys" are necessary for business, but actually they're a wonderful excuse to take his rewards now.

Tony Berman is slightly naive when it comes to people; he will always look for justice and is often an arbitrator because of his gifted tongue. The more insecure he is in a situation, the more he relies on his verbiage. Impulsive, he loves practical jokes, testing his own luck and on occasion he takes a junket to Vegas. A follower of positive thinker Zig Ziegler, his philosophy is if you believe in it enough it'll happen. Tony's sure it will happen for him. Why not? He's a bullshitter, but an ethical one, and anyone with his integrity has got to have God on his side.

Having placed Tony Berman in the first condo, the next question became who to place next door to him. Tony is only as good as the character we could put him up against. Who did I know who was Berman's antithesis? What character could we place in the second condo who would present the greatest conflict? Who would prove his greatest foil?

A friend of mine had the opposite qualities of Berman. He always played by the rules, didn't believe in shortcuts, and through junior high and high school consistently made the dean's list. Not once did he overstep his bounds, not even for the experience. He graduated with honors, went to UCLA, then USC, found a wonderful wife (one of my dearest friends), bought a little house, then a bigger one. Today, they are very successful. Here was a wonderful character because he represented the opposite philosophy of Berman. One was "go for it—life is a gamble," and the other was "don't rock the boat; play by the rules and you'll get there." Can you imagine the conflict between these two characters and the limitless storylines they could provide?

We created our second character using my friend as a prototype. Again, we exaggerated and intensified basic traits, then went to work creating an entirely different person. We named this character Michael Kellegrew.

Michael Kellegrew

An attorney, a little wheel in a large firm for the last six years, he is perhaps the brightest member of the three couples. Knowledgeable in even the most obscure subjects, he is not a braggart, abhors risk, is very low-key and matter-of-fact. He deals best with issues in the clear-cut black and white, feels he owes it to you to tell you the dismal truth, and could talk endlessly on the inequities of life. While driving through Beverly Hills, Kellegrew, instead of awing the houses, wonders how many of the residents are involved in lawsuits. His idea of good reading is, "How to Prepare Yourself for the Oncoming Recession."

At this point, we went to work creating a character for the third condo. What kind of person would drive both Berman and Kellegrew crazy? We couldn't think of anyone, so we created a character from scratch. He's the kind of guy who doesn't care if he ever sees Europe. No stress, no sweat, no angina at forty. He's smart, but doesn't like to stretch it. He cherishes his weekends off. Life is good. Don't hassle or resist the flow. This type of person would provide great conflict for our other two characters, who at this stage are not content. To make matters worse, he makes more money than both of them because he belongs to a union. We named our character Jim Owen.

Jim Owen

He is not as intellectual as Mike or as intuitive as Tony, but probably the most sensitive of the three. Jim studied two years to become an engineer, then decided he could make as much money hanging drywall. Who needed ulcers, angina at forty, or getting laid off? He enjoys the outdoors and the physical labor even though he has to tolerate a moronic boss. He's policitally aware, well read, but prefers Clint Eastwood to Cronkite, and if he never tours Europe he'll live. His contentment with life could drive an ambitious soul to drink, but Jim feels, "Who needs motivation when you've got a good union?" He's incapable of airs, keeps friends from all walks of life, and on occasion brings his street buddies home.

Now we began matching up our characters with their perspective mates. For Berman, we needed a woman who completely reacted to his extravagance, the kind who goes to "Cost-less," buys cheap booze, and puts it in expensive bottles. She is certain her husband's risk taking will someday ruin them.

Chris Berman

Curvy, wide-eyed, exuberant, she looks at every new experience as an adventure. A top saleswoman in her field, she's secure in her work but not in her personal life. Blunt to a fault and incapable of holding a grudge, she blurts before she thinks, lacking tact and certainly forethought. Chris will always have her umbrella waiting for a rainy day—her husband's excessive spending and prolific generosity have taught her to stash grocery money. Her secret bank account attests to the fact that no man is ever going to leave her high and dry. Hysterical outbursts and routine fights are a part of this woman's foreplay.

For Kellegrew, we needed a woman who was constantly frustrated by his overly cautious nature—a lady who wants to have fun; an instigator with a little bit of the devil in her.

Lynda Kellegrew

A secretary for most of her married life, Lynda doesn't want to work, but wants "things" and is not beyond pushing Mike to get them. She's fun-loving, extremely social, outwardly possesses a great disposition, and when alone with Mike, she goads him to loosen up and be more like his friends. Why can't he let go? Why can't they have more fun? Lynda's escapades and angelic face make her somewhat of a dichotomy. Mike feels that if it were not for his stable influence, she may have gone out of control.

In the third condo, we matched our hard hat with a Jewish princess. They are the only couple who aren't married. And they have a physical relationship that utterly shakes the foundation of the complex.

Lori Daniels

Intelligent, but not ambitious, she does things—and well— out of necessity. Lori has held a multitude of jobs, and at the moment is an instructor at a Nautilus salon. An active member of NOW, this lady doesn't have to fight for independence like Chris—it comes naturally. Lori's parents, who sent her to USC, wanted her to marry a doctor. Jim isn't exactly what they had in mind, but she moved in with him anyway. She has no complaints, there's a terrific physical attraction between them, and as she often says, "Jimmy doesn't brown-bag it in bed."

After developing our couples, we added two secondary characters: (1) A maid who works from condo to condo, and (2) a low-rider grounds keeper.

Maid

A good listener but a better talker, who's frequently making moral judgments. A hundred percent for the person she happens to be with at the time, she professes loyalty but when slightly nudged will spill her guts.

Grounds Keeper

This macho forty-year-old, given to headbands, tight T-shirts, and biker boots, upturns the soil and waters from his Harley.

We sold "Common Ground" to NBC. It was the characters that sold this project. They made the concept come alive. They made the concept work. Unfortunately, the series never went to air. There were top-level management changes, and when the prior regime went, so did the enthusiasm for our project. Timing is crucial in this business.

The Bible

The bible is a written presentation that explains what the pilot is all about. These written presentations run about seven to fifteen pages and essentially are a pitch on paper. They tell the reader exactly what it is the creator/writer expects of the series—that is, what it's about, the mood the writer wishes to convey, and the format the show will revolve around. The presentation is usually followed by a handful of TV guideline stories (a short three- or four-line description for each show that indicates the series' ongoing potential to buyers).

In selling a pilot, it is the bible that sells, not the script. A script, no matter how good, cannot convey the overall scope or umbrella perspective the writer intends the series to take. To better understand what the bible, or pilot presentation, is all about, it is best to show rather than to explain.

"City Lights," a pilot I developed with Pamela and Earl Wallace, incorporates the elements we have discussed. In the first paragraph, we create the mood we wish to convey for the series. Into this backdrop, enter our two main characters, Deke and Jordan. By their descriptions, we are immediately aware that they are opposites and prove a great contrast.

"City Lights"

> *San Francisco.*
> *The very special feel of The City after night falls.*
> *An urgent jazz track underlies upscale images of sleek cars, hot fashion and fast money. While on the streets faces*

tell another story . . . ham-and-eggers hustling the side-
walks, one-time porno queens tricked out to ten-dollar-a-
pop whores, and fan-tan parlor shills working the back alleys
of Chinatown. And a damp mist settling in from the Mission,
across North Beach and up Nob Hill, with a foghorn moaning in the distance . . .

A gleaming pearlescent '57 T-Bird squeals to a halt in
front of City Night Court, and out springs a smashing young
woman of twenty-six or so in a low-cut Christian le Croix
evening gown. She hastens toward the entry. This is JOR-
DAN ABERNATHY, who, we'll see, is in her own way more
"now" than Madonna.

The guy hustling her up the steps, in a ratty sweater and
baggy ducks, is an Australian of about the same age by the
name of DEKE WINBY. His deceptively laid-back demeanor
cloaks a gristly, rugged nature.

The courtroom docket is chock-a-block with miscreants of
every sort, from tourist-mugging thugs through the nightly
quota of Tenderloin hookers to crack-peddling gang members. And all the regulars perk up as Jordan makes an entrance worthy of Garbo—they know it's showtime.

Now we discover that Jordan Abernathy—her night at the
opera rudely interrupted by Deke—is here on business:
she's a fast-rising criminal defense attorney. Fresh out of law
school, a young San Francisco aristocrat with high-octane
connections, she's set on making a name for herself à la
Melvin Belli.

Deke is her investigator. But unlike that other Aussie,
Dundee, he's a generation removed from the Outback and
reptile poaching, and there's not a naive bone in his body.
We'll learn that Deke is a twenty-eight-year-old maverick
raised in the slums of the big city of Sydney who evolved into
a streetwise private eye. And as we meet him, he's an exile
on the run in San Francisco from the mob in Australia.

Clearly, these two—Deke and Jordan—have almost nothing in common—except their youth and a deep-seated rebel
streak. So why does she keep him on retainer, and why does
he stay there?

Well, for one thing he's a hell of an investigator. More
than once he's turned a case around and added another
notch to her curriculum vitae. And, due to his unlicensed
circumstances, he works cheap.

And maybe it's also got something to do with that gnaw-

ing physical attraction between them. They both like to play with fire, and the chemistry between these two could cause a meltdown.

But mostly it's because she owes him. More about that momentarily.

But this night Jordan's client is a former pro football player fallen on desperate times, a drinking and brawling buddy of Deke's. Arrested for public intoxication, he bit off a piece of a cop's ear, chewed and swallowed. For a moment—playing things by ear (so to speak)—Jordan is hard-pressed to come up with a defense. Then, in a stroke of brilliance:

"Your honor, I would point out to the court that this man is destitute. He's been living on the streets for weeks and has no resources whatsoever."

"What's that got to do with anything, Miss Abernathy?" responds the judge.

"Well," says Jordan, playing to the audience, "He hasn't had a thing to eat for three days."

The courtroom erupts in laughter, and Jordan knows she's going to get some ink in the early-morning edition of the Chronicle.

That's Jordan Abernathy—the postfeminist achiever personified, ready to take a big bite out of the Nineties, and she'll be as outrageous, theatrical and audacious as it takes. Jordan revels in the spotlight and thrills at seeing her name in the headlines.

This girl wants to be a star.

Next we introduce the arena or franchise of the show—that is, these two unlikely types work together. Jordan, a defense attorney, is out to make a name for herself. Deke is somewhat of a sleazy private investigator, totally unaffected by style or pretense.

We now know what the story is about. Our concept is clear: an upscale ambitious San Francisco attorney and a salty, sexy Australian private eye who she keeps on retainer. With the concept defined we now move into our characters.

The Characters

DEKE: A laid-back rogue who doesn't play by the rules and could care less what the world thinks of it. His mother disappeared early and his merchant seaman father was mostly gone.

He was taken in and affectionately raised by the outcasts of the seamy side of Sydney—bookies, hookers . . . you name it. Those down on their luck and depleted in funds—but never in heart. To this day he passionately defends the underdog and has too little patience for the games of the upper crust.

His hangout is a dive down in the Tenderloin called The Limetown Pub. It's more than a bar; it's where he takes his phone calls, showers and hustles some change on the side at darts, at which he's a demon.

His best friend and confidant is the Limetown barkeep, REGGIE, an incurable romantic who has committed to memory every line that Dashiell Hammett ever wrote about The City. Reggie invariably has a Hammett-esque slant on whatever case Deke and Jordan are working.

Deke flagrantly drives a wreck of a pickup that was probably a Jeep or something in an earlier incarnation, and—to Jordan's delight—will walk into a society party dressed any damned way he pleases.

Home is a derelict tug moored to a pier that once had a name . . . definitely the wrong side of the wharf. But for Deke, water is home and at night he can look out across the bay and imagine the lights of Sydney.

JORDAN: An Abernathy, a name that reeks of San Francisco society. She only knows the best. Mom, a well-known San Francisco Superior Court judge, was one of the first women to battle her way to the bench.

An outspoken feminist, ALISSA ABERNATHY was a difficult role model for Jordan to live up to. Although she inherited Alissa's brains, drive and ambition, Jordan tends to be rejective of the deadly serious philosophy and rhetoric of her mother's circle of friends.

For her part, Alissa thinks her flamboyant and unrepentantly sexy daughter is something of a loose cannon on a heaving deck, and sparks are always flying between the two.

Like Deke, Jordan also has a view of the bay, but it's from her Russian Hill condo. You'll find her at Nob Hill cocktail parties, in a box-seat at Giants opening day, sailing on the Bay, or wowing the glitterati at the opening of the opera season . . . and rarely in the company of the same man.

That is, when she's not scheming up some outrageous legal strategy for another one of her headline-grabbing cases. Remember the woman who sued the city claiming that the trauma of a cable car accident turned her into a nymphomaniac? For such a case Jordan would kill (and Alissa would die).

What drives Jordan? Maybe it's simply reaction against Alissa, who has been a highly intimidating, if loving, force in her life. Or perhaps she's still vainly seeking the approval of the ne-er-do-well father she never knew. Or maybe she's just so full of life and fun that even The City can hardly contain her.

In any event, she's going for the brass ring her way—and she's invariably surprised to discover that the men in her life either fall insanely in love with her, or are completely intimidated.

Deke Winby, with his solid core and common touch, is the single exception. He understands Jordan. He's the net beneath her high-flying trapeze—her anchor in reality, sometimes conscience and dependable strong shoulder to cry on when those rare moments occur. Jordan—in that one quiet moment when nobody's watching—might secretly like to be pulled off by her hair. And Deke is the one man in her firmament strong enough to do it. Except that's not his style.

So what was it that brought this unlikely pair together?

At this point in the presentation we *briefly* give the background on how these two unlikely characters got together. Some bibles do not require this explanation, but in this case the reader would certainly be curious so it must be addressed. Notice how this background was left for later in the presentation. Though the backstory would play out later in the series, it is not what the series is about.

When Mrs. Reese Wainright appeared at Jordan's office in a gingerbread Victorian at 122 Case Street looking for a defense attorney to prove fraud in a recent divorce settlement, Jordan smelled front-page headlines.

The American-born Mrs. Wainright had been the wife of a well-known Australian publishing magnate, and insisted her ex was hiding assets in their recent property settlement—the case was jet-set glitz from the get-go. And so she winged to Sydney in search of her only witness, an accountant who Mrs. Wainright insisted had the "real" books.

Enter Deke . . . a Sydney private eye who had a reputation that defied censored explanation. Jordan finally tracked him down at his second home—the racetrack—and he signed on for a sizable fee.

There was only one snag—it turned out that Wainright was hiding more than money. Deke uncovered his heavy ties with the Australian mob, and unwittingly ended up a witness to the murder of the account–witness.

Deke, with a contract on his head, barely escaped Australia with his hide. Which is how he ended up in San Francisco—or, as he tags it, "The wrong city by the Bay"—broke and on the run.

Jordan, feeling more or less responsible for Deke's plight, helped him get set up, then hired him for the odd investigative job. In no time their cockeyed chemistry clicked, and the rest is history.

Deke and Jordan—bantering, bickering, poles apart all the way—are an unbeatable team.

Next we move into the format—that is, how the show is presented each week. Every show revolves around an ongoing format. Here the writers clarify and capsulize their vision—the dos and don'ts of the series.

The Format

"CITY LIGHTS" is an action/character venue, not a courtroom drama. The obligatory courtroom scenes will serve to explicate and polish off story points, as well as showcase Jordan's flamboyant approach to the practice of law. In other words, the drama will lie in the interaction of the characters and not in courtroom thrust and parry.

This section is followed by the quick storyline—to whet the reader's appetite, to instill in the reader's head the limitless potential of the series.

EPISODES: Usually involving a murder, but not every time out, will exploit the whole panorama of the city Herb Caen once tagged Baghdad-by-the-Bay, and will be people oriented. For instance, street artist/bag lady Contessa Moon discovers her sketches on napkins, paper bags and wrapping paper are being sold for big bucks in a major gallery and tries to raise a stink . . . shortly thereafter the gallery owner turns up dead, and Contessa is jailed. Deke and Jordan saddle up.

A movement to turn Alcatraz into a gambling mecca brings the mob to town. When Chief Withered Ear claims The Rock belongs to his tribe, Jordan takes his case for the headline value in it. Soon someone starts trying to kill the client and Deke suddenly has his hands full keeping the old reprobate alive.

When Mr. San Francisco (read Cyril Magnin) is murdered, it's discovered he left his fortune to the cabbie who drove him from his suite at the Fairmont to his club every day. The cabbie, a friend of Deke's, is booked in a flash and Jordan leaps to his defense, leaving the well-connected family of the departed aghast.

And many other storylines that mine the terrain from the hot-tub/BMW/Lucas-land of Marin, through the rich subcultures of the Castro, Tenderloin and Chinatown, to the badlands of Oakland and the aging radical-chic of Berkeley . . .

In the end we briefly bring it back home and hit the reader with yet another marketable aspect of the series—that is, a man and a woman with clashing personalities and underlying sexual tension (basically, this step is like closing the sale).

Above all, "CITY LIGHTS" is a contemporary romance. Deke and Jordan are both strong-willed and extremely independent people, yet they've forged a bond that bridges their social, economic and cultural differences.

And they're both solid enough, if and when they come to terms with their feelings, to make it together.

End

Pilot presentations vary in format. As long as they are concise, entertaining, and clear, nothing else matters. Too much detail and too many pages will give the reader too much room to find fault. It is better to whet the appetite than to overfeed. When writing these presentations, think of your series as a motion picture, and you are creating the promos for the movie houses. Promos only show the best, the most marketable, the most theatrical. They are presented in such a way that we get the overall picture, we know what the story is about, and we have a semblance of order.

Remember, selling is the art of seduction. What's sexier: someone only partially clad or someone broad stark naked? Don't overkill.

A Word From Writer/Producer Jay Tarses

"The Days and Nights of Molly Dodd" was hailed by many critics as a revolutionary breakthrough when it first premiered on NBC in 1987. "Molly," wonderfully played by Blair Brown, is about a thirty-eight-year-old single working woman living in New York and divorced from an irresponsible jazz musician for whom she still harbors feelings. Molly has no children, a lot of problems with men, a mother who won't let up, and an uneventful career. This well-written, offbeat slice of life, which is filmed without a laugh track, is the creation of writer/producer Jay Tarses.

I first worked for Jay when he was teamed with writer/producer Tom Patchett. They were producing the "Tony Randall Show," and gave my partner and me our first break into half-hour comedy. After writing the Randall segment, we wrote two episodes for the next sitcom they created, "We've Got Each Other." Among their numerous credits, Patchett and Tarses went on to create "Open All Night," a half-hour sitcom about a couple who owned a convenience store, "The Chopped Liver Brothers," a sitcom about a pair of stand-up comics in which they took the starring roles, and the critically acclaimed "Buffalo Bill."

In 1982, the team broke up. Tom Patchett would later become the creator/producer of the successful series "Alf." Jay Tarses went on to create and produce "The Faculty," "Slap Maxwell," and "Molly Dodd," which originally aired on NBC and was later picked up by Lifetime Television Network in April of 1989. The show has since been renewed for an additional twenty-six episodes. Jay now commutes to New York where the entire cast and crew of "Molly Dodd" is now shot. I was able to catch him on the West Coast during some editing sessions.

MADELINE DIMAGGIO: Molly Dodd is a sensational character. How did she happen? Where did she come from?

JAY TARSES: Molly Dodd was born during lunch with Brandon Tartikoff (entertainment president of NBC). Brandon said to me, "I want to do a show about a woman." I said, "I'll do it if I can use Blair Brown." He said, "You got it. I like Blair." I'd just done a pilot with her for ABC called "The Faculty," about school teachers, which I thought was wonderful, but which ABC thought was too dark. So it didn't go. But we had a great rapport and I wanted to work with her again. I met with Blair and we started discussing what kind of woman Molly was going to be. We began to draw guidelines. I would do all the writing. Blair would be the model.

MD: The model?

JT: Well, Blair's not Molly, but they do look exactly alike. Whereas Blair's a successful person, Molly's not. Blair knows a lot about the single life in New York because she lives it.

MD: I read your first script and loved it. It was an incredible departure from anything I had seen on the air.

JT: I wanted to write scenes that didn't necessarily smack of sitcom, that were just people talking about the things that people do talk about. I didn't want to make specific points. I wanted to tell a story about a woman surviving in New York City. That's all I wanted, including the swirl of people around Molly. People who walk into her life and out of it, the men, her job, her family, and how she copes with everything. People are all the same. It doesn't matter if we're men or women. Everybody feels alone at some time; everybody feels the effects of relationships. Everybody feels despair, joy, hope, sadness. I wanted the show to be open-ended and to move in small increments, rather than have big epiphanies in every episode.

MD: How did the network handle that?

JT: They didn't understand it. They didn't like the format. When I wrote the script and turned it in there was sort of a puzzled silence. We had a meeting to discuss the script, and I told them as best I could what I was trying to do. And they told me as best as they could that they were puzzled. But they gave me a thirteen-show guarantee, which they don't like to give, anyway.

MD: What do they usually give?

JT: Maybe a pilot. And then if they like the pilot you shoot it. If they like that, they'll give you an order for a few. They gave me thirteen, so we called the first script a prototype. I shot the prototype and they didn't like it. They wanted me to do some reshooting, so I did. I compromised. I gave them what I thought they would like to make the show work for them. I had a thirteen-show deal. I didn't want to fight with them the whole way.

MD: Was it the network that coined your show a dramedy?

JT: Somebody called it a dramedy because they needed a catch word. Since they couldn't put the show in a convenient box, they invented a box and called it "dramedy," which isn't even a word; it's two half-words. Dramedy sort of had a bad connotation after a while, because it was usually a show no one knew what to do with. But I never thought what I was doing was that unusual. I thought it was interesting.

MD: But it was unusual in that it breaks from the traditional mold of sitcom humor and glitz.

JT: Molly is like a jazz riff. It has its own music. It has its own spirit. And it's mainly because of Blair's spirit, which permeates everything. It has good writing, it's well directed and well lit by Steve Dubin. Pat Williams composed a great score—it's just a nice little movie. If you like it, why analyze it. And people *did* like it at first. When we first went on the air we got terrific ratings and the reviews were wonderful.

MD: What happened?

JT: Tartikoff didn't believe in the show. He kept calling it "inaccessible"; it would never reach a huge audience. He wanted it to be funnier. But we still got really good numbers, good reviews, so he was forced to renew us. But rather than renew us for the fall, he renewed us for thirteen more shows, and put us on the following March and scheduled us erratically. NBC kept putting up as many obstacles as they could, hoping someday we'd trip over one. Eventually, we did. A show like "Molly Dodd" will never get a mass audience. It will never get the Thursday night "Bill Cosby"–"Cheers" audience. It's not a lot of people's cup of tea. It's a very specialized kind of a show, but it should be allowed to exist. "St. Elsewhere" existed for seven years without an audience. That's kind of what "Molly Dodd" was.

MD: The most recent demographics show that the largest viewing audience is made up of women Molly's age.

JT: That doesn't make a bit of difference. Women eighteen to forty-nine loved the show. People I like and respect loved the show, but it didn't get big enough ratings. I can't reach those Nielsen people. That's not the audience I get, but that's the audience they need. The networks are in a different business than I am. They're in business to make as much money as they can from their sponsors. They're in the business of getting the highest possible ratings. They'll do a satan worship show if the numbers are big enough. I can't do that. Maybe I should be on PBS or something, I don't know.

MD: Haven't you found a good place on cable now?

JT: The Lifetime Channel has been great. They wanted us. They made us feel as if we were the answer to whatever prayers they had, and it's a good feeling to not feel like somebody's stepsister.

MD: The narrative in "Molly Dodd" is much longer than in most TV scripts, but there's such a feel to it. None of it is excess. I love the segment where she gets up in the morning and decides whether or not to shave her legs.

JT: We've struck a chord with women. They'll come up and say, "How did you know that? How can a man write that?"

MD: Then you don't think gender matters when writing about the female psyche?

JT: We've had scripts written by women that have been awful, and we've had scripts written by men that have been wonderful, and vice-versa.

MD: I'm glad to hear that. It's frustrating to me that the networks seem to always want female storylines from women writers. One of my favorite films, *An Unmarried Woman,* was written by Paul Mazursky.

JT: And I think women have incredible insight into men. Zane Grey was never out west and he wrote great westerns. You don't have to necessarily be dead to write about dying.

MD: Is your show staff-written?

JT: No. This year it was just myself and Eric Overmyer, who is essentially a playwright, on staff. It's all outside scripts. The writing I don't do, he does. And then we farm out scripts to a lot of New York-based writers, mostly playwrights.

MD: Because the quality is better, or because they're more accessible?

JT: It's because they can write this show better than traditional sitcom writers. It's not a sitcom. It's a very peculiar show. And playwrights seem to have these weird angles and these interesting slants on things. The essence of "Molly Dodd," the thing I always wanted to do with the show, is make sure the audience doesn't know what's going to happen next. So in order to keep that, we need to utilize a different kind of writer.

MD: Do you read spec scripts?

JT: No. If it comes through an agent, someone will read it. I can't legally do it. But sometimes I do; sometimes it sneaks through the cracks. Sometimes it'll be somebody who knows somebody who knows somebody else who'll call and ask me to do it. Or I'll be doing an interview with somebody, or it will be a social thing and somebody will just get me to. I like pleasant people, and sometimes somebody pleasant will say, "Hey, gee, listen, would you like to read my script?" And sometimes you just do it; you just read it.

MD: What do you think about the half-hour sitcom writing today as compared to ten years ago?

JT: It's probably the same. The writers work just as hard, and they're just as clever. I guess there's good writing on the "Cosby Show," whatever he doesn't do himself, and maybe "Cheers," and maybe the first season of "Wonder Years." But there's plenty of bad writing out there, too. There was a time when Patchett and I tried to find and develop a lot of writers. There's certainly room for good writers.

MD: How did you break into the business?

JT: Patchett and I were a comedy team.

MD: When did you decide you first wanted to write?

JT: We always wrote our own material, so we were writing as well as performing. It was just a logical extension. We weren't making a huge amount of money as performers so we thought we'd try to write scripts. We sent spec scripts out to the coast.

MD: Which was the first to sell?

JT: I think it was the "New Dick Van Dyke Show," the one that took place in Arizona. Then we did some "Sandy Duncan" shows. And then we started writing a lot of variety shows and specials, "The Carol Burnett Show," "The Jackson Five," "Diana Ross," all those kinds of things. We still wanted to be performers. We just accidently got into writing.

MD: You've worn just about every hat there is to wear in this industry. Do you still consider yourself first and foremost a writer?

JT: Yeah, absolutely. Writing's hard, and I've often thought about not doing it, but it's what I am. It pays the mortgage.

MD: What about directing?

JT: I don't love it—I like it. In a TV situation you really don't have as much control when you're a director. You can't light it. The director of photography does that. Once you say "action," the bullet's out of the gun. You can pretend to be one of these great visionaries, but really your job is to make sure everybody hits his mark, and that the actor's words are said properly.

MD: Really? I've heard so often that film is the director's medium.

JT: If you have the time to do two pages a day. But this is television. We have deadlines. In the movie business it's like a one-year schedule. On "Molly," we shoot six or seven pages every day. A script runs twenty-seven or twenty-eight pages. In a movie, there's time to work with the actors, pull out a performance. That's why Blair is so terrific to work with. She's very sympatico with me, knows all the nuances. With her, I know the words are going to sound perfect.

MD: You're the creator/producer of "Molly Dodd." You've written and directed many of the episodes. You're even in town to do editing.

JT: I do it all. I'm a hands-on kind of guy.

MD: What is a typical day like for you?

JT: A typical day in New York, I get up, hop on the subway to our studio in Queens where we shoot interiors of "Molly Dodd." Then I'll go and work on a script, or rewrite somebody else's. Then I whip down to the set and watch rehearsals. If there's problems, or if the actors can't say their lines, I'll fix them. Then I go upstairs and solve the U.S. trade deficit.

MD: If you were out scraping around today, what would you do to break in? What advice would you give to new writers?

JT: Don't give up. I think there is so much room in this business for people to earn a living. It depends on what they want. If they want to earn a living as a writer and they have a modicum of ability, if they're good, if they're decent, and if they don't give up they'll find a way. There are a lot of ways to earn a living in this business. Anybody can make it. Everybody that I started out with is still around, unless they're dead. They all drive big cars, they have houses with electricity, and some of them aren't neurotic. The point is, you can find a way to make it in the business. You can find a way to survive somehow.

MD: So just keep writing?

JT: Keep doing something; just keep pumping it out. You never know how it's going to happen. It's different every time. Try to meet people. Try to find somebody who likes what you do. If you're pigheaded enough and determined enough, there are ways to get your stuff read, there are ways to get your stuff produced, and there are ways to become successful if you stay with it. Eventually something will happen. I don't know what, and I don't know how, but I do believe that most people can get in. Many people who have worked for me as gophers and secretaries are now actual functioning writers and producers, or are working in some capacity in the industry. But they're in the business because they stayed with it and kept punching.

11

Writing the Two-Hour Movie

In order for the movie script to be purchased it must first be a good reading experience. A good read is one in which you are compelled to turn the page. It is a story that immediately grabs you. The characters are alive. The dialogue is lean. Every line serves a purpose; every scene progresses the action and gives greater depth to character. The narrative and locales instill pictures in your mind. There is powerful plot progression, powerful turning points, and a strong beginning, middle, and end.

Recently, I reread *Body Heat* for the third time. Each time I read this script I'm transported, and an hour passes before I realize that I haven't refilled my coffee cup. Creating a script with this kind of direction and focus is a monumental battle for the novice as well as for the veteran writer. I've critiqued many speculation scripts written in the hopes of an eventual sale. Too often these scripts wander off track. It is as though somewhere the writers have forgotten what they are writing about. Other times I find myself excited by the material, only to discover that the script shifts gears and topples into that no-writer's land called the "mess in the middle."

The script, unlike a horse, can't afford to lose momentum in hopes of a last push for the finish line. It must remain consistent throughout. How does the writer give a script this needed direction and focus? Where does a good movie script begin? It begins with structure, the single most essential element of all screenplays. Attempting to write without thoroughly understanding structure is like driving blindly around looking for a house when you could ask for directions. Structure keeps the screenplay on track. It is the foundation on which everything is built.

The Basic Three-Act Structure

Movies for Television and feature films run approximately 105 to 120 pages. These scripts rely on the basic three-act structure. These acts are invisible; they are not delineated. If we were to diagram the screenplay as a 120-page unit, or 120 minutes, it would look like figure 9.

Act I is the act of the setup. The setup establishes the main characters and the circumstances of the story. Just as in our half-hour and one-hour scripts, the setup supplies us with everything we need to get the story going.

The Setup

Establishes the tone, the texture, and the place of the movie.

Establishes the main players.

Establishes a problem for the main character and his or her dramatic need.

At the end of this twenty-five-page to thirty-five-page unit of action, a turning point is introduced into the story that totally shifts the action around. Act II, the confrontation, is a forty-five-page to sixty-page unit of action. It is here the character meets the majority of obstacles. As the act progresses, a problem or problems are resolved, but these lead to greater complications. At the end of the confrontation, another turning point occurs that turns the story around and catapults the action into Act III.

The Confrontation

Presents obstacles to the character's dramatic need.

Creates the rising conflict and action of the script.

Raises the stakes for the character.

Develops tension and/or suspense.

The third and final act is the resolution, a twenty-five-page to thirty-five-page unit of action. It is here that the story builds to a climax and is resolved.

The Resolution

Presents a moment of discovery and change for the character.

Builds toward the climax.

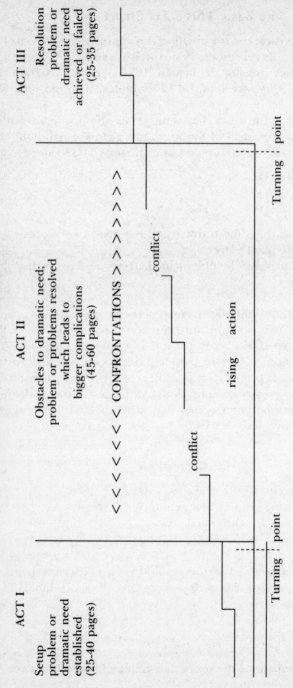

THREE-ACT STRUCTURE

ACT I

Setup
problem or
dramatic need
established
(25-40 pages)

ACT II

Obstacles to dramatic need;
problem or problems resolved
which leads to
bigger complications
(45-60 pages)

< < < < < < < CONFRONTATIONS > > > > > > >

conflict

conflict

rising   action

Turning — point

Turning — point

ACT III

Resolution
problem or
dramatic need
achieved or failed
(25-35 pages)

(*Note:*
The verticle lines are imaginary divisions and only serve the
purpose for the writer. These acts are not delineated on the
script page.)

Figure 9.

Allows the character to achieve or not achieve his or her dramatic
need.

Allows the story to be resolved (usually the last three to five pages
of the script).

At this point in the book it might prove beneficial to reread chapter
2. The Tools of Teleplay Writing absolutely apply to the M.O.W. and
feature film. In episodic television we are somewhat limited in our use
of locales and narrative. But now, with the two-hour movie, we have
free reign and we can use these tools to their full potential. We are
no longer limited by preset locations and formats, or existing characters. It is now all ours to create: our imaginations, our craft . . . and
our blank page.

By now, you should be looking at scripts differently. Reading in
script format should be more comfortable to you. And you will note
the same commonly used camera techniques turning up again and
again. Various elements and components of scene construction
should now be familiar. Ask yourself:

Do we care about the characters?

How do the writers successfully or unsuccessfully use exposition?

What are the visuals they choose to incorporate?

Where does one scene end and the next begin?

What is the length of the scene?

Imagine yourself sitting in the audience eating popcorn. What
keeps you interested? Entertained? And last, but certainly not least,
become aware of what *isn't* said. Does the writing show things instead
of talk about them? Does it indicate rather than explain?

Act I: The Setup

To help us better understand structure, let's walk through various
excerpts from "If the Shoe Fits," a screenplay I scripted with Pamela
Wallace. "If the Shoe Fits" is a high-concept, updated version of
Cinderella. In it, our heroine, Kelly, a struggling shoe designer, works
as a gopher in a couturier fashion house. Kelly is rather plain; in fact,
when we first see her the only thing we notice are the red boots she
wears, which are her own creation. Let's review page one again.

**(PLEASE NOTE: Correct script formatting is absolutely crucial
for writers in presenting and submitting scripts. For the sake of
space, and to properly show script development, the format of the**

following excerpt has been condensed. For proper formatting guidelines, please refer to chapter 13.)

We open on visual images of New York City. Here we create the mood and overall feeling of the piece—the lyrical, magical sense that we have entered into a fairytale. We meet Kelly as she is ushered along with the crowds, just another inconspicuous soul, dwarfed by the city.

Next we meet the outrageous, punky Wanda, who we will later learn is on a mission.

"IF THE SHOE FITS"

FADE IN:

EXT. 5TH AVENUE—WORKDAY MORNING

In the Kingdom of Manhattan on this frosty new day of the winter holiday season, a sea of peasantry heaves and surges amid the chaos and clamor of the traffic-choked boulevard, far below the gleaming towers and burly parapets of the mighty rulers of the realm.

CAMERA FINDS AND GOES WITH one such workbound toiler, an honest lass by the name of KELLY GARRETT, as she's carried along by the tide of folk . . . Bright and sprightly in a small-town girl sort of way, she carries a shoe bag. Her attention is occasionally caught by:

SHOES

All sorts of them . . . on the feet of the young and the old, newsboys and stockbrokers, sales girls and shopkeepers, cops and cowboys, panhandlers and pretzel-benders . . . And all of them, in some way large or small, reflecting the personality of their wearers.

Shoes . . . striding and sliding and gliding, scuffing and shuffling and bustling, plodding and jogging and tripping along . . . vivid testimony to the enduring truth that, whatever our station in life, we are all as one where the sole meets the sidewalk.

BACK TO KELLY

But the wildest, most outrageous of all these shoes are on the feet of our heroine . . . red taffeta boots—sequined, beaded, jeweled and feathered—a fantasy realized. They're a vivid contrast to the rest of Kelly—her face, her hair, her clothes—which are frankly nondescript. At first glance she appears plain. But her shoes suggest there's more to her than meets the eye.

INT. BUS

CLOSE ON a gigantic bubble—pink, glistening, so huge it would turn
any kid green with envy. Suddenly it BURSTS—but miraculously it
doesn't glomp onto the face of the chewer, WANDA.

  Wanda is nothing if not eccentric; curly red hair flopped up in a big
bow, a sheepskin vest, bicycle shorts over tights and boots. In short,
Wanda would put Cindy Lauper to shame. One long earring skims her
shoulders; a mass of tiny crystal falling stars that sparkle in the winter
sunshine.

STREET

The metro bus pulls over and Wanda fights her way out. She's clutching a map of the city, and is obviously completely lost.
Ahead in the crowd, a SLEAZY-LOOKING YOUNG MAN grabs a
purse from an ELDERLY WOMAN. As she screeches, "Purse
snatcher!" he turns and runs smack into Wanda, dropping the bag.

A POLICEMAN appears and collars the scuz.

> ELDERLY WOMAN (to thief)
> Scum! I hope you rot in jail!

Wanda hands the woman her purse.

> ELDERLY WOMAN
> Thanks.

> WANDA
> Say, you wouldn't know the way
> to Soho, would you?

> ELDERLY WOMAN
> I don't talk to strangers.

She walks off in a huff. Wanda turns to another PASSER-BY:

> WANDA
> Excuse me—

That person brushes past her shaking his head impatiently. Wanda
tries a young MOTHER pushing a baby pram:

> WANDA
> What a darling child. Say, I'm
> trying to get to Third Avenue—

> MOTHER
> Drop dead.

Just then Kelly materializes in the vicinity:

KELLY
Just go down to the corner and turn
right. It's only three blocks.

Wanda turns, stares at Kelly—seems to recognize her:

KELLY (continuing)
Is something wrong?

WANDA
No. Turn right, three blocks.
Thanks, thanks a lot.

KELLY
You're welcome.

WANDA
Maybe I can do something for you
someday.

Kelly smiles and moves on. Wanda calls after her:

WANDA (continuing)
Hey, I like the boots!

Wanda moves off toward the corner, passing a rather spacey bag lady
who repeats "Happy New Year" to everyone passing her—and is uni-
versally ignored.

WANDA (continuing)
Happy New Year to you, too—

As Wanda is swallowed up by the crowd, the bag lady stares open-
mouthed as a fifty-dollar bill, seemingly from out of nowhere, floats
down at her feet.

BACK TO KELLY

We FOLLOW her red boots as they trot up the steps into the rather
awesome entrance of the House of Payton, bastion of the eccentric,
egotistical, world-famous designer, Elliot Payton.

She goes in, and the big doors close behind her.

■ ■ ■

As mentioned in chapter 9, there are three areas in which we can
reveal characters in film: through their personal, professional, and
private lives. A series of scenes (a sequence) revealing Kelly's professional life follows. We introduce more of the main characters and
plant essential story beats.

We establish Kelly's work place, the House of Payton, and her
dramatic need to be recognized as a shoe designer.

We introduce the subplot: Victor Floyd and Irene Spencer (assist-
ants to designer Payton) are involved in a sordid affair, and are
out to steal his latest creations.

The sequence ends with Kelly's hustling and bustling as a gopher,
further establishing her lowly job and the lack of appreciation for
her.

Notice how the cutting between locales creates the quick pacing.

The notation (o.s.) refers to a character speaking off-screen. We
hear them but cannot see them.

INT. HOUSE OF PAYTON—DESIGN SALON—DAY

About an acre of bustling floor space . . .
A middle-aged supervisor, AUDREY, with an eye jaundiced by experience, passes as Kelly enters.

> AUDREY
> Did you bring them?

Kelly removes a shoe box from the bag she was carrying. She opens
the lid.

A SHOE

This is no ordinary shoe—it's the work of an artist, a fantasy realized,
something a contemporary princess, like Cher, would wear. The kind
of shoe the famous master shoemaker Vivier designs—all faux jewels,
sequins, feathers, silk and satin and velvet.

> KELLY
> Well—?

> AUDREY
> Well what? It's a dream! How did
> you ever create something like this?

> KELLY (winks)
> Dorothy's ruby slippers.

> AUDREY
> They're absolutely magical!

> KELLY
> With wings on your feet dreams
> can come true.

> AUDREY
> You're gonna knock Payton's socks off!
> Go for it, kid. But remember—if

> AUDREY (continued)
> you want his attention, you've gotta
> get in his face.

> KELLY
> Right. Get in his face.

KELLY'S WORK STATION

The tiniest of cubbyholes . . . As Kelly comes in and starts to put her things down, a CO-WORKER appears:

> CO-WORKER
> Don't bother to sit down—Payton's
> got half the models in Manhattan
> upstairs waiting to be prepped.

> KELLY (surprised)
> Right now? What should I bring?

> CO-WORKER
> Who knows? He's crazy. Bring
> everything.

The Co-Worker moves on. Kelly grumbles:

> KELLY
> Everything—

And as she starts to scoop things up . . .

ANGLE

GOING WITH the fundamentally contemptible VICTOR FLOYD and the greedy and underhanded IRENE SPENCER. They're talking urgently under their breaths:

> IRENE
> Do you have the camera?

Victor nods, surreptitiously REVEALING a microfilm camera squirreled away in his vest pocket. Then:

> VICTOR
> I got a message from Kim. He's
> not happy. He wants a meeting.

> IRENE
> A meeting? That's dangerous. If
> we're ever seen with him—
> (and)
> When?

> VICTOR
> Tonight!

She gives him an electric look, and . . .

ELEVATOR

As Victor and Irene enter . . . stand there all businesslike as the doors close.

INT. ELEVATOR

Irene instantly stabs the stop button, throws herself passionately on Victor:

>   VICTOR
> Irene—!

>   IRENE
> Don't deny me, Victor!

>   VICTOR
> Never, sweetest, but here?

>   IRENE
> Danger turns me on! Penetrate me,
> Victor!

And as a mad grope begins . . .

KELLY

Approaching the elevator, carrying an awkward armload of huge sketches, swatches of fabric, various kits and accessories. Trying to balance her burden, she manages to punch the button, but nothing happens.

INT. ELEVATOR

It's getting hot and heavy . . . Victor has his hand up her skirt, Irene's going for his fly—gasping with passion she hauls him around against the control console . . .

BACK TO KELLY

Odd noises coming from within.

Impatiently she tries to hit the button again, but her sketches slip from her arms. As she stoops to pick them up, the elevator doors open to REVEAL Victor and Irene in a clench.

It's an instant before Victor realizes their exposure and pulls violently away. By the time Kelly has gathered up her things, the two lovers have pulled themselves together again.

As Kelly awkwardly wedges into the elevator, her sketches and things protruding at awkward angles:

>   IRENE
> You're late, Garrett.

> KELLY
> Sorry, Mrs. Spencer.
>
> VICTOR
> You should have used the service
> elevator.
>
> KELLY
> Sorry, Mr. Floyd.
>
> IRENE
> Will you get that out of my face!
>
> KELLY
> Sorry, Mrs. Spencer.
>
> And, as the elevator doors close again . . .
>
> VICTOR (o.s.)
> God, you're clumsy!
>
> KELLY (o.s).
> Sorry, Mr. Floyd.

■ ■ ■

A sequence is a series of scenes strung together for a specific purpose. In the sequence above our purpose was to establish Kelly's place of work.

Sequences can be as short as a couple of scenes or as long as a forty-minute unit of action. There is no set number of sequences that belong in a screenplay. It is simply a matter of what the story dictates.

I prefer thinking in terms of visual sequences rather than isolated scenes when developing the screenplay, because it opens up visual possibilities of using many pictures instead of just one locale. Be mindful, however. Don't inadvertently throw in sequences that are extraneous or used as filler. Every scene must serve a purpose to further progress the action.

A very short sequence follows that introduces Mike Powers, our romantic lead (the modern-day Prince). The sequence consists of three very quick scenes.

EXT. STREET—MANHATTAN—DAY

An open Jeep is weaving in and out of traffic. Behind the wheel is MIKE POWERS, about thirty, bundled up in a sheepskin coat topped off with a Met's cap. In a word, he's a hunk—but a frustrated one, and not just with the traffic. He's a man at war with the world and himself.

INT. JEEP—MOVING

Mike seems to be talking to himself.

> MIKE
> Look at all those schmucks locked
> up in their cages . . . that's all
> a car is, you know . . . look at
> 'em. Heck—windows rolled up
> tight . . . heater blasting . . .

We PAN AWAY to REVEAL a huge Chesapeake Bay retriever curled up in the passenger's seat freezing to death, his paws crossed over his snout. This is HECTOR.

> MIKE (continuing)
> . . . might as well be in a coma . . .

He blasts the HORN.

> MIKE (continuing)
> Move it!

Hector gives him an alarmed look . . . Just then he gets a horn BLAST from the cab behind, leans out to shake his fist at the offending driver.

EXT. PAYTON BUILDING—DAY

As Mike pulls up in front of the Payton Building and double parks, blocking traffic behind him. Ignoring the HONKING horns, he jumps out of the Jeep, leaving the keys in the ignition. Hector bounds from the vehicle, follows Mike inside.

A moment later a young GOPHER-TYPE runs out, gets in the Jeep and drives it toward a sign marked PARKING.

■ ■ ■

Each scene in the sequence that follows (page 180) plants important story points and progresses the action forward. In Scene 1 of the sequence:

"Gopher" Kelly is surrounded by, and must answer to, a bevy of
    beauties.
Kelly squirrels away material for her shoes.
Mike is bored by the beautiful models, all of whom are very aware
    of him.
Victor and Irene are Payton's right- and left-hand whips.

Notice the narrative on which the sequence opens. It is colorful, highly visual. It suggests many images without telling the director how to shoot them. The blocks of narrative are separated into paragraphs, which are easier on the eyes and help denote various activities going on at the same time. In Scene 2 of the sequence:

> Mike and designer Payton have been searching frantically for the right model for the Payton Girl layout.
>
> We plant Kelly's feelings toward Mike. She doesn't like him but at the same time cannot help but be attracted to him.
>
> Mike, though he outwardly appears to have everything, is frustrated with his life—in a sense as frustrated as Kelly.
>
> In the last beat of the sequence (page 185), Kelly and Mike are for the first time brought together. She is struggling with her feelings toward him.

Note camera angles are used here because we are working in such a vast space. The backstage incorporates many areas, there is much activity going on, and the angles point us in the direction where we, the audience, must look.

INT. PHOTO STUDIO—BACKSTAGE

A madhouse. A dozen or so models are being prepared for display—garbed, shod, coiffed and made-up. Any given model has two or three stylists at work on her at once.

In a dazzling sequence, we SEE one breathtaking image after another . . . thick manes of wild, full hair blown by wind machines . . . pouty, moist lips . . . sculpted cheekbones . . . it's enough to make the average woman utterly depressed.

And it does. We SEE that at the bottom of the chain of command is Kelly, a workhorse among thoroughbreds, scurrying here and there at the behest of almost everyone, fetching supplies, pinning a hem, touching up makeup.

We also SEE that she's got a little bag into which she squirrels away little bits of discarded fluff, feathers and sequins, and costume jewelry . . . and then she notices . . .

ANGLE—MIKE

As Mike walks through the photo studio, all the women are aware of him. As he passes, the models speak to him and he responds without looking—he "knows" their voices.

> DANIELLE
> Hi, Mike.

> MIKE
> Hi, Danielle.

> BLAIR
> Hello, Mike.

> MIKE
> Hello, Blair.

> SHELLY
> Mike, hi.

Mike just waves—then disappears—Hector following on his heels. Prowling amid the chaos are Irene and Victor in a high state of agitation:

> IRENE
> This delay is intolerable! I won't
> stand for it!

> VICTOR
> You're going to have to crack the
> whip, Irene.

> IRENE
> You're right, Victor. (then, to all) I'm warning
> all of you! If those girls aren't out there in
> five minutes there will be some new faces in
> the unemployment line tomorrow.

INT. PHOTO STUDIO—LATER

DOLLYING ALONG a lineup of the same fabulously beautiful models we saw being prepped earlier.

REVERSE ANGLE

Scrutinizing them is Mike Powers . . . Hovering over him is none other than ELLIOT PAYTON. He's in his mid- to late fifties, and his state of volatile agitation seems to be perpetual.

Following a fawning step or two behind him are Irene and Victor. We SEE Hector curled up asleep on a sofa in the b.g.

Kelly and Audrey are moving ahead of them, adding final desperate touches to the models.

As Mike stops in front of each model, Irene jabs Victor and he sneaks out his tiny camera and SNAPS a shot.

> MIKE
> Shallow . . .

PAYTON (astounded)
> Shallow!

And another:

MIKE
> No . . . soul—

PAYTON
> Soul? Soul—?!

ANGLE—KELLY/AUDREY

Audrey is eyeing Mike hungrily:

AUDREY
> Why didn't Santa Claus bring me one
> of him for Christmas?

KELLY
> Who, Peter Pan? Are you kidding?
> He's so arrogant, and egotistical.

AUDREY
> Yeah, but once you overlook that . . .

Kelly eyes Mike, annoyed by her own attraction to him.

ANGLE—MIKE/PAYTON

As Mike scrutinizes another model:

MIKE
> Only beautiful—

PAYTON
> Only beautiful?!

MIKE
> Is there an echo in here?

In a sudden fit of temper, Payton erupts:

PAYTON
> Get them out! All of them!

IRENE
> Yes, Mr. Payton, of course,
> Mr. Payton!

She starts to hustle the girls out.

PAYTON
> And bring in the next batch!

VICTOR
> Yes, Mr. Payton, of course,
> Mr. Payton!

Victor bustles off.

ANGLE

As Payton turns to Mike in total exasperation:

> PAYTON
> Michael, what is it you want?!

> MIKE
> If I knew, it'd be easy.

Payton stares at him:

> PAYTON
> I'm paying you a thousand dollars
> an hour and you don't know?!

Mike drops wearily into a director's chair, surrounded by an assortment of sophisticated camera gear:

> MIKE
> So, do us both a favor—fire me.

> PAYTON
> I can't. This will be my crowning
> achievement—the look for the last
> decade of the 20th century. I won't
> have anything less than the best for
> this spread. Unfortunately, you're it.

> MIKE
> I see your problem.

> PAYTON
> The problem, Michael, is you. Not me.
> Not the models. You've been impossible
> for weeks. What's going on?

> MIKE
> I don't know.

> PAYTON
> You've got everything. Money. Fame.
> Unlimited access to the most beautiful
> women in the world.

> MIKE (angrily)
> It's not enough! I'm fed up with
> this town, my work (he starts to pace),
> the hustle. Sometimes I think I should
> just cash out and go live in
> the mountains! Get back to reality.

> PAYTON
> Reality is overrated. (then) You're a classic
> example of the "only child" syndrome. Spoiled

> PAYTON (continued)
> from the cradle—handed everything on a
> silver platter—and disadvantaged by a unique
> talent. Know what I think, things have come
> too easily for you.
>
> MIKE
> What things?—There's nothing
> substantial in my life.

Payton stares at him:

> PAYTON
> Michael, you're beginning to sound
> like marriage bait.
>
> MIKE
> Marriage? Me? Don't be ridiculous.
>
> PAYTON
> I know all the signs. I've been there
> three times. (then) The next time I feel like getting
> married, I'm going to find a woman
> I don't like and buy her a house.
>
> MIKE
> You make a lousy wise old fart.
>
> PAYTON
> Fine. But time is running out and
> I still don't have my Payton Girl,
> thanks to your sudden case of angst.
> The world waits while you fiddle.
>
> MIKE
> The world could give a shit, Elliot. (then,
> sighing) Oh, all right. I'm as tired of this as
> you are. Maybe the girl I'm looking for
> doesn't exist. Go ahead—you pick the face.
> Let's get this spread in the can.
>
> PAYTON (beaming)
> That's more like it!

Just then the next batch of models is herded in.

ANGLE

Kelly is tagging along with the file of models, tucking in a blouse here, adjusting a curl there. Spotting Mike, she is distracted in spite of herself and bumps into Irene, who snaps:

> IRENE
> Garrett, will you just get out
> of the way!

As Kelly moves away from Irene, she knocks over one of Mike's big Hasselblads. He barely saves it from crashing.

> MIKE
> Hey, be careful, okay? That's a
> very big-ticket piece of equipment.

Her reply is curt.

> KELLY
> Sorry—

> MIKE
> It's okay.

Then, turning to go, she manages to bump into the camera again. Once more, Mike barely catches it in time.

> MIKE (continuing)
> Miss—

> KELLY (mortified)
> Garrett. Kelly Garrett.

> MIKE
> Well, Miss Garrett, is there
> something about this particular
> camera you want to destroy, or
> is it cameras in general?

Just then in the b.g. Payton turns excitedly:

> PAYTON
> Michael, come here! This may
> be her!

He goes . . . Kelly, boiling with mixed feelings, watches after him.

■ ■ ■

In the brief scenes that follow, a possible Payton Girl is chosen—a Ferrari of a brunette named Bashia. Mike agrees to run a few photo sheets on her to see what they've got.

Later that afternoon, Kelly makes a bold attempt to have her work noticed. This series of scenes is tied together by a single purpose—that is, to establish Kelly's dramatic need to be a shoe designer.

The fact that Kelly comes forward provides a window into her character. Though she must take orders imposed by her low-level job, she has guts. She's ambitious and has aspirations of getting somewhere.

Notice how the conflict creates the dialogue and necessary exposition to move the story forward.

Again, this arena is large with simultaneous activities. The camera angles are not directing, but rather telling us where we must look to advance the plot.

INT. PAYTON'S OFFICE SUITE—LATER

Kelly emerges from the elevator clutching her shoe box, crosses through a set of tall wooden doors into the anteroom and plants herself before an ICE-BITCH of a SECRETARY.

> SECRETARY
> Yes?

> KELLY (firmly)
> I'd like to see Mr. Payton, please.

> SECRETARY
> Who are you?

> KELLY
> I happen to be one of his employees.

Cold silence from the ice-bitch. Kelly starts to lose it:

> KELLY (continuing)
> Uh . . . Kelly Garrett—

It's going . . .

> KELLY (continuing)
> From . . . uh, well—design.

It's gone. And . . .

ELEVATOR FOYER

As Kelly finds herself ejected and the big wooden doors closing behind her.

A beat . . . all the spirit seems to drain out of her. She crosses to the bank of elevators.

But just then all three elevators open as one . . . out boils a caravan of models, seamstresses, tailors and schleppers pushing racks of clothes. They all head for Payton's office.

It's a moment of decision for Kelly. At the last possible instant she falls into the parade funneling through the big doors.

INT. ANTEROOM

As the Secretary waves the caravan on through, we SEE Kelly's red boots beneath a rolling rack of clothes headed into Payton's office.

INT. PAYTON'S OFFICE

Payton reigns in the middle of mass confusion, rejecting this sketch or
that fabric while fielding phone calls and shouting orders.
Intimidated, for a moment Kelly fades back into the woodwork.

ANGLE—VICTOR/IRENE

As Payton appears on the verge of approving a garment for the "look":

> IRENE (hisses)
> Whip it out, Victor!

Victor snakes out his microfilm camera, fires off a shot from behind
Irene's back . . . then quickly tucks it away again.

BACK TO SCENE

As Kelly musters her grit, steps into the fray surrounding Payton.

ANGLE

Payton's wrath is building as Kelly presses forward; nothing satisfies
him . . . he's reached the point of hurling garments to the floor and
ripping sketches into shreds.

> PAYTON
> This is supposed to be a winter
> coat?! I might be able to sell it
> to an Arab for a camel blanket! (and) The lapels,
> Henri! How many times do I have to tell you—
> the lapels! (and) And you, Gladys—here's what
> I think of your pathetic little lingerie sketches!

Which brings him to Kelly, who is almost trembling in fear. He stares
at her blankly. The room falls silent. He looks around:

> PAYTON (continuing)
> Who is this?

> KELLY
> Kelly Garrett, Mr. Payton. I have
> some shoes for you to look at.

We see the color has drained from Irene's face; Victor looks on equally
aghast.

> IRENE
> My God—

Payton still doesn't quite get the picture.

> PAYTON
> Shoes? I'm not looking at shoes.

Kelly starts fumbling with the lid to her shoe box:

> KELLY
> I know, Mr. Payton . . . But, you
> see, I designed them myself . . .
> in my spare time . . . at home . . .
> And I thought if you could just look
> at them—

He stares at her in dismay:

> PAYTON
> You mean you're an amateur? In
> my office—

> KELLY
> No! I'm a designer—I really am!

But Payton bellows:

> PAYTON
> Who is responsible for this! I
> want to know who is responsible
> for this right now!

> KELLY (terrified)
> Please, if you'll just look—

But it's too late; Victor and Irene have pounced and already are hustling her from the office:

> IRENE
> This is unpardonable, Mr. Payton!
> It will never happen again!

> KELLY
> But—

> VICTOR
> Quiet, you little vermin! (and) Appropriate
> measures will be taken, I assure you, Mr.
> Payton!

And then . . .

OUTER OFFICE

As Victor and Irene haul Kelly through the anteroom, much to the Secretary's surprise, and . . .

ELEVATOR FOYER

. . . out through the big doors.

> IRENE
> How could you?!

> VICTOR
> The audacity!

> KELLY
> I only wanted to show him my shoes—!

> IRENE
> Shoes? You want somebody to look
> at your shoes?! I'll be happy to
> look at your shoes!

She snatches the shoe box from Kelly, rips it open despite her protests, and yanks out the half boots:

> IRENE (continuing)
> What do you think, Victor?

> VICTOR
> Ha! Ludicrous—!

> IRENE (maliciously)
> But maybe with some modification,
> eh? For instance—

She starts to rip off some of the feathers and baubles:

> KELLY
> No—!

> VICTOR
> And that silly buckle—!

He joins Irene's frenzy of destruction; Kelly watches helplessly as her creation is trashed. Finally, Irene hurls the shoes to the floor.

> IRENE
> There—! So much for your *shoes!*

> VICTOR
> Just one other thing, Garrett—

> IRENE
> If anything like this ever happens
> again—you're fired!

And they turn and head back into the office with a satisfied stride. A beat, then the stunned Kelly kneels to pick up the shoes from the floor, trying to hold back her tears.

ANGLE—ELEVATOR

Just then the elevator doors open and Mike and Bashia step out.

> BASHIA
> . . . you have no idea what this
> means! *Me,* the Payton Girl!
> Although I've always known I had
> something—even when I was a
> little girl . . .

> MIKE
> I'm ready for some food. What are
> you in the mood for?

> BASHIA
> Whatever you are, Mike—

Mike notices Kelly and stops to help her.

> MIKE
> What happened? Drop something?

He quickly scoops up the remains of the shoes, stuffs them in the box and hands them to her.

> MIKE (continuing)
> There you go.

And he and Bashia disappear into Payton's office. HOLD as Kelly stares miserably after him. And then . . .

EXT. HOUSE OF PAYTON—DAY

As Kelly emerges from the building—hurries unhappily up the avenue.

ANOTHER ANGLE

As the garishly attired Wanda emerges from the crowd in the f.g. watching after Kelly. She pops a bubble.

A COP appears, eyeing her suspiciously.

> COP
> Move along—no soliciting.

Wanda realizes she been taken for a hooker, gives him a look.

> WANDA
> Well I never!

She moves off in a huff. HOLD ON Cop watching after her as he's nailed by a big glop of pigeon shit from above.

■ ■ ■

On page 191 in the setup we establish Kelly's wish—that is, to be more beautiful. The entire screenplay pivots on this wish. We also introduce our last main player, Kelly's roommate, Rita.

INT. KELLY'S FLAT—NIGHT

Rita has brewed some tea, is pouring for both of them.

> KELLY
>
> I look at all those incredibly
> beautiful models—they don't
> even have to lift a finger . . . (and) When I
> came to New York I believed that if you
> wanted something badly enough, and worked
> hard enough to get it, somehow it would
> happen . . . I really believed that! (then) But it
> all boils down to how you look! I read this
> study that beautiful people make more money,
> get promoted faster and are considered
> smarter. Smarter!

> RITA
>
> Maybe you ought to have some tea, okay—

> KELLY
>
> You should see the new Payton Girl.
> Dumb as a post—but she's beautiful! (then) If
> I were beautiful, do you think Payton would
> have had me thrown out of his office! And
> men—do you think I'd be sitting home
> playing Monopoly with you on New Year's
> Eve?!

> RITA
>
> We don't have to play Monopoly.

Kelly shakes her head, crosses out onto the small balcony.

EXT. BALCONY—NIGHT

Rita joins her.

> KELLY
>
> That's not the point. If I were
> beautiful, life would just be so
> much . . . so much—

> RITA
>
> What?

> KELLY (explodes)
>
> Easier!

> RITA
>
> Yeah, but you're not. You're
> just . . . you. No offense.

Kelly regards the panorama of city lights, shakes her head:

> KELLY
> I know, I know. (then) Can you imagine what
> it would be like being drop-dead head-turning
> gorgeous?
>
> RITA
> I can't imagine seeing daylight
> through my thighs.

■ ■ ■

A quick succession of scenes follows the above that advance both the main story and the subplot:

Payton calls Mike and tells him Bashia won't work.
Irene and Victor meet with their "deep throat" connection.

We are moving now to the first major turning point in the script where Kelly reiterates her wish.

EXT. KELLY'S FLAT—NIGHT

A gusher of water exploding skyward from a broken hydrant . . . a beat, and then the water inexplicably quits gushing, and INTO FRAME bops Wanda, as flamboyant as ever. She pauses, glances up at Kelly's window. The light is on.

INT. KELLY'S BEDROOM—NIGHT

A makeshift cobbler's workshop that Kelly has set up near a window. She's wearing a leather apron, has her hair tied back under a kerchief and is repairing the shoes Victor and Irene destroyed. Kelly gets up, stretches tiredly, then catches her reflection in a mirror. She looks awful.

> KELLY
> I wish that just once—just for
> one day—I could be beautiful.

BACK TO WANDA—STREET

She smiles, pops her gum as she moves down the street.

INT. FLAT—ON KELLY

As she works at her cobbler's bench.
Through the window the CITY LIGHTS suddenly and magically FLARE with a brief surge of power.
HOLD, and then . . .

DISSOLVE TO:

Morning. Kelly is asleep at her workbench. The early light shines through the window and we SEE

THE SHOES

Even more magnificent than before. There is almost a mystical glow to them.

■   ■   ■

The Act I turning point of "Shoe" happens on page 194. At this point the action of the story is turned to a new direction. Once Kelly is transformed by Wanda, we are catapulted into the next act—we know our setup is now complete. We know what the story is about: Kelly is being transformed into a beautiful woman, and with the beauty comes power.

The following sequence was a bit tricky in its execution. It was important to show only bits of the makeover so as not to kill the surprise in the end. Therefore, the use of various camera angles was necessary. Though the sequence runs about five pages, its transition on film would be very fast.

EXT. 5TH AVENUE—MORNING

As Kelly is headed for work amid the bustle when suddenly a hand reaches out and stops her:

> WANDA (o.s.)
> Hey, come here. I need to talk
> to you—

And we REVEAL Wanda standing outside the door of the ultra-chic Le Salon.

> KELLY
> Me? What about?

> WANDA
> Look, I'm trying to get a job in
> this place and I need someone to
> make-over. Show what I can do.
> You know, a test case. And you're
> perfect—sort of a nondescript type.

> KELLY
> I'm running a little late—

She starts to move along, but Wanda blocks her way:

> WANDA
> It's free! Oh, come on, please?
> Please? Please! (and) Do you know what a job
> in Uni Maguro's salon would mean to me? My
> career would be set! I'd never have to worry
> again—
>
> KELLY
> I have to get to work. I'm already
> in trouble—
>
> WANDA
> So I'll give you a note from your
> doctor. Premenstrual syndrome—
> something very hormonal like that.
> Except you'll have to help me with
> the spelling. (and) You've got to! It's the only
> way Uni will see my work!
>
> That Kelly can relate to:
>
> KELLY
> The only way—?
>
> And . . .

■ ■ ■

The make-over sequence consists of fast paced visuals showing bits of Kelly's transformation so as not to kill the surprise in the end. Wanda highlights and wraps Kelly's hair, applies make-up with the precision of a surgeon, mousses and blow-dries an incredible mass of locks with the finesse of a Benihana chef—and all the while as she babbles and boogies to the music of U2. Finally, she tells Kenny to throw back her head and look in the mirror. Kelly is pole-axed by the face staring back at her . . . revealed is an absolutely stunningly beautiful woman who is only vaguely reminnicent of herself. She tries to say something, but can't, then faints dead away. Wanda revives Kelly with smelling salts, sticks her in the company limo, and has her delivered to work.

Act II: The Confrontation

The confrontation is the largest unit of the screenplay (forty-five to sixty pages), and the most difficult to execute. Often Act II can become the "mess in the middle." Here many scripts lose their momentum and pacing.

In structuring this unit I like to break it into three parts: beginning, middle, and end—just as we did the screenplay. Ask yourself what is the overall thrust needed for each unit? In "Shoe" it broke down as follows:

BEGINNING: Kelly is happy with her makeover and it changes her life.
MIDDLE: Kelly and Mike fall in love, but because of a major complication he loses her.
END: In the last portion of the confrontation, which builds to the second turning point, Kelly loses the effect of her makeover and must adjust to being her old self again.

For each unit of the confrontation there is usually one pivotal scene or sequence on which the entire unit hinges. The key sequence in unit one is Kelly being mistaken for a model and being chosen as the long-awaited Payton Girl.

Notice the fast pacing of the sequence. The scenes are quick and cut between many locales. The following provides good action while at the same time accomplishes our story needs.

EXT. HOUSE OF PAYTON

As the limo pulls up and Kelly steps out, crosses to the entrance.

INT. HOUSE OF PAYTON

As Kelly strides through, people turn and do double-takes. And now we're SEEING Kelly starting to begin to love it.

ANGLE AT ELEVATOR

As Kelly waits . . . the door opens, REVEALING Mike Powers and Payton, backed by Victor and Irene. Mike and Payton are in mid-argument.

> MIKE
> Don't blame me—now you're the
> one who can't make up his mind!

They all emerge, pushing past Kelly almost—but not quite—without seeing her. She steps into the elevator.
Then suddenly Mike and Payton pull up short, staring at each other—it's like they've simultaneously been rapped upside the head with a nine-pound hammer:

MIKE/PAYTON (in unison)
It's her—!!

They lunge back toward the elevator . . . but the doors have closed.

PAYTON (bellows)
Get her—!

MIKE
The stairs—!

And they all lunge for the stairs.

SERIES OF CUTS

Mike and Payton, followed by Victor and Irene, race up the stairs . . . but when they come out on the second floor the elevator is still going up.

More stairs . . . Victor is trailing badly, Irene desperately pulling him along.

THIRD FLOOR

Audrey awaits the elevator . . . It arrives, doors open and she steps in to join Kelly.

Doors close just as Payton and Mike erupt out of the stairwell. Elevator continuing up; they dash back for the stairwell . . .

INT. ELEVATOR

As Kelly gives Audrey a look:

KELLY
Hi, Audrey—

AUDREY
Hi . . . Do I know you?

KELLY
Yeah, sure. I mean . . . yeah—

AUDREY
I'm sorry. I'm terrible with names,
but I never forget a face . . .

Kelly can't believe it . . . she really is totally changed.

MORE CUTS—THE PURSUIT

More stairs yet . . . now Victor and Irene are gasping, Victor clutching his chest. But on the fourth floor, the elevator is still going up.
As Mike and Payton hurl open the door to lunge back into the stairwell, they flatten Irene and Victor, who are trailing badly now.
Until . . .

FIFTH FLOOR

As the elevator doors open and Kelly steps out into the design salon. Just then the stairwell door flies open and Mike and Payton erupt into the corridor. Gasping, they pull up, staring at the surprised Kelly.

> MIKE
> It's her. It really is.

> PAYTON
> Yes. Absolutely perfect.

> KELLY
> Are you talking to me?

About now, Victor and Irene topple out of the stairwell, nearly ready for paramedic attention.
Payton composes himself, crosses to her:

> PAYTON
> Oh yes, my dear. And we have such
> wonderful things in store for you.

And we . . .

> DISSOLVE THROUGH TO:

INT. ELEVATOR FOYER—HOUSE OF PAYTON—DAY

All three elevators open at once. Out boil another caravan of seamstresses, tailors and schleppers pushing racks of clothes.
At the head of the procession is Kelly being swept along by Mike and Payton, followed by Victor and Irene. Payton ventilates as the whole melange tumbles toward his office.

> PAYTON
> Would you please give her some room!

There's a milliner, carrying feathers, flowers, bits of rhinestones, tulle, ribbon, etc. An assistant with the accessory tray, like a pirate's treasure trove of jewelry, hair combs, etc.

Another wearing a pin cushion on her wrist and scissors hanging from a ribbon at her waist . . .

> KELLY (to Mike)
> Will somebody tell me what's
> going on?

> MIKE
> Lady, you're about to become a
> very valuable commodity. (and) By the way,
> what's your name?

Kelly gives him a look, then eyes some of the stunning models who are attached to the entourage:

>   KELLY
> . . . Chelsea. Just call me
> Chelsea.

INT. PAYTON'S OFFICE

As the crowd boils in . . . Payton plants Kelly in the middle of the room.
The others fall silent. Payton eyes her from here and there, this way
and that.

>   PAYTON
> Yes—yes—yes!

We see Mike on the phone in the b.g. as Payton turns to the dressers:

>   PAYTON (continuing)
> Well, don't just stand there!

Kelly looks horrified as a crowd of people starts to swoop down on
her:

>   KELLY
> Hold it—!

They all stop abruptly.

>   KELLY (continuing)
> I haven't agreed to do this.

>   PAYTON (stunned)
> What?! What's that got to do
> with it?!

>   KELLY
> I'm not a model.

>   PAYTON
> Of course you're not. You're the
> Payton Girl.

>   KELLY
> Mr. Payton, you don't understand!
> I wouldn't know where to start—

>   PAYTON
> Let me worry about that—

>   KELLY
> No—!!

He stares at her:

>   PAYTON
> You can't be serious.

He turns to Mike:

> PAYTON (continuing)
> She can't be serious, can she, Mike?
> Talk to her!

Mike hangs up the phone, joins them, maneuvers Kelly aside just as he did Bashia earlier.

> MIKE
> Okay, Chelsea, what's going on here?

> KELLY
> Look, that's not my real name—

> MIKE
> Of course it isn't. C'mon, honey,
> now what's your problem?

> KELLY
> And I'm not your honey.

> MIKE
> Right. Sorry. Chelsea, do you
> get what's going on here? Do
> you know what Payton's offering?

He gestures toward the group of models who are looking enviously on:

> MIKE (continuing)
> Any one of them would rip your
> heart out for a shot like this.

Kelly glances in that direction:

HER P.O.V.—MODELS

. . . the same ones she waited on earlier—they're absolutely glaring at her.

BACK TO KELLY

We can see she smells payback time:

> KELLY
> You mean—you want me, not them?

> MIKE
> You got it!

Kelly glances at Irene and Victor. They're waiting with baited breath just like everyone else in the room. They smile ingratiatingly at her. And Payton most of all . . . he looks like he's waiting to hear the results of a biopsy. The worm has definitely turned.

> KELLY
> Well . . .

Everyone hangs on her next words:

                           KELLY (continuing)
        Then I'll do it.

                          PAYTON (instantly)
       Strip her!

ANGLE

As the mob undresses Kelly in an instant, then slips one of Payton's boldest creations over her head—something incredibly chic, romantic, and avant garde, with a full-tiered skirt.

                          PAYTON
       The sleeves—!

An assistant goes up to Kelly and rips off the bouffant sleeves, leaving only narrow straps.

IRENE

As she jabs Victor, who whips out his camera and snaps a quick picture.

                          PAYTON (continuing)
       Leg! Give me leg!

Someone rips the seam halfway up to Kelly's thigh, and Irene jabs Victor again.

BACK TO SCENE

Payton is wild-eyed now:

                          PAYTON (continuing)
       Too much skirt!

Someone rips off one of the underskirts and Payton wraps it around her shoulders as a cape.
He grabs the neckline, pulls it down and pins it in a deep "V."

IRENE/VICTOR

When she jabs him again, he turns on her in impotent fury and jabs her back. Angrily she jabs him again, harder.
He's about to jab her right back when suddenly the obsessed Payton appears and they freeze. Payton stares at Irene for a moment, then snatches an earring from her. Irene YELPS in pain as he turns abruptly away.

BACK TO SCENE

Payton pins on the earring to finish off the dress. Then he stands back and stares at her intently for one long moment.

```
                    PAYTON
            Now, I need a vision—

    Another moment, and then:

                    PAYTON (continuing)
            I've got it—!!
```

Payton's vision becomes a photo shoot that afternoon in the snow-covered countryside of New York. Kelly is a stunning image of white-on-white. Wearing a baroque gown and an ermine cape, she sits astride a white Arabian horse against the wintry backdrop. But all is not as it appears.

There are problems for Kelly—there must be or we will not have our needed conflict to carry this act. With each consecutive scene/sequence, we present her with obstacles. The beats that provide the building conflict and raise the action are as follows:

The photo shoot at first goes miserably; Kelly is stiff and unnatural.

Frustrated, Mike calls lunch. He drives Kelly to his nearby mountain retreat, hoping to relax her.

En route, the Jeep gets stuck in the snow.

The tension heightens as they trek by foot to the cabin.

Mike discovers he's left the keys in the ignition.

He slips and falls off the icy roof in an attempt to get through the window.

Later, in a quiet moment with their defenses down, Kelly and Mike discover they like each other. As the rest of the shoot goes smoothly, we sense their powerful attraction.

As we build to the middle portion of the confrontation, the romance has begun between Mike and Kelly, presenting bigger complications and raising the stakes for Kelly. It is not she, but rather Chelsea, who Mike loves.

In the second unit of the confrontation we place obstacles in Mike and Kelly's romance. Again, it is conflict that carries the action forward.

The night of the shoot, Mike expects Kelly to attend an annual New Year's Eve gala thrown by Payton at the Plaza Hotel.

Kelly has nothing to wear when she arrives in the city, and it's too late to shop—all the stores are closed.

Wanda loans Kelly a designer gown off the window mannequin at Le Salon.

Kelly, delivered by horse and carriage, makes a grand entrance at the Plaza.

As midnight approaches (midpoint in the confrontation), we cut between two events happening simultaneously: Mike and Kelly's romance (main story), and the party at the Plaza; Irene and Victor (subplot), as they break into the vault at the House of Payton and steal the proofs from the day's photo shoot.

The pivotal sequence in this unit happens when Mike and Kelly are separated. The events are set in motion when Wanda, who's boogying in the Village, overhears Uni (her boss) telling his friends about a party at Le Salon after the big apple comes down, ushering in the New Year. Wanda panics—she has a half-hour to get Kelly's dress back on the mannequin. To raise the tension, we set this action sequence against the countdown at Times Square.

Notice the contrasting imagery and the paced cutting between three events. There is the raucous crowd at Times Square, the very formal, sophisticated gala at the Plaza, and a banged-up VW as it races through the streets.

Writing a screenplay is like creating a tapestry. It is burlap and silk, sharp and muted colors. Pacing must also vary and create contrast. Too much of one thing, whether fast or slow, becomes monotonous and lulls an audience. It's like a symphony all played in crescendo, or waiting for a Jaws that never comes above the water.

In the following, we begin with fast-paced cuts. The pacing slows down significantly at the Plaza, then speeds up again with the chase.

EXT. TIMES SQUARE—NIGHT

The crowd is getting louder, more excited as midnight approaches. All eyes are up and waiting for the big apple.

HIGH ABOVE THEM

The big apple hovers, waiting suspended for the countdown.

EXT. STREET—MANHATTAN—NIGHT

As Wanda's beat-up orange Volks whips PAST CAMERA . . . Suddenly a police car pulls out in pursuit, lights flashing—

—and barely covers a hundred feet before another car sails through an intersection and smashes into it.

INT. VOLKS—MOVING

Wanda eyes her rearview mirror, pops a bubble. And only pours on more coal. And . . .

INT. PLAZA BALLROOM—NIGHT

As Mike and Kelly dance . . . this time the music is slow and dreamy. They can't take their eyes off one another.

> MIKE
> Look, tomorrow's a brand new
> year. Everything's going to
> look different to you.

> KELLY
> I've been trying to tell you all
> day that I'm not the person you
> think I am.

She looks up at him:

> KELLY (continuing)
> You wouldn't recognize the
> person I really am.

> MIKE
> You're wrong about that.

> KELLY
> I didn't seem to make a big
> impression before. And I
> haven't changed. Not really.

He's drawn her closer and closer . . . they're about to kiss:

> MIKE (softly)
> I would recognize you anytime
> . . . anywhere.

They kiss . . . Then:

Wanda pokes her head out from behind a potted palm.

> WANDA
> Pssst—! Kelly—!

Kelly stares at her in dismay; Mike doesn't quite get what's going on.

> MIKE
> Who's that?

> WANDA
> Come here! I've gotta talk to you!

Kelly gives Mike a completely flustered look:

> KELLY
> Just a minute, okay?

She crosses to Wanda.

ANGLE—WANDA/KELLY

In the b.g. we can see that Mike's agent, Evelyn, has found him again.

> KELLY
> Wanda, what is it?

> WANDA
> We've gotta go, kiddo. Uni's
> coming back to the salon any
> minute!

> KELLY
> You mean leave? Now?!

> WANDA
> Now! If I don't get this stuff
> back before he gets there, I'm
> done for!

> KELLY
> But . . . I've got to say good-bye!

> WANDA
> No time! I've got the car double-
> parked outside. Come on!

Kelly glances back toward Mike, but Wanda is already pulling her away.

ANGLE—MIKE

He spots Kelly leaving.

> MIKE
> Hey—

> EVELYN
> But Mike—

> MIKE
> Later, Evelyn—

And he takes off after Kelly.

ANGLES

As Wanda pulls Kelly through the crowd . . . Mike pushing after them, trying to keep an eye on Kelly's fast-retreating back.
Until . . .

EXT. PLAZA HOTEL—NIGHT

The orange Volks is indeed double-parked. Wanda puts Kelly in, then scrambles in behind the wheel.
She pulls out just as Mike emerges from the Plaza, races into the f.g. He glances after the Volkswagen, then hails a cab:

> MIKE (to cabbie)
> Follow that—whatever it is!

The cab races away in pursuit of Wanda.

VARIOUS CUTS

Wanda careening through traffic . . . The cab in pursuit. Until . . .

INT. VOLKS—MOVING

As Wanda comes to a screeching halt. Traffic is choked around Times Square.

> WANDA
> Come on—it'll be faster on foot!

She and Kelly jump out, plunge into the crowd.

ANGLE

As the cab pulls up . . . Mike jumps out, takes off on foot after them.

EXT. TIMES SQUARE—THE COUNTDOWN

The big apple is still high above us but coming down. The crowd is wilder, louder, even more outrageous.

Through the horns and rattles and sea of VOICES we catch glimpses of Wanda and Kelly . . . and Mike pushing his way after them.
Now the countdown begins . . . 44 . . . 43 . . . 42 . . . 41 . . .

MORE CUTS

As the countdown continues . . . Mike seems to be gaining a bit on them—But then suddenly Wanda ducks into an alley:

> WANDA
> This way—

We see Mike pass the alley.

ANGLE

As Kelly's heel gets caught in a grate and her shoe comes flying off. She pauses, but:

> WANDA (continuing)
> Forget it, woman, we gotta go!

As the countdown continues . . . 19 . . . 18 . . . 17 . . .
Mike pulls up . . . in desperation he starts to retrace his steps. Pauses at the mouth of the alley.
Counting . . . 5 . . . 4 . . . 3 . . . 2 . . . and—

THE BIG APPLE

As it hits down. The crowd EXPLODES in celebration. People throw themselves at each other . . . SCREAMING, blowing NOISEMAKERS, kissing and hugging. Firecrackers are going off and total pandemonium reigns.

ALLEY

Empty, except for Mike. Kelly's shoe is in the f.g. Mike approaches, stoops to pick it up.

HOLD a long beat . . .

■ ■ ■

The Act II turning point happens on page 207. Here, the story completely turns around and catapults us into the third act. In the following sequence, Kelly wakes up and discovers she is back to her old self. At first she reacts, but after some hard thought she comes to a decision. Kelly has her moment of discovery. And because of it, she grows, and we indicate a change in her character.

EXT. LE SALON—MANHATTAN—NEW YEAR'S MORNING

As the sun comes up, the dress Kelly wore the night before is safely back on the mannequin.

INT. KELLY'S BEDROOM—DAY

Kelly is asleep in her bed. The woman we SEE in a flannel nightgown bears no resemblance to the stunning creature of the night before. Kelly is back to her old self. Her makeup is gone, her hair—which was a magnificent mane—has now gone flat and limp. Even the color seems to have faded.

As she awakens, the events of the previous night come to mind, and a languorous smile comes over her groggy face.
She pulls herself out of bed, humming the tune she danced to with Mike, as she passes the mirror en route to the bathroom.

MIRROR

She briefly glances at her reflection and continues on her way.
Then suddenly she stops. It registers. She peers back at the mirror and
stares in complete dismay as reality sets in.

ANOTHER ANGLE

A beat . . . then in sudden panic she dives for her makeup, throwing
cosmetics in a heap on the counter while at the same time plugging in
her hot rollers. Then she pulls up:

> KELLY
> Wanda—!

(And . . .)

LIVING ROOM

As Kelly hastens in, dives for the telephone. She starts to frantically
thumb through the phone book—then abruptly stops.
She sits there for a moment, completely confused and at a total loss.
Then we GO WITH her as she rises and slowly crosses to another
mirror.

She stares at her reflection for a long moment. We SLOWLY
TIGHTEN TO her, and then . . .

EXT. STREET—MANHATTAN—STILL EARLY MORNING

As a huge New York City street sweeper RUMBLES PAST
CAMERA . . .
As it passes we REVEAL Kelly, walking toward us, is the only other
living thing in the Manhattan canyon-bottom. The streets are a mess
in the aftermath of New Year's Eve.

VARIOUS ANGLES—KELLY

Bundled in a coat and scarf, we GO WITH her as she pensively prowls
the streets. Streamers and ticker-tape bedeck the trees, the boulevards
are oceans of confetti, discarded party favors, hats and empty bottles
of booze.

Elsewhere she passes a horse-mounted New York COP, slouching in
the saddle, looking a little hung-over himself.

As Kelly moves along, we sense that she's beginning to sort things out.
As a piece falls into place here and there, she pauses to reflect on her
image in a store window . . .

Until finally she stops. She pulls herself up with conviction. Taking a
deep breath, she turns and strides firmly back the way she came.
And we . . .

INT. KELLY'S APARTMENT BUILDING—DAY

As Kelly arrives at her door—it's locked and she's forgotten her key. Annoyed with herself, she BANGS on the door, calls:

>   KELLY
>   Rita! Rita, let me in! I forgot
>   my key!

We hear a muffled response from within . . . a beat, and then a groggy Rita, a robe wrapped about her, opens the door, hardly looking at Kelly:

>   RITA
>   My God, what are you doing up
>   so early—?

She starts back for her bedroom, then freezes:

>   RITA (continuing)
>   Eeeek—!

She slowly turns, looks at Kelly in dismay:

>   RITA (continuing)
>   It's you—I mean really you!

>   KELLY
>   Yeah. It's me, all right.

>   RITA
>   But what happened?!

>   KELLY
>   I don't know.

Rita collapses in a chair:

>   RITA
>   Oh my God—this is terrible.

And we . . .

INT. KITCHEN—LATER

Where Kelly is brewing tea. Rita has parked at the dinette table:

>   RITA
>   Despite the way you look, this is
>   not a hopeless situation. We'll
>   find Wanda again—

>   KELLY
>   No. I thought of that. I'm not
>   going back to her.

> RITA (stunned)
> Are you crazy? You have a six-
> figure career riding on the way
> you look!

> KELLY
> That's the point. I don't want it
> on those terms. (then) I thought about it a lot this
> morning. Chelsea wasn't me.
> This is me. (and) It's almost a relief. I couldn't
> have kept it up anyway.

> RITA
> What about Mike?

His name drops on her like a load of bricks:

> KELLY
> He wants Chelsea. She's gone.
> And let's face it—Kelly Garrett
> wouldn't fit into his life. He
> told me as much last night.

> RITA
> Look, when you go back to work,
> just give him a chance.

> KELLY
> No. I'm not going back to work.
> I'll go in tomorrow and pick up
> my stuff . . . and then I'm going
> home and try to sort things out.

Rita stares at her. Kelly sighs:

> KELLY (continuing)
> I should have done it a long
> time ago.

Rita shakes her head in dismay:

> RITA
> You're quitting . . . ?

> KELLY
> Yeah. I'm quitting.

■ ■ ■

Act III: The Resolution
At this point in the screenplay we begin building toward the climax.
We must present our characters with yet more obstacles, each build-
ing upon the other until we reveal their ultimate solution. Here, the
stakes are raised even higher in both the main story and the subplot.
As we begin the act:

There has been a frantic search for Chelsea.

All Mike has been left with is a single shoe.

The shoe design has left Payton completely overwhelmed. He has
decided to scrap the original layout and recreate his look starting
with the new shoe. Now he must find the shoe's designer. And,
they must reshoot Chelsea.

Victor and Irene have already passed on the microfilm of Payton's
originals to their connection in Taiwan, and it is too late to stop
production. The couple is now in serious trouble, and thugs are
after them.

The first of the two pivotal scenes leading to the climax takes place
when Mike and Kelly come together for the first time after she has
been changed back to her old self. Below, she has come to the House
of Payton to retrieve her things. Mike does not recognize her and we
feel, as Kelly does, that all is lost. Notice the narrative. The activity
with the camera and the business with the eye help create and punctuate the dialogue.

INT. PHOTO STUDIO

Mike is packing up some camera gear as Kelly appears in the doorway.
She watches him for a moment.
A beat, then he notices her:

> MIKE
> Oh, hi there—

He pauses . . . then does something uncharacteristic: he remembers—

> MIKE (continuing)
> Garrett, isn't it?

> KELLY
> You remembered—

> MIKE
> Yeah . . . Garrett, give me a hand
> here. Let me have that tripod—

Kelly's momentary hope is dashed. Mike gives her another look:

> MIKE (continuing)
> Well—? You do work here,
> don't you?

She hands him the tripod.

> KELLY
> No, as a matter of fact. I just
> quit.

> MIKE
> Yeah? Well . . . uh, thanks.

> KELLY
> I'm just sort of saying good-bye
> to everybody—

> MIKE
> I guess it's a trend—Elliot
> can't seem to hang on to anybody.

> KELLY
> What do you mean?

> MIKE (dismisses it)
> Ah, nothing—(and) Well, good luck, Garrett—(then) Any-
> thing the matter?

Kelly is blinking back a tear:

> KELLY
> Nothing . . . something in my eye.

> MIKE
> Here. Let me take a look. Come
> over here in the light.

He takes her to a window.

ANGLE

As he tilts her chin up:

> MIKE (continued)
> Look right at me—

He's looking into her eyes, about to lift her eyelid when something
seems to strike him.

> KELLY
> Is something wrong?

Mike shakes it off.

> MIKE
> No. Just, uh—No.

He looks into her eye clinically from a couple of angles:

> MIKE (continued)
> Garrett, you ever want something
> and you didn't even realize it
> until it was too late?

> KELLY
> Yes. I suppose everyone has.

Mike shakes his head, releases her:

> MIKE
> Don't see anything. I guess you
> blinked it out.

> KELLY
> What is it you wanted?

> MIKE
> Same old story. A lady. She's
> gone. And I don't see any way
> of getting her back.

> KELLY (a beat)
> Maybe you're standing in the
> kitchen.

> MIKE
> Pardon me?

> KELLY
> Somebody told me that once. What
> you want can be very close—like
> in the living room. But you're in
> the kitchen. You're just in the
> wrong place and you can't see it.

Mike shakes his head, chuckles:

> MIKE
> I'll give that some thought. Do
> some remodeling or something.

A beat, then:

> KELLY
> Well, I'd better go.
>
> She turns, starts out:
>
> MIKE
> Hey, Garrett, I mean it—
> good luck.
>
> She pauses, looks back at him:
>
> KELLY
> You too.
>
> And then she goes. We HOLD Mike a beat, and then . . .

■　■　■

The second pivotal moment in the script (below) is a short sequence in which we find Mike alone. Here, he makes his discovery that pushes us to the climax.

There is a rule in film: *If you can show it, don't talk about it.* Here, we show it all. There is no need for dialogue—the visuals tell the story.

> INT. PHOTO STUDIO—HOUSE OF PAYTON—DAY
>
> Mike has everything gathered up; he slings some camera bags over his shoulders, starts to go.
> But he pauses as he passes a table. There are some scattered enlargements spread out. He picks one up.
>
> INSERT—PHOTO
>
> It's a close-up he shot of Kelly as Chelsea.
>
> BACK TO MIKE
>
> He eyes it regretfully for a moment, then tosses it back on the pile. He's halfway to the door before it registers—he freezes . . . allows the camera bags to slip off his shoulders and clatter to the floor. Then he turns and rushes back to the table, grabs the photo.
> He stares at the photo for a long beat, races for the darkroom.
>
> INT. DARKROOM
>
> As Mike hurls this and that about . . . he finds the proof sheet he's looking for . . . zeroes in on the particular photo.
> He slips the negative strip from its sleeve, slams it into the enlarger.

He kills the lights, snaps on the machine in the eerie red glow of the safelights.

ANGLE—ENLARGEMENT

As Kelly's features come into focus.

MIKE

He hasn't got it yet . . . doesn't quite know what he's after. He cranks open the aperture.

ENLARGEMENT

Kelly's features jump up to a larger size.

MIKE

It still hasn't clicked. He opens up the aperture even more.

ENLARGEMENT

Now he's zeroing in on her eyes . . . Mike gives it another crank . . . another yet—Kelly's eyes FILL FRAME.

MIKE

A long beat . . . finally it hits him like a Mack Truck:

>   MIKE
>   Garrett—!

And we . . .

■ ■ ■

The stakes rise for Mike: He has made a discovery, but has it come too late? There is a new sense of urgency.

Mike and Payton arrive at Kelly's apartment and discover she's gone.

Wanda, dressed as a metermaid, tells them she just gave a cabbie a ticket for double parking. He was waiting to take two ladies to La Guardia airport. She thinks they said "United."

Mike's Jeep races through the streets.

At the airport, both our main story and subplot come together.

Notice the fast-paced building to the climax. Again, it's the visuals—the cutting between locales, the action narrative—that tell the story.

EXT. LA GUARDIA AIRPORT—TERMINAL "A"—DAY

The taxi is parked along the passenger loading curb. The cabbie hands
Kelly the remainder of the luggage and they . . .
Disappear inside the terminal.

CAMERA ANGLES OVER TO:

EXT. TERMINAL "B"—DAY

An oddly dressed man and woman are hustling along a concourse,
pulling a large amount of luggage with them.

CLOSE ON COUPLE

It's Irene and Victor both dressed in drag—and looking in fear over
their shoulders. They hurry to the gate.

> IRENE
> This is all your fault, Victor.

> VICTOR
> You're the one who wanted a house
> of design.

> IRENE
> Only after you seduced me!

> VICTOR
> I seduced you?!

> IRENE
> If I wasn't running for my life
> I'd call your wife and tell her!

Then, as they hurry past the sign—"ICELANDIC AIR"

> VICTOR
> Where is it we're going?

> IRENE
> Someplace that begins with an "R."

ANGLE—TAIWANESE MOBSTERS

As Irene and Victor disappear in the distance, THREE SUMO WRES-
TLER-TYPES dressed in black suits, packing guns, appear. They
pause, and, in unison, straighten their ties. Then they move on after
Irene and Victor.

EXT. LA GUARDIA—TERMINAL "A"—DAY

The Jeep pulls to a SCREECHING HALT, double parks. Mike and
Payton bail out and run inside.

INT. TERMINAL "A"—DAY

Mike races past the UNITED AIRLINES ticketing counters toward the departure monitors. Payton is trailing behind.

INT. UNITED AIRLINES—MONITORS

Mike slides to a halt, glances up at the screen.

ON SCREEN

Listed among the departures is FLIGHT 728—GATE 12 to CHEY-ENNE, WYOMING, the MONITOR FLICKS—"BOARDING"

INT. UNITED AIRLINES—GATE 12

Rita and Kelly are standing at the boarding ramp. They embrace. Over the P.A. system we HEAR:

> P.A. (V.O.)
> This is the last call for flight 728.
> All passengers holding confirmed seats
> should be on board.

> KELLY
> I'll write.

> RITA
> It's not going to be the same
> without you. (then) I'm really going to miss you.

> KELLY
> Hey, knock 'em dead, you hear.
> Broadway needs you.

Kelly hurries down the ramp so both can avoid tears. Rita watches her disappear, turns and leaves.

EXT. UNITED FLIGHT 728—DAY

The engines roaring.

INT. UNITED AIRLINES—GATE 12

MIKE

As he rushes toward the gate. Suddenly he stops.

HIS P.O.V.—THROUGH THE WINDOW

The ramp has been dropped. Kelly's plane begins moving backward toward the taxi apron.

BACK TO MIKE

Realizing it's too late.

ATTENDANT

Sorry, you just missed it.

Winded, Payton catches up. He sees the look on Mike's face—and it says it all.

EXT. GROUND CONTROL—DAY

Standing among the crew in United overalls and ear covers is Wanda directing Kelly's plane.

INT. UNITED TERMINAL—DAY

Mike and Payton silently walk past the boarding gates and toward the exit.

BACK TO WANDA

Flailing her arms directing the plane over the powerful engines. And then, right on cue, she blows a huge bubble—it bursts.

QUICK CUT TO:

ANGLE AIRPLANE WHEEL

As the tire explodes and goes flat.

INT. UNITED TERMINAL—DAY

Mike and Payton are heading down an escalator, heads bowed, looking dejected.

ESCALATOR—MIKE'S P.O.V.

A pair of flamboyant shoes, moving past them on the "UP" escalator.

BACK TO MIKE

For an instant it doesn't register. Then he reacts.

MIKE

Kelly!

He jumps over the railing onto the "UP" escalator, pushing his way past startled people.

PAYTON

He's stuck on the "DOWN" escalator, watching Mike race after Kelly.

BACK TO MIKE

As he pushes his way past the crowd—he's lost sight of Kelly. And then . . . he spots her in the distance.

> MIKE
> Kelly!

She stops, turns.

HER P.O.V.

Mike winded standing at the top of the escalator. He begins walking toward her.

> MIKE (continuing)
> Or should I say Chelsea?

A moment . . . and then Kelly manages to find her voice.

> KELLY
> She doesn't exist anymore.

> MIKE
> It doesn't matter.

And then he moves even closer:

> MIKE (continuing)
> I didn't fall in love with Chelsea.

After a long moment, Mike pulls Kelly to him and kisses her, long and hard, the kiss so hot . . .

■ ■ ■

The resolve of a screenplay (wrap-up beats following the climax) should run no longer than three to five pages. A resolve that runs too long kills the climax and overall impact of the script. "Shoe" runs 111 pages. The short resolve happens on page 110 of the script.

Here, we show the solution—the culminating result of the story. It is a happy one; Mike and Kelly are together. The shot at the end suggests that Kelly has not only found love but she will someday be recognized as a shoe designer (her dramatic need). Payton is present and of course our last shot is of her shoes.

EXT. CHURCH—NEW YORK—DAY
ANGLE—JEEP

Double-parked as usual.

Mike and Kelly come out of the church, having just been married. Kelly is a radiant bride.

A crowd waiting outside throws rice at them. We SEE that Rita and Payton are in the wedding party.

ANGLE—ACROSS THE STREET

As a city bus pulls out of town, and in the back window is Wanda. She watches the newlyweds and pops a huge bubble.

BACK TO MIKE AND KELLY

As Mike and Kelly get in the Jeep, with Hector waiting in the backseat.

AND AS THEY PULL AWAY

We SEE . . .

SHOES

Kelly's shoes—the ones she wore to Payton's party—tied to the back of the Jeep.

FADE OUT

THE END

■ ■ ■

Movie of the Week

Movies of the Week run 120 minutes and consist of seven acts. *Never write a spec M.O.W. script that is broken down into seven acts.* Instead, write a spec motion picture (feature film) script that can be marketed to television.

Since there is little difference between television movies and feature films, many two-hour scripts are marketed in both areas. By breaking your material into seven acts, you are limiting yourself to only the television market, leaving four networks open to you: ABC, CBS, NBC, and Fox. If these networks reject your script, you have absolutely nowhere else to take it—you can't take your television movie and try to pass it around as a feature film script. Once readers, executives, or producers spot seven acts, a light bulb goes on that flashes "TV," and they are automatically turned off by your project.

There are literally hundreds of independent producers looking for small movies. Why do yourself a disservice and cut yourself off from this market? Today, it is actually easier to sell a spec motion picture script to television than it is a seven-act M.O.W., because the networks can break down and change your material in the ways they see fit.

My agent recently told me of a client who sold a feature film script to television. The story was about a young man whose father gets hit in the head, goes crazy, and lands in a mental institution. The boy tries to bring his father back to reality, and is ultimately forced to break into the institution, take his father, and run away with him. The network decided that the boy should be a girl, that the institution should be a prison, and that the father should be crippled instead of crazy.

Script changes are a part of the industry, especially in television where it's everybody's job to have their finger in the pie. There will be story meetings where you can negotiate some of the script changes or make suggestions, but the writer must be willing to make concessions, especially in the beginning. Some of the suggested changes you may like; others you may hate. At this point you can do one of two things: bemoan the industry, or be happy you are working and move on to the next assignment.

The Seven-Act Structure

Let's briefly look at the seven-act breakdown. If we place seven acts into the basic three-act structure, they would be divided for the most part as they are in figure 10. (*Note:* These acts *are* delineated and placed on the page.)

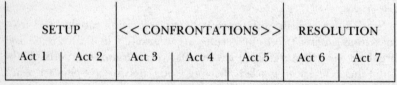

SEVEN-ACT STRUCTURE

SETUP		<< CONFRONTATIONS >>			RESOLUTION	
Act 1	Act 2	Act 3	Act 4	Act 5	Act 6	Act 7

Figure 10.

The usual length of an M.O.W. runs anywhere from 101 to 115 pages. If these acts consisted of equal lengths they would average approximately seventeen pages per act. Again, these numbers are only a gauge—the same kind we've been using throughout this book to help us stay on track. The fact is that the acts are not consistent.

Let's use two very well-written Movies of the Week as examples: (1) "An Early Frost," scripted by Ron Cowen and Daniel Lipman, is the story of a young attorney who discovers he has AIDS and must confront his family; (2) "Something About Amelia," delicately scripted by William Hanely, deals with father–daughter incest. Compare the act breakdowns for both of these TV Movies:

"An Early Frost": Length 105 Pages

Act I	Act II	Act III	Act IV	Act V	Act VI	Act VII
23 pp	18 pp	15 pp	11 pp	10 pp	9 pp	13 pp

"Something About Amelia": Length 106 Pages

Act I	Act II	Act III	Act IV	Act V	Act VI	Act VII
26 pp	11 pp	19 pp	12 pp	15 pp	6 pp	12 pp

Since the acts in an M.O.W. can run as long as twenty-five to thirty pages, and as short as five to six pages, it is impossible to give definitive guidelines. In both of the above movies, Act I ran longer than the other acts, which often happens because Act I is the setup act and there is more to establish. This is not a hard-and-fast rule, however.

Movies for television are essentially "small" (low-budgeted) motion pictures. They incorporate the same elements and tools of writing that we have discussed throughout this book.

What Is Meant by *High Concept*?

The term *high concept,* a catch phrase used throughout the industry, means an idea that can be easily grasped, promises to be entertaining or controversial, and can be defined in one or two lines. Network executives believe that high concepts, whether comedy or drama, are synonymous with good ratings (although we know this isn't always the case). The small difference between M.O.W.s and feature films is that M.O.W.s tend to rely exclusively on high concepts or the sensational to pull in big ratings.

As I sit here at my computer the network TV lineup of M.O.W.s includes the controversial Roe vs. Wade docudrama on the landmark Supreme Court decision regarding abortion; "Guts and Glory," the movie about Col. Oliver North and the Iran Contra scandal; "Bionic Reunion," which needs no explanation; "The Trial of the Incredible Hulk," ditto; and "Trouble in Paradise," starring Raquel Welch. Welch is shipwrecked on an island with a drunken sailor. Need I say more? Everything in television points to ratings.

A while back, writer Pamela Wallace came across an article in the newspaper on various marriage seminars popping up all over the country, teaching singles how to find and connect with the right mate. She stashed the article in her desk, thinking that somewhere in it was an idea for a story. About a year later, we found ourselves having lunch and discussing the fact that we were both divorced, juggling careers, and raising children. Obviously, we weren't alone. There were men and women all over the country in the same situation. And times were changing. Divorce statistics were down, social diseases were up, and it had even been announced that Hugh Heffner was getting married. The problem for unattached singles was no longer the fear of committment, but rather where and how to find the right person to commit to.

By the end of lunch, we had decided to develop an M.O.W. that we later titled, "How to Get Married Or Your Money Back." It was a comedic look at singles and the matrimony game. In it, the two arch enemies, a female sportscaster and a macho jock, both busy with careers and tired of being single, discover to their horror that they have turned up at the same seminar on "How to Get Married," which comes with a marriage manual and a money-back guarantee. Running into each other is bad enough, but things get worse when they find they have been paired as partners in a postclass project. They must meet regularly as a support couple and help each other in their search for the right mate; thus, each will better understand the psyche of the opposite sex.

"How to Get Married Or Your Money Back" is an example of high concept. First, the idea can be described in one or two lines. In this case, the one-liner became our title. Next, it was an idea that promised to be entertaining and have mass appeal. When we laid the idea on friends, we had a great response. The unattached said they would stay tuned to learn how to meet the opposite sex and find the right person. Confirmed singles were interested in seeing how someone could manipulate a person to the altar—just so it *wouldn't* happen to them! Married friends responded positively, identifying with the pangs of courting and the endless strings of disasters leading to the altar.

We took "How to Get Married Or Your Money Back" to a production company, who in turn set us up at the networks to pitch. The idea made it to the top of CBS, where it was eventually nixed. They felt it was too close to a project being developed by Gloria Steinem on single women and marriage. Our instinct was right. The idea was high concept enough to make it to the tower.

High concept also applies to feature films where the term has become synonymous with big box office. *Three Men and a Baby, Big, Back to the Future, Lethal Weapon,* and *Splash* are only a few examples of high-concept box-office hits.

If you're looking at the Las Vegas odds for either the M.O.W. or the feature film, your biggest shot for a sale is with a high-concept script—at least at first. This is not to say you should compromise the quality of your writing. The scripts I have mentioned were all very well written. What I am saying is that high concept is what producers want. It is what the market thrives on: Just turn to the movie page in your newspaper or open the *TV Guide.* Know it, consider it, and then write what you must. There have always been those very bold souls who break from the commercial, write a hit, and invariably all of Hollywood jumps on the bandwagon. Also, ask yourself when plotting your idea:

Do we care about the hero or heroes? Are we fascinated by them?
Is their dramatic need strong enough?
Have we placed enough obstacles in their path?
In the course of the story, do they change or grow?
Will the audience identify with the characters and plot?
Does the story have commercial appeal?

One of the biggest complaints among producers today is that scripts lack passion. In the end, you are the only guide. Let your passion dictate; listen to your inner self. You must care about your subject—it will show on the pages.

12

Developing the Two-Hour Movie and Movie of the Week

Developing the two-hour script is almost identical to the procedure used for episodic television scripts (review chapter 8). However, since we are working in a much larger structure, there are three additional steps, as shown in figure 11.

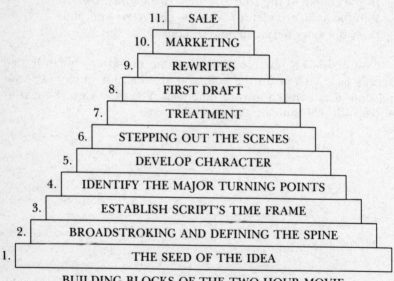

11.	SALE
10.	MARKETING
9.	REWRITES
8.	FIRST DRAFT
7.	TREATMENT
6.	STEPPING OUT THE SCENES
5.	DEVELOP CHARACTER
4.	IDENTIFY THE MAJOR TURNING POINTS
3.	ESTABLISH SCRIPT'S TIME FRAME
2.	BROADSTROKING AND DEFINING THE SPINE
1.	THE SEED OF THE IDEA

BUILDING BLOCKS OF THE TWO-HOUR MOVIE
Figure 11.

Step 1: The Seed of the Idea

We begin formulating a notion or the basic premise.

Step 2: Broadstroking and Defining the Spine

We plant the seed to see if it takes, asking ourselves necessary questions that elicit the correct responses. It is here that we identify the *spine,* the one- or two-line description of what the story is about. We call it the spine because it is the central idea or core of the story.

For examples, "A lost alien is befriended by a young boy who helps him find his way back home" *(E.T.).* "A teenage boy moves to L.A. and is harassed by a school gang; with the help of an elderly Japanese maintenance man, he learns karate and defends himself" *(The Karate Kid).* "A happily married woman's husband deserts her; in her struggle with unmarried life, she discovers love and independence" *(An Unmarried Woman).* Inherent within these descriptions are character, need, conflict, action, and resolve. Remember, if you can't define it, you can't write it. While preparing and writing the script, repeat the spine over and over to yourself to keep from wandering off target.

Step 3: Establishing the Script's Time Frame

This step gives clarity to the script. *Hannah and Her Sisters* opens on a Thanksgiving dinner, with all the characters having gone through major changes in the interim, and ends at a subsequent Thanksgiving celebration.

Does your story take place in one night, as does *After Hours,* or does it span the six months of a football season? In *Heaven Can Wait,* writers Elaine May and Warren Beatty open with Joe Pendleton at a pregame practice, and end with him in the body of another man making the winning touchdown at the Super Bowl. James L. Brooks, in *Terms of Endearment,* chose the time context of a young woman's life.

A movie is a series of fragments, a blueprint of visual impressions that give the illusion of a complete story when strung together. By clearly defining the time frame, the writer identifies the necessary bits and pieces needed to tell the story. A vague time span leads to poor decisions and no guard rails to protect from going on a tangent.

Step 4: Identifying the Major Turning Points

Attempting to write without knowing where you are going is no better than driving around blindly looking for a house when you could ask for directions. The screenplay consists of three acts (refer to diagram, page 170). Act I is the act of the setup. At the end of this twenty-five- to thirty-five-page unit of action, a major turning point is introduced into the story that totally shifts the action. Another turning point occurs at the end of Act II, the confrontation, a forty-five- to sixty-page unit of action, which again swings the story around and propels it into the third act, the resolution, the last twenty-five- to thirty-five-page unit of action.

By identifying the major turning points first, you can effectively shortcut your work. In essence, you are determining your destination before mapping out your route. Doing so will help keep you on track and will give your script a clear and direct line of focus.

Step 5: Developing Character

Structure holds the story in place, but it is character, scene by scene, line by line, that takes you through the script. Once you have determined the spine, time frame, and turning points of the story, the character, if fully developed, will tell you how to get there.

An underdeveloped protagonist results in a one-dimensional script, whereas intense character work not only opens up the screenwriter visually but also develops other aspects of the script. The people in your character's personal life and professional life become characters in your story. Their routines and the places they frequent become your locales. *Note:* Character development *does not* have to wait until step 5. Some screenwriters may choose this step before they identify the turning points or even the spine of the story. It is crucial, however, that character work is completed before step 6.

Step 6: Stepping Out the Scenes

With the character work now complete, we step out the scenes and/or sequences leading to the major turning points. At this point, we know where to go. It is now a matter of determining how to get there. For this purpose it is useful to use index cards. Each card represents a scene and/or sequence. On the card, place the locale, who is in the scene/sequence, and why the scene has to be there. If the card does not provide us with new, pertinent story information or character revelation it is excess and does not belong in the script (see chapter 8).

When you complete the stepping-out process, you can step back and see the general sweep of the script. Since the cards can be shifted around easily, this step is the place to make needed structural revisions.

Step 7: Treatment

Here, we write the narrative version that describes what is taking place in the scene. What are the characters doing? How does the pertinent information come out? What are the inner components of the scene or sequence that make it work? (Again, see chapter 8).

As you write treatment, ideas and dialogue will come to you more freely than when you are writing in script format. At this stage, you're letting ideas out without the burden of having to execute them in script form. How something is said is not important here. It is rather *what* is said, and the natural progression of the scene itself. You can work on treatment just like an artist works on a drafting table—cut and paste—and make the necessary revisions before you begin the first draft.

Step 8: First Draft

The foundation has been laid; now you begin writing in script format. You have seen examples of script formatting in the various excerpts of screenplays and teleplays we have studied throughout this book. (For margin and tab settings, see chapter 13, Teleplay Form.)

At this point in the development process we already know the story structurally works. We know the progression of scenes and/or sequences, what pertinent information must come out, and we have even envisioned in treatment how it plays out. Now, the most important thing is to just write. Get it down on paper. But, don't let your inner critic get in the way. Perfectionism leads to procrastination, which leads to paralysis—and the premature editing of a potential gem. Remember, the first draft exists to be rewritten.

Step 9: Rewrites

Here, we trim, cut, and perfect our script. Corrections are made, points are clarified and defined, characters are intensified, and dialogue and narrative are tightened and sharpened. It is time for the inner critic to go to work. Great scripts happen in the rewriting. Be ruthless with your own material. You are finished rewriting only when you know you are not capable of making the script any better at this particular time in your life (see page 134).

Step 10: Marketing

Creativity *doesn't* stop when the script is done. Now the writer becomes a salesperson.

Step 11: The Sale

Here, all your efforts pay off.

Miniseries and Adaptations

I am often approached by new writers who tell me they have a sensational idea for a miniseries. If you write to sell, and if you choose to invest your energies in areas that could reap rewards, don't even consider writing the miniseries. Even if you do have a sensational idea, your talents will be better spent churning out good two-hour movies.

Writing the miniseries is like hitting the ceiling. There is no higher place for the television writer to go. It is the coup de grace, the Olympic gold medal, the pot of gold at the end of the rainbow.

First, consider how few miniseries are made. Next, consider their exorbitant costs. Writers of miniseries are the elite, hand-picked by the networks, and are in the top echelon of produced television writers. Rarely, if ever, are miniseries derived from original material anymore. They are almost exclusively adapted from other sources, primarily from successful novels.

I must send out another word of warning on adaptations. In my various lectures and workshops, new writers will excitedly tell me they've come across a very obscure novel that would make a great M.O.W. or feature film—they absolutely must adapt it. "How do you go about doing this?" they ask. Never attempt to put one word on paper until you've contacted the publishers or the Copyright Office in Washington, D.C., to learn the status of the book. If the copyright has not run out you will have to make arrangements with the author, the author's agent, or whoever owns the copyright. This procedure may involve money or it may not.

I must also advise you, however, that trying to sell an obscure novel idea to the networks is like trying to sell empty calories to a serious dieter. If the material is dated, they will be turned off even more. The novels the networks want are the big sellers that have already proven themselves. They in turn pay a handsome price to obtain the rights to these novels, and again hand-pick the writer to script them. For new writers breaking in, it is unquestionably better to develop and write original material.

Perhaps it is best to think of the miniseries and/or adaptations as goals to aspire to. They are possible goals, yet highly unlikely if your plan is to shortcut the necessary steps in getting you there.

A Word from Writer/Producer Earl Wallace

Earl Wallace not only holds the distinction of receiving a 1986 Academy Award for the motion picture *Witness,* which he scripted with William Kelly and Pamela Wallace, but of adapting the longest running miniseries in history, *Winds of War* and its sequel *War and Remembrance,* in conjunction with producer Dan Curtis and author Herman Wouk. The miniseries were based on Herman Wouk's novel about World War II, which follows a family through the dramatic events of the war in both Europe and the Pacific. I talked with Earl about the scripting of this immense project and the necessary steps his career took leading up to it.

MADELINE DIMAGGIO: Writing *Winds of War* and *War and Remembrance* was a titanic undertaking. Together, both miniseries run forty-eight hours. How did a project of this magnitude begin?

EARL WALLACE: *War and Remembrance* was a direct outgrowth of *Winds of War,* which Paramount committed to back in the seventies. It began as a very risky venture because they knew it was going to be very expensive, and since the combined resources of ABC and Paramount would probably not be enough to carry it, they would probably need foreign financing. Ultimately, *Winds* ended up costing in excess of $42 million, I believe, and a portion of this did come from European sources, Paramount put up a certain amount of backing, ABC put up the rest. The point is that if *Winds of War* hadn't happened, *War and Remembrance* would not have happened either.

MD: How was it determined you were to be the writer?

EW: Dan Curtis, the producer, began adapting *Winds of War* with Herman Wouk, I believe in about 1980–1981, and it became apparent to him very shortly that the job was simply too big and he asked me to come in to perform a story editing function.

MD: Were his original intentions to write the screenplay on his own or with Herman Wouk? How had he anticipated doing it?

EW: The original deal called for Herman Wouk to do it—what Herman brought him did not meet Dan's needs. It was not Herman's ability as a storyteller or even necessarily as a screenwriter that posed the problem. The problem was that what he was giving Dan did not enable Dan to put it on the screen. They were dealing with Herman's book for Chrissake—it's not like there was any deficiency in the dramatic material—it was the way it was being presented.

MD: What was your function as story editor?

EW: First, we sat down and decided how to attack the book. A key thing to remember in terms of producing a script for *Winds* is that it was a very large melodrama. It was laid out very well and the characters were not complex. This was not a problem of solving huge story disasters—it wasn't a problem of creating new characters—it was simply taking the material that was in the book as it was and laying it out in screenplay fashion.

MD: How did you go about this? What was the working arrangement between you and Dan? Who determined how it was to be laid out?

EW: The working process was very simple. I would sit down with a chunk of Herman's book and do a draft—you know, put it in screenplay form. Dan would take the first draft and make his notations, add what he could, and then we would both sit down with it together and produce a final shooting draft—for that particular section of the book that we were working on.

MD: Did you work from a step?

EW: No, we never did, because as I said there were not any mechanical story problems that had to be solved. It was simply a matter of taking the book and dramatizing it. We would look at sections of the book and say we can't include this particular segment—we just don't have time for it, so we threw it out. These were the kinds of decisions we had to make along the way. We were committed to reproducing the book. For that reason, we had minimal problems with Herman Wouk and the network.

MD: Did Herman Wouk approve the scripts?

EW: He didn't really have script approval—that's almost impossible for a novelist to get—even Herman Wouk. But he got everything else.

MD: Such as?

EW: The key to ABC's safe deposit box! He made the most awesome deal in television history.

MD: How long did both projects take you to write?

EW: As I recall, the work on *Winds of War* took about six months and ran eighteen hours. *War and Remembrance* took a couple of years and ran thirty-two hours. I got story editor credit on *Winds of War*, and written-for-television credit for all of *War and Remembrance*.

MD: How many scripts did you write? How did they break down? And how did they break down as far as running time?

EW: Originally, we broke it down into three-hour scripts—six three-hour scripts for *Winds of War*, and ten three-hour scripts for *War and Remembrance*. Since the project was of rather huge stature, we conceived the episodes as rather substantial—you don't want to kick off an hour here, two hours there, etc. It should be consistent. In the final analysis, Dan broke it down into three-hour episodes and two-hour episodes.

MD: Did this affect the structuring of the script—going between two- and three-hour episodes?

EW: Not really, because it didn't change the script that we wrote. Dan just broke it off—two hours here, three hours there, because the dramatic ending seemed more appropriate. He did some shifting of scenes but that was in the editing room. The way we laid it out, as I said, was basically in three-hour episodes. Dan went out and shot it, saw what he had, and decided how he wanted to see it aired. He wouldn't ordinarily have had that power, but because of last year's writers' strike—and ABC realizing they didn't have anything for the November sweeps—they needed something desperately. Dan had no desire to air anything before 1989, but he agreed to have *War and Remembrance* ready if in return he could carve it up the way he wanted it—so they cut a deal.

MD: What would you say is the biggest problem of adapting a novel?

EW: Every novel is different. You attack every one of them differently. You try to find a film story in it, then break it down into acts and apply your craft as you know it.

MD: Is there an incredible amount of cutting involved?

EW: Again, it depends on the novel. With Herman Wouk's books it was mostly a matter of excess—you know, trimming fat from the story. If you were talking about adapting *The Great Gatsby,* you'd have a whole different set of problems.

MD: Did you have a say in casting or in any aspect of the production other than the writing?

EW: No, and that's not atypical, either. You have to bear in mind that with a project this size, when the final curtain fell over the two projects, they had invested almost $150 million. If they are going to unload that kind of money, they're not going to leave casting to anybody but the networks and the producers.

MD: Were there any consessions or compromises you had to make to appease the network as author or producer in writing these scripts?

EW: This was an unusual experience in that we were committed to getting the book on the screen. Herman had a very powerful deal so he could have imposed enormous problems—he didn't—and ABC was also very committed. The only real controversial elements were the holocaust interviews.

MD: What kind of research did you need, other than what was already in the book?

EW: We interviewed survivors of the holocaust who were located through the Simon Weisenthal Center, which worked with us very closely and was enormously helpful. We looked for things—for instance, Dan had a sequence which involved Babi Yar and the massacre of the Jews in the early days of the war at Kaiv in Russia. Herman had done an enormous amount of research on this for himself, but only a small portion appeared in the novel. We needed to say more—here's how this event unfolded from beginning to end. We needed to go back and relive it through the eyes of the people who witnessed it.

A woman in her seventies who had survived the holocaust agreed to answer questions and talk about her experiences. She recounted an incident in which she and another young woman were pulled out of Auschwitz and sent to the cities to help clean up the rubble created by allied bombs. The woman who was with her had recently given birth to a baby which she somehow tried to smuggle out in a shoe box. The German guards discovered it and murdered the child in front of her. They did it in the most brutal way you can imagine. The woman telling the story relived it after many years and just crumbled in front of our eyes. You can hear about a lot of these stories and you can read about them, but I don't think you can truly comprehend or grasp them until you witness something like that. It was a very traumatic experience in a lot of different ways.

MD: What would you say the difference is between adapting a massive book like *Winds of War* and *War and Remembrance* to a smaller novel?

EW: The only other adaptation I did was another big book entitled *Love and Glory.* The original title was *Women in the Army,* but that was a truly horrible book that had no real story. It was more of a bad essay on the women's army during World War II. In this case it was a matter of keeping four or five of the characters, throwing out most everything else in the book, and working basically from only the concept. During the course of my writing, the regime changed at CBS. We had agreed the book would be a big, broad, sexy melodrama with a lot of color and as much humor as we could throw into it. The new president decided he wanted to do it more seriously and make it shorter. This was when I already had five or six hours into the script. It was terrible. Ultimately, it did not have a happy ending. I believe they're making it again.

MD: You have worked in every medium—film, episodic television (both staff and free-lance), M.O.W.s, miniseries, and feature films. How do they differ?

EW: Features, M.O.W.s, and minis are not all that different—you just have a little more time with a miniseries. Screen writing is basically screen writing viewed through different glasses. Features see through one glass, the miniseries sees through another—but the craft is essentially the same. Nobody will really want to hear that, but it is. Film writing is basically story writing, embellished with such qualities as touches of humor, touches of character, heavy dependency on pace— it can move in a variety of different ways. *The Way We Were* does not have the same pace as *Butch Cassidy and the Sundance Kid,* but pace is equally important in both scripts. These types of games you have to understand—if you don't you shouldn't be in the game anyway.

MD: How does this type of writing differ from writing episodes or being on staff in episodic television?

EW: Staff work, as far as I'm concerned, is the writer's nightmare—it has its own energy attached because it's meatball screen writing to a large entent. You must maintain a weekly air date and the responsibility runs heaviest on the writers to keep those scripts coming in. At the same time, you're dealing with preproduction and the ongoing problem with the show that's in production, along with a variety of people like the director and the stars. So the problems never end.

MD: Could you tell my readers the steps you took in television that led you to the miniseries?

EW: I took a class at UCLA in screen writing from Wells Root, and one of the assignments was to write an original one-hour episode. I wrote a "Gunsmoke." Wells knew a writer for the show, a fellow who has since passed away by the name of Ron Bishop, and they decided to buy the thing.

MD: Then you sold the first script you wrote?

EW: I had written a couple of little things, but I was on the outside of the industry and I knew I had to find some pipeline inside. When I found in the Extension guide that Wells Root had been a working screenwriter and had numerous credits, I knew he had to know people, so I took his class. It actually worked out that way. I sold that script and then the following year I wrote three or four more "Gunsmokes" and then rewrote three or four more. The following year I went on staff. When "Gunsmoke" was canceled, I had a lot of credentials. I went out and did episodes—"Baretta," "Quincy"—and a couple of series that didn't get on the air. I got involved with Dan Curtis way back then. He was doing some two-hour things for NBC—"The Melvin Pervis G-Man" series. It was about an FBI agent back in the thirties running down people like Dillinger and Ma Barker. All of a sudden in a very short period of time I found myself doing two-hour. When you get to that plateau in television, you've made a major stride. Even though "Melvin Pervis" was a series, it was a quasi M.O.W. Then I began doing other two-hour projects and M.O.W.s. I worked as story editor on a show called "Bronc." Dan Curtis and I liked each other a lot so I always ended up going back to him at some period of time. We did a three-hour western called "The Last Ride of the Dalton Gang," and some other projects. When *Winds of War* came along and he found himself in over his head, he came to me because we were very close at the time.

MD: What would you tell a new writer who wants to break in?

EW: If you really want to be a film writer move to L.A. and keep writing—that's all you can do. Along the way maybe you'll make some connections. Unless you are intimately related to somebody you have to be here and you have to keep writing.

A Note on Collaboration

This industry is not one in which you will shine alone. Film is a highly collaborative art form. Once you sell, at every stage of the television and motion picture development process there will be meetings. It is a given that you will have input from other professionals. The scriptwriter provides the bare bones, the skeleton, so that everyone else can come along and attach the flesh. Good television and feature films simply do not happen because there is a good script. It is a collaborative effort where everyone working is committed to the project. They all come together with their individual expertise and everything clicks.

I personally am very fond of the collaborative process. It's truly exciting to think how many jobs a single script employs. Hundreds of people will, in a period of time and space, make a living off the writer's singular idea. You wonder as you write who will be cast, who will direct, edit, costume, compose the music, play the music, who the crew and the extras will be, and even who the caterers will be. On and on it goes. Don't leave when the movie is over. Watch the credits at the end of the show. You will be amazed by just how collaborative this field is.

Many scriptwriters collaborate in Hollywood also. Writing teams are very common. Throughout this book I have mentioned my various collaborative projects. Obviously, though I have sole credits, I am one of those beings who seems to gravitate toward a partnership. I have been on both sides of the fence, and each has its advantages and disadvantages. It depends on your personality. *Writers must know themselves.*

I am social by nature. I like bouncing ideas off creative minds, and at times I need the validation of my own ideas. This is a very sophisticated way of telling you that I'm a bit insecure. That's okay, I'll admit it—it puts me in the ninetieth percentile of people working in this industry.

If you are considering a writing collaboration there are some very important issues you must address. Sharing the writing process is like walking down the aisle together. At first, both people are very trusting and idealistic. But like a marriage, when difficulties arise egos get involved and feelings get hurt. If there is not an open line of communication the partnership can turn very sour. Nothing will kill the creative process faster and breaking up can be as difficult as it is in a marriage.

If you choose to write with a partner, and the script you write sells, you are very obligated to remain with that partner on your next assignment. Producers and story editors are buying a team and they will not settle for half of it. If you build a career with your partner, then choose to break up, it will be like beginning all over again. For some inexplicable reason, the Hollywood mentality assumes that whichever partner isn't in the room is the one who did the work—this is especially true in episodic television. I am adaptable and accepting of my industry, but on this particular point I get a little crazy. It is not uncommon for the ex-member of a team to go to a meeting and have someone ask, "So who really wrote the script?"

This problem is so prevalent that my agent jokingly told me once that writers should make prenuptial agreements. They should decide in the event of a breakup who will take credit for which script—sort of like divvying up the kids—and each must have permission from the other to take her name off the scripts she didn't retain. Once you are established in the industry this problem doesn't exist. A name artist will collaborate on certain scripts while her career remains independent of her partner's and the project.

If you choose to work with a partner, if you are seriously writing to sell, and if you want to establish yourself as a team, here are the ground rules for building a successful collaboration:

1. Communication is key. You must trust each other's opinion. Listen, and be willing to compromise. Egos must get out of the way. Everything has to be geared toward the good of the project.

2. Is the other writer as committed as you are? What if midway through the project he decides to quit? Or what if he must relocate? Will the rights then revert to the writer who completes the project? Discuss this situation and get backup plans *on paper*. This written agreement can be done between the two of you. You don't need an attorney; you simply need something in writing.

3. How much time is your partner willing to invest in the project and the partnership? What about the expenses? Writing is not a cheap proposition: There are copying fees, supplies, mailings, business lunches, research expenses. Is your partner financially committed as well?

4. Decide whose name will go first. This point sounds a bit trite, but later it can become a big issue—one of my partners and I once flipped a coin! Maybe you should decide what sounds best. In any case, decide in the beginning.

5. Choose a partner who compliments you, one who possesses strengths where you are weak and vice versa. The point of a good partnership is that you write better faster. Two idea people can discount one another. The same is true of two organizers—it's like two sides of a positive magnet coming together. It is the differences between you and your partner that make for a powerful team.

6. Know the personal life of your partner. Writing takes a lot of time. In fact, you may spend more time with your partner than with your spouse. With this many hours spent together, the line between professional and personal becomes very thin. Will your partner's spouse, boyfriend, or girlfriend begin resenting the time you require? Will yours?

   It is very important that you let your significant other know the commitment you have made and the time that it will entail. Other people will be very affected by your decision.

7. Find out who, between the two of you, has the most powerful verbal skills and let that person be the "front" man or woman. Two writers trying to outtalk each other at a pitch session just won't do. Let one do the talking; let the other chime in when necessary. One is the driver; the other is the navigator.

8. Decide who will do what writing task and when. If either of you falls short, the other should be able to call the neglectful partner on it and pinch hit.

9. Spend a week or two discussing your writing arrangements so that before you begin nothing is assumed and everything is clear.

With the ground rules laid, collaboration can be a supportive, exhilarating experience. When you face rejection, you will have someone with whom to commiserate. You'll also have someone to share the highs, the excitement, and the achievements. When one of you is down, the other can pick up. When one of you is off, the other can take over. A good partnership is creatively satisfying. Good ideas, when bounced off another creative mind, become even better; they shine brighter and intensify.

"If the Shoe Fits" was one of those experiences. Pam, Earl, and I would meet for breakfast and discuss where we wanted to take the script, then individually go off and do it. There were no surprises. Nobody pulled any punches. We each knew what was expected of us and we did it. The writing went incredibly fast and the process was great fun.

A Note on Research

As a writer, your responsibility is to get the facts straight. Therefore, research is crucial. But again I must warn you that some subjects warrant thorough investigation; others can be an excuse for writers *not* to write. All too often, I have come across writers who have overresearched. They have too much. The problem then becomes what to use. Some writers attempt to stick everything they have learned into a script. It's as though they're saying, "This took a lot of time, so you're going to hear all of it."

One writer found herself in a terrific dilemma. She had researched a public individual for close to seven years. One day, she came to me practically in tears. She had accumulated two-hundred to three-hundred pages of material on this person, including clippings, fact sheets—the whole bit. "Where do I begin?" she asked. I told her there was absolutely no way she could get all of this information into a screenplay, that she would have to decide what portion of his life to use as the focus. She insisted that anything less than all of it would be doing this person a disservice because his life was so full. By now, I'm certain, so is her closet. Do only what research is necessary. Be practical about it. There is nothing wrong with shortcuts.

When I completed my screenplay, "Belly Up," I sent it to friends. Why? There were specific areas in which I needed some help. My protagonist, Alex, bet with his cronies on the golf course. Instead of taking up golf, I simply sent my script to someone I knew who bet on the golf course. He gave me golf talk—the kind of slang used while making wagers—and I placed it in my script. Later, an established male producer told me, "You write like a man." (I guess he meant this as a compliment.) I smiled, lest I not get an option. It turned out that he was a heavy bettor on the golf course. In fact, I think half the reason I made it to his office is that he wanted to talk about golf. "That's exactly what we do," he said. I laughed it off and acted as though I had been raised on the golf course. Unfortunately, he still didn't buy the script. May he rim his next putt.

I also gave "Belly Up" to an attorney friend. I wasn't aware of all the nuances involved in bankruptcy, so I needed a bit of legal advice.

Next, I gave the script to a female accountant. Lindsay, my female lead, was such, and I wanted to know if what I wrote was accurate.

There is a saying that we are all just five people away from the one person we need to get to. Think of the vast area of research you already have at your fingertips. And don't be afraid to use the phone. If you want to know about the life of an architect, why not simply pick up the phone and take an architect to lunch. You will be amazed at how cooperative people can be when they discover what you are doing.

Be creative with your research as well as with your writing. The universe has provided you with convenient resources. If, after you exhaust the shortcuts, you need more, then it's time to go to your local library and search for books, reference works, and periodicals.

I have a good relationship with my local librarian. She knows I'm a writer and at various times we've talked about my projects. Often, when I'm swamped, I can call her and find what I need waiting for me at the reference desk when I arrive. When you tell people you write and share your enthusiasm, they also get caught in the process. You will find there are many knowledgeable people who are willing to share information with you.

I have talked to morticians, police officers, physicians, historians, designers, bomb squads, cosmetic companies, gold assayers, prison pharmacists—all sorts of fascinating people. By merely picking up the phone, introducing myself, and explaining what I am doing, I am able to get exactly the information I need.

The Writers Guild of America lists sources in its monthly bulletin for obtaining accurate information on a variety of subjects. Since these telephone numbers are subject to change, it would be best if you check the Writers Guild's most recent bulletin, or subscribe to the *Writers Guild of America Journal* (see appendix A).

13

Teleplay Form

When I first began writing, I disassembled a friend's "Hawaii-Five-O" script, took out one of the pages, stuck it in my typewriter, set the margins and tabs according to what was on the page, and I never looked back. Years later, when I began teaching, students asked me what the necessary settings were (the format), and I had to go back and look them up!

What began with my eyeballing the page eventually became second nature to me. To this day I keep a teleplay and a screenplay within reach so when I get stuck on some formatting technicality I can pull them out for help.

Recently, I bought a book on script formatting and sat down to study it. Had I done this fourteen years earlier I never would have attempted script writing! The book was ridiculously complex, overly detailed, and read like a computer manual, which I've never been able to make too much sense out of either. Reading this book was like going to a golf pro who tells you seventy-five different things to do with your swing. You're so busy trying to remember all seventy-five things that you end up missing the ball! With this in mind, I will try to keep it simple: As I give you the guidelines, peruse the script examples in this book so you can see them in application.

Script Formats

One-Hour and Two-Hour
The formatting for one- and two-hour scripts is identical with one exception: In episodic television, all acts are numbered and delineated on the pages, whereas in the motion picture format (screenplay format), the acts are imaginary and serve only to help the writer—they are *not* delineated on the pages.

General Rules

Use pica type only. Elite print is too hard to read and not acceptable for submission.

Line up the paper on the left edge of the typewriter marked "0," then set the margins and tabs as follows:

Number of Spaces from Left Margin (0)		Right Typing Margin
20	Scene description (narrative)	70
30	Dialogue	65
35	Parenthetical description	50
40	Character name	NA
75	Page numbers	NA

Be sure to eye the right margin—it should be jagged. A right-justified margin won't do.

The page number is placed four to six lines down from the top of the page.

Act numbers (for television) are centered, and are about eleven lines down from the top of the page, with the title of the episode or M.O.W. centered two spaces above.

All scene settings (INT., EXT.) start at the left margin.

Most angles are on the left margin.

All description (narrative) starts at the left margin, is single-spaced, and written in lowercase.

Double space is used between the scene settings and the description; between the description and the character's name.

Dialogue begins on the line directly under the character's name.

Triple space is used for a new scene setting.

The word *continued* used to appear at the bottom right of the page, to indicate the scene was continuing. Today, it is considered somewhat out of style. If you want to use it, the tab setting is 65.

Cut to (tab 62) is no longer necessary to indicate a quick change of scenes, but sometimes is used for effect.

The Half-Hour Situation Comedy Format

All of the above settings for margins and tabs are identical. The only changes are as follows:

All dialogue is double-spaced.

All scene descriptions are capitalized and set at the left margin. Some shows will place parentheses around the descriptions, others will not. With many shows, scenes will begin fifteen spaces from the top of the page.

It is important to order a sample script for the show you choose to write for since formats can vary slightly from show to show.

Camera Definitions

Below is a list of camera angles and terminology from the script examples used in this book.

FADE IN: The way every teleplay/screenplay opens. The camera goes from black to an image, from nothing to a picture.

CAMERA FINDS: The camera moves in on a particular portion of the big picture.

CAMERA GOES WITH: The camera moves with the character or thing; for example, a character moving from one room to another, or a car driving down the street.

ANGLE/ANGLE ON: What the camera is focused on. It is the subject of the shot and can be indicated in various ways (also ON/ CAMERA ON:). It can also be done by simply capitalizing the subject, such as SHOES (see page 172).

BACK TO SCENE/RESUME: The camera returns from an angle to its original shot, where it was before.

ESTABLISHING SHOT: Used to establish where we are, or what the camera is looking at (page 27). If the writer chooses, the script can also read, for example: EXT. CENTURY CITY— ESTABLISHING—DAY.

STOCK SHOT/(STOCK): Film footage that has already been shot. It is in the can and kept on file to be used over and over.

FULL SHOT: A very big picture. The camera takes in a large area.

P.O.V.: A person's point of view—what he, she, or they are looking at. This term can also indicate the camera's P.O.V.

FADE OUT: Used at the end of a teaser, the end of an act, and at the end of the script. It means the screen gradually goes to black; the image disappears. As with FADE IN, it is always spelled out, capitalized, and can appear on the left or the right side of the page (commonly, the left side).

DISSOLVE: Takes place when the image on screen is fading out while a new image is fading in. Dissolves are often used to denote a time lapse.

SOUND EFFECTS/SOUND FX: Almost always capitalized in script format.

TWO SHOT: Two people are in the shot. There is also a THREE SHOT. I find it simpler and less directorial to name the subjects in the shot.

CLOSE ON/CLOSE UP: The camera closely examines some detail of the picture for emphasis or clarity.

VARIOUS ANGLES: This suggests many shots, but the writer is essentially saying that the decisions are up to the director.

CUT TO/CUT (INSIDE–OUTSIDE) TO: Cutting between shots and scenes is automatic and should not be spelled out. Use this technique sparingly and only for emphasis—that is, when the CUT is making a particular point or statement.

QUICK CUT TO: Again, this is only for effect. The quick cut makes a statement; it serves as an exclamation point.

PAN/PULL BACK TO REVEAL/MOVING SHOT/DOLLYING: The camera moves slowly from one side to another, is following the movement of a single subject, or is pulling back to reveal additional information.

REVERSE ANGLE: The reverse position of the previous shot. If, for example, the P.O.V. of the camera is a line of beautiful models, we REVERSE the angle and see who is scrutinizing them (page 181).

INTO FRAME: Exactly what it says. Something or someone comes into the picture.

WIDENING: The shot becomes bigger, reveals more of the picture.

SERIES OF CUTS: These suggest a series of many pictures that are somewhat interchangeable.

VARIOUS CUTS/MORE CUTS/VARIOUS ANGLES: In some cases the writer may need to specify (list the shots); in others the writer may only need to suggest examples.

HOLD: To stay, or hold, on the picture for an effect.

INSERT: A close shot of something that is placed or inserted into the picture. On page 214, the series of photographic enlargements are actually inserts and could have been stated as such: INSERT: ENLARGEMENTS.

It is helpful to understand camera angles and on some occasions it is necessary to use them. Remember, however, that too many camera angles and misuse of camera angles is a tip-off that you are an amateur. Use them sparingly and make sure they are used properly.

The Submission Script

Rules for Submission—All Scripts

Script covers should not have embossed lettering or fancy graphics.

The cover should consist of heavy colored paper and three holes punched with clasps holding the script.

The title page should look clean, simple, and balanced. The title should be centered and placed twenty to twenty-five lines down from the top of the page.

Episodic Television

The title of the series comes first (line 22), capitalized and underlined. Follow with the title of the episode three lines down (typed in lowercase). Skip five lines, then center "Written By:"; skip two more lines, then type your name:

<u>FANTASY ISLAND</u>

"Night of the Tormented Soul"

Written by:

Madeline DiMaggio

Movies of the Week and Feature Films

The title of the story is capitalized and underlined, followed by "An Original Screenplay" (if original) down five lines from the title; "By" down two lines; your name two lines below that.

<u>BELLY UP!</u>

An Original Screenplay

By

Madeline DiMaggio

For all half-hour, one-hour, and two-hour scripts, your agent's name, address, and phone number is placed in the lower right corner. If you don't yet have an agent, list your own address and phone number.

All scripts should look professional. They must be typed in the correct format. There can be no typographical errors. Keep your original. Send a clean photocopy.

What Not to Do

Never indicate what the draft of the script is, first, revised, final, or otherwise. It is assumed that the script is the writer's final work draft. Scripts should not be submitted before this point.

Never put a date on the script. It sometimes takes years for something to sell. Why let readers know how long the material has been floating around? A date will only "date" your script.

Don't number your scenes. Numbering is done by the production department after the script is turned in. It is never done in the writer's draft.

Don't include a cast list.

Don't include a set list.

Your character descriptions should never include your ideas or comments on casting. There is no such thing as a "Clint Eastwood type." Leave casting to the casting directors.

Keep descriptions vague enough so that many actors can step into the role. Keep it castable.

Protect your material with the Writers Guild Registration Office, but don't place the registration number on the title page (proof of amateur paranoia). Keep the number in a well-protected place. It provides proof of authorship and the date your material was registered. In the event that your material is plagiarized, your attorney can subpoena a records representative of the WGA to appear on your behalf. Scripts may be registered by mail. For information and procedures for WGA registration, see appendix B.

14

So It's Written—
What Do I Do Now?

I have discovered through my various workshops and speaking engagements that writers are often more interested in marketing their scripts than they are in writing them. "How do you break into the business?" they'll passionately ask. "Tell me what to do." "How do I bust this impossible barrier?"

At this point, I respond with a question of my own: "Where are you in terms of writing your script right now?" "Well," they'll answer, "I haven't written it yet, but when I do, how can I get it sold and how much money will I make?"

The most crucial and most important marketing tool you will ever possess is your completed script. All the doors you will ever open lie within the quality of your own writing. It shows on the pages. A great script may not sell, but I promise you it will open doors to an eventual sale if:

1. The writer has some knowledge of marketing and obtaining an agent.
2. The writer continues to write and produces high-quality material.
3. The writer perseveres.
4. The writer is determined.
5. The writer hangs in there long enough.

With each "if," literally thousands of would-be screenwriters drop out and the competition narrows. In the end it is passion and persistence that win. There is no question that once you sell, this field can be highly lucrative. If, however, money is your sole motivation, there are other fields that promise more expedient and promising pay-offs—like brain surgery, for example. After many years of intense training you're making a fabulous and consistent income.

In screen writing, you are always "in training," and your income will never be consistent. Once you hit it big, you could income average the years spent out of work, those wee hours rewriting, the endless hours of thinking about your storyline, characters, plot twists, and turns, and so forth. Subtract the costs you've incurred for copies, postage, and marketing, and it possibly will come out to minimum wage. Possibly. This information is not to discourage you, only to make a point. Steven Spielberg was driven by the passion to make movies, not by the passion to make dollars.

Make your first concern the quality of your script. Marketing cannot begin until you hold the polished draft in your hand. Make it the best you've got.

Marketing Strategies

Everybody who ever broke into this industry has a different story on how they went about it. Tales of marketing strategies and landing that much-needed break are about as diverse and creative as the writers who tell them. No matter how you proceed, eventually you have to find an agent. There is a remote chance you could sell a script without an agent. It is impossible, however, to have a career without one. Agents are crucial.

A Word from Mitchel Stein

Mitchel Stein is the writers' representative for the Shapiro-Lichtman Agency.

MADELINE DIMAGGIO: Why does a writer need an agent?

MITCHEL STEIN: You're not considered real in this town without one. Having representation means your material is of a high caliber. Further, in order to submit to the studios your work needs to come through an agent. But it's a catch-22—agents don't want to represent you unless you're currently represented or you have had something produced. And, it's difficult to be produced unless you have representation. It's an unfortunate rule.

MD: But not an infallible one. Many new writers find representation.

MS: True. Every year agencies take on a handful of new writers. Often, though, they come through a personal recommendation. I have found that for every hundred spec scripts I read, maybe there is only one that I like. Unsolicited scripts usually don't pay off.

MD: Is an outside writer better off writing a spec feature film or a spec episodic?

MS: It depends on where your immediate interests lie. If you want to write episodic television, sitcoms for example, then you should have a couple of samples from existing shows, especially from a show that is perceived as challenging and popular within the entertainment community. Also accept the fact that your script will be poorly received at the show for which you've written the spec.

MD: How do you know what's popular in the community, by the ratings?

MS: No, by the general buzz. By the quality and sophistication of the writing. For example, "Frank's Place," which did miserably in the ratings, was very highly regarded as an intelligent show. "Molly Dodd," and "Slap Maxwell," while they did poorly, were also thought of as intelligent shows. "Designing Women," and "Newhart," are currently well thought of. Further, shows fall in and out of favor within the community and so do the sample spec scripts. There was a time when "All in the Family," "Barney Miller," and "Taxi," were *the* shows to spec. Then it became "Cheers," and "Family Ties." Today, if you wrote a "Cheers" or a "Family Ties," you'd be wasting your time. The people who have to read and evaluate these spec scripts have read thousands of them by now, and they can't bear the thought of reading another dated show. They would much rather read a spec "Rosanne," "Wonder Years," or "Murphy Brown." Those are the only comedies that I can recommend to you now. But, let's see what the new season brings.

MD: When you say "they," who are you referring to?

MS: I'm talking about the studio executives, the network executives, and the writing staffs of the shows.

MD: You mentioned that the writer should never expect to sell a sample script of an existing show to that show. Why is that? Would the staff from an existing show rather read material from another show?

MS: The producer reading a sample of his own show can find too many things wrong with the script. Producers know their own show too well, with all its subtleties and nuances, that are nearly impossible for an outside writer to capture. The bottom line is, don't give them so many excuses to say "no." Send them a show where you both have equal insight and appreciation.

MD: Sometimes you hear of writers selling without agents. How does that happen?

MS: It's difficult. It happens usually through a connection, such as an executive at one of the studios or a network who will champion you. If it's a network executive, he might call an agent and tell him he's found a new writer and see if they'll read his work and see if it might be somebody they'd want to represent. A studio executive may do the same thing, but he's more likely to pass the material on to an executive producer and get their opinion. Regardless, it's because there is an existing relationship however distant and remote.

MD: What about M.O.W.s and feature films? Do small production companies have readers?

MS: Yes, everybody has readers, and everyone is looking for new material and exciting new writers. It's just a question of access. Without an agent you're forced to sign a release form. However, that makes it much easier for them to steal your ideas, though you hear very rarely of someone being ripped off. On the other hand, I know a writer who is currently working on a television show. It's been years since he's been back to work. He filed a lawsuit against a very big-name producer, and he won. The repercussions were that the client was a bad apple, and that he didn't play the game. Word was, you don't want to hire him, he's trouble.

MD: It's a small community, isn't it?

MS: Very small. When you get right down to it there are few writers and even fewer agents. Right before the Writers Guild strike, the WGA hosted for all writers' representatives an evening at Chasen's. They offered us dinner to make sure that we'd show up. They told us why they were striking and what they expected of us. There were about ninety agents present and I would say that represented about eighty percent of all the literary representatives in the business.

MD: How does a new writer know which agencies to submit to? Do some specialize in certain things? How do they find out?

MS: The WGA provides a list of agencies that will accept unsolicited material. From the outside trying to get in, you don't know which agency is best suited for you. It's a crap shoot. You just want an agent, period. Once you've got representation it's either working or it isn't. If your agency isn't handling your specific needs, it's now much easier for you to get interviews with other agencies.

MD: What is a packaging agent? Do only the bigger agencies do packaging?

MS: A packaging agent puts many of the elements of a show together before it's presented for sale. Usually, these elements can include a writer or a piece of material, a star, a director—anything that a buyer will recognize as essential to the success of the project. If the buyer absolutely needs a specific element, then perhaps they will pay a packaging fee. And everybody does it, or at least tries to. When successful, packaging can be very profitable.

MD: And all these people will be through your agency.

MS: Not necessarily, but why not? If we control the package, our clients don't pay any commission to us.

MD: So the writers don't have to pay the standard ten percent?

MS: Correct. They save the ten percent, and the agency still does well. As a packager, we get a percentage of the production budget and back-end profits. The monies can be substantial. Typically, a TV packager gets an initial three percent of the production budget. If an episode costs a million dollars to produce, three percent is quite significant. And it could go on for years at twenty-two episodes per season.

MD: So agents push packaging?

MS: Sure, but in reality packages are few. Most studios are reluctant to recognize them, and there is a paucity of star–writer–directors that can demand that a packaging fee is paid.

MD: Are producers and story editors on staff more likely to hire writers from their same agency? I mean obviously one would be more inclined to give these writers a break, right?

MS: In theory, no. In reality, yes. One particular agency, for example, currently appears to have a lock on all the comedy shows at one studio. Is it a coincidence? Who knows? However, it is difficult to get any of my clients on these shows. You keep hearing new names out of nowhere. So-and-so is now a new story editor. A lot of times you've never heard of these people. Why? Because the agents are shoving their clients in through their producers. They don't make any money on these people now, but they're grooming them, getting them ready for next season when they can take a new talent to market with some impressive current credits.

MD: Is it deadly to send a synopsis with a teleplay?

MS: Absolutely! It's the worst. It encourages readers not to read your script. They'll judge your work based on the quality of the synopsis and maybe then ten pages of your script. It's too easy for them to pass.

MD: What do you look for in a script? What do you consider a good read?

MS: Great dialogue, interesting characters, and the semblance of a sound structure. I also like to see a lot of white on the pages. One thing that turns me off more than anything is when I open up a script and there is page after page of single-spaced, detailed descriptions and camera directions, like "pan to so-and-so," or "zoom to the left." Don't tell me how I'm supposed to visualize the scene. And don't tell the director how to do his job. It's just extra clutter on the page.

For example, two guys are walking down the street and they spot a girl. One writer's description tells us "she's five foot four, wearing a long flowery dress, she's got striking orange hair, she's wearing tall red heels," and on and on. I don't need the exact picture. Another writer might say, "They see a girl and she's a knockout." It's one line. Let it be my fantasy. Don't tell me unless it's important to the story.

MD: Are you better off writing a Movie of the Week or a feature that you could pass off as a Movie of the Week?

MS: Never, ever, ever write a script with the intention of selling it as a Movie of the Week. Not ever. Just write features, and write them structurally sound. If someone wants it for television they'll help you change it for the medium. Besides, everybody loves to give input and help "improve" your story.

MD: Let's say a writer does a really good half-hour sitcom and they are referred to an agent. What's the next step? Does the agent bring them in and talk or will they usually want to see more sample writing?

MS: If you want to write sitcoms, have at least two comedy samples. If your sole intention is to write drama, have a couple of samples of different shows, and preferably, shows of different styles. It's important to demonstrate a range in your ability. An agent is looking for ammunition to sell you, and the more you provide the agent, the easier you make his job.

MD: Are you pretty much stuck in the genre you choose to write in? In other words, if a writer turns in a good comedy, does that mean they can only be marketed in comedy?

MS: No, but if you're writing "The Equalizer," or "Wiseguy," don't ask your agent to start selling you to "Golden Girls" without a comedy sample. He's got to have the appropriate material to submit.

MD: Is writing for cable the same as writing for network television today?

MS: If "cable" means that you're writing for Showtime, HBO, Disney Channel, yes. It doesn't matter where you're writing. If you're writing, you're writing. It's the caliber of what you're doing that's important. HBO's movies tend to be prestige pictures. Showtime is looking for film noire projects. Next week they'll want "Meatballs." You can't second guess them. People spend their days calling the networks, trying to find out what they want.

MD: What are the chances for the new writer to sell a television pilot?

MS: Remote at best. Save yourself the trouble and write some good sample episodes. If you want to write television pilots then get known as a good television writer. Accumulate credits and staff experience so that the studios and networks are seeking you out. That's when you have a real shot. Of course, there are always exceptions. A great pilot is a great pilot, although it almost has to be of a higher quality when coming from an outside neophyte.

MD: What if you submitted a great idea in the form of a treatment? Couldn't you have one of your hot writers attach themselves to the project? Wouldn't this help push it through?

MS: Yes, but I'm not in the business of selling unsolicited ideas. I'm in the business of finding employment for my writers. If a writer is that hot, ideas and projects are already being offered from the studios with money offers. It's just too hard for an outside writer to compete with the established buyers.

MD: What about collaboration?

MS: There's nothing wrong with a collaboration as long as you are committed to working with that person indefinitely.

MD: Indefinitely?

MS: Indefinitely! Because the moment the collaboration splits up, your jointly created material is nearly worthless. People will assume your partner wrote it. It's unfortunate, but it's like starting over again. You may have a body of credits, but they're going to want to see an original solo writing sample.

MD: What's the difference between a writer being persistent and a writer being a pain? What do you expect from your clients?

MS: I think it's imperative that the writer know how to push their agent's buttons. You have to know the fine line between motivating them and turning them off. Some people who call me once a month are a pain in the ass. Some people who call me twice a day are being persistent. It depends on the personality, the relationship. People skills are as important as writing in this business.

MD: What about living in the area?

MS: If you're going to write episodic television you should live nearby. If you don't, get a local phone number anyway. It's difficult and expensive living far away since part of the process in getting employment is being available for meetings, often with only a moment's notice.

MD: Does the client have to do their own marketing?

MS: No, but it sure helps. Agents have many clients; the writer has only one. Some writers sit at home and never call and wait for the phone to ring. Others call up saying they've just spoken to a producer and to please send a script over to them. We hope that the writer will be out there as much as we are.

The New Cable and Syndication Market

Before writers can successfully begin to market they must know all the avenues open to them for a sale. Since the beginning of television, programming has been monopolized by the big three networks: ABC, CBS, and NBC. Not only have viewers been limited to these three sources but television writers have had little choice as to where they could take their material.

I am very glad to say times are changing! Today, the average American household has more than thirty television channels to choose from. We now have Pay-TV, which reaches an estimated 52 million subscribers, and basic cable and independent stations. As these new markets grow they are competing with the networks by offering first-run original programming. This is great news because it means more jobs for writers. Each day we are being presented with new outlets, both creatively and economically, in which to pursue our work.

One of the most pertinent and respected production companies in the cable industry today is actress/producer Shelley Duvall's Think, Inc. Entertainment. Recently, I had lunch with Alene Terasaki, the company's director of series and specials, to discuss the direction of cable and the new markets.

A Word from Alene Terasaki

MADELINE DIMAGGIO: What exactly is meant by "development"?

ALENE TERASAKI: My job is to look for scripts and ideas that we can develop into a movie, a television series (pilot), or a miniseries. One of the great advantages of my having been at HBO is that I got the opportunity to do everything—comedy series, variety, miniseries, cable movies, dramatic series. Had I gone with a commercial network, I would have been very much specialized in only one area.

MD: In what way does pay cable differ from commercial television?

AT: Pay cable is attracting more and more of what you would call mainstream feature film writers, directors, and actors. It's not PBS. Cable tries to appeal to a mainstream audience with things they would get to see in a movie theater, not things they would tune in to at 8:00, 9:00, or 10:00 P.M. on ABC, CBS, or NBC.

The primary service that pay cable offers you is features, movies, and "event" programming, or what I think the networks call "stunt" programming. They want things that will get consumer press attention, and enhance the value of the subscription. Even if the subscriber doesn't watch the Spinks fight, they know it's on HBO. Even if they don't tune in to "Motown," they know it's on Showtime. The subscriber knows that it's on and that they couldn't see it elsewhere. HBO's "Comic Relief" is another one. They want to do that with their scripted programs as well.

There are more outlets for material in cable and more specialized markets. They'll take shows in cable that would be considered too narrow in their appeal for network television. That's exactly what I'm looking for. That's what happened to "Molly Dodd," which went to Lifetime cable.

When I say pay cable wants things you wouldn't see on commercial television, that doesn't mean trash sitcoms set in whorehouses—you might want to find things that are more sophisticated. One example is HBO's "Tanner 88," a multiple half-hour comedy which ran a fictional candidate for president. It was written by Garry Trudeau and directed by Robert Altman.

MD: Does cable attract names that would not ordinarily go on network television because it is so specialized?

AT: From a creative point of view, you have a lot more latitude. Movies don't have to be written with seven-act breaks for commercials and you're not restricted in terms of language and content. There is no standards and practices department at HBO, only a legal department. I think I'm in on the leading edge of a very creative area of television.

MD: With cable reaching 52 million households, how do you see its popularity changing the future of network television?

AT: I can't imagine what the impact will be, to tell you the truth. Networks are probably always going to get the lion's share of the market. But in terms of creative freedom, inventiveness, the opportunity to take chances, and to do things that have some substance, cable presents really exciting possibilities.

MD: How many cable companies are there?

AT: Somebody was saying the other day that there are 27 cable services—that's an enormous number. But let's go through some of them. There are the pay services: HBO, Showtime, Cinemax, The Movie Channel, Disney Channel—of those, the people who commission a lot of original programming are HBO, and Cinemax (HBO develops for Cinemax), the Disney Channel, and Showtime. Then there is Turner Network Television, which is advertiser-supported, and commissions a significant amount of original programming. There's Nickelodeon, Lifetime, ESPN—MTV does a little bit of original programming—Arts and Entertainment very little, and The Discovery Channel which specializes in documentaries.

MD: What's the difference between cable and first-run syndication?

AT: Syndicated shows are aired by independent stations not usually network-affiliated. They put together a syndicate of stations which air nonnetwork shows that are original, for example, "She's the Sheriff," "Star Trek—The Next Generation," "Entertainment Tonight," "Friday the 13th," "Freddy's Nightmare," "War of the Worlds," "Arsenio Hall," etc. "Tales of the Darkside" was very successful. "Oprah" started out as a syndicated show.

MD: In other words, we watch "syndication" on our regular stations.

AT: Yes, but it's in a nonnetwork time slot, or they preempt something that comes from a network feed and put that show on instead because they think they're going to get more viewers and advertising revenue.

MD: And with cable you "buy" in. You pay.

AT: Yes. You can get basic cable, which is just "x" number of stations, for example, CNN. The difference between first-run syndication and original programming on cable is content and the method of delivery. One of them comes to you through a service that's available only on cable; the other over the air on your antenna.

MD: You said your job is to look for scripts and ideas you wish to develop. Is there anything Think Entertainment is looking for in particular?

AT: No, not really. We're trying to cover the entire cable market. I think our company, probably better than any other, understands cable because we've spent so much time in it. That is our franchise, to sell and produce for cable.

MD: For pay cable movies, what story lines would you say have the best shot for a sale—if you were forced to look at Las Vegas odds?

AT: It depends on the market, of course, but I would look for stories that appeal to a slightly older, not teenage, audience that have the kinds of things you see in movie houses. Also stories with strong male appeal because so much of network television is aimed at females.

MD: Such as action adventure?

AT: Yes, although action adventure tends to be expensive—so suspense thrillers, sometimes courtroom dramas, stories like *Jagged Edge,* and *Fatal Attraction.* And controversial material—*The Chicago Seven Conspiracy Trial, Nightbreaker* (about atomic testing), and *Mandela.*

MD: What about comedy? How does it fare on cable?

AT: It has to be the right kind. The reason there are so many adolescent comedies around is because there is still that adolescent market in features—*Police Academy, Animal House,* and *Bill and Ted's Excellent Adventure. Mr. Mom* did really well on HBO when it aired. They watched it over and over—a solid part of the pay cable audience spends a lot of time at home because they have children in the house. They identify with that kind of story. *Irreconcilable Differences* also did very well. These are the types of things they're looking for, shows like *Finnegan Begin Again,* which was an original HBO production with Mary Tyler Moore and Robert Preston in a May–December romance. It was really sweet. People loved it and gave it high ratings when they were asked to evaluate it.

MD: What do you consider a good "read"? What do you look for in a script?

AT: A good story and good characters! I guess what I look for are stories that seem to come out of the writer's experience. There's a texture and sort of a verisimilitude that makes me feel I've been brought into a real world. If I can see that world from the inside, if it's alive for me, if the people are alive, then I'm really attracted to that writing. I don't know how else to put it. It's very subjective. Something that writers have to understand is that different genres require different skills. Sitcom writing is wonderfully skillful writing. It's very different from writing a feature comedy or a one-hour detective show. When you read a quality script you can really see the craft going on and understand it.

MD: Have you ever read scripts that don't come to you by way of an agent? Do you read unsolicited material?

AT: I'm not allowed to take unsolicited material. It has to come from an agent or attorney, or by referral.

MD: If a script came across your desk with that special ability you mentioned, would you be willing to work with a new writer? It wouldn't matter if they had no credits?

AT: Absolutely, but for me to spend time with the writer I would have to really like the material. I would have to feel that, if it were re-worked, it would be salable. Salability doesn't always have to do with whether something is good or not. Recently I read a first screenplay, and even though I knew it probably wasn't salable (the story was very soft), and we didn't option it, the writer showed so much talent that I've been working with him, suggesting rewrites, and have recommended him to others.

MD: Can you explain what you mean by a "soft" story?

AT: It's what the audience would not find easily recognizable. It's not the kind of story they've seen before. Harder pieces, or concept-driven pieces, seem to me to be things that fit into genres, like action adventure, detective, western, romance, etc. When I say "soft," what I mean is we're being asked to tune in, watch, and fall in love with only the characters.

MD: Was *Moonstruck* soft?

AT: Yes, it really was. I think it became so successful because John Patrick Shanley created the most fabulously wonderful characters. If you tried to describe the story in a log line, what is it? "Aging Italian girl falls in love with the brother of her fiancé." That's a little bit harder log line, but it misleads you. What was the story about? "A love story set under the full moon in Brooklyn?"

MD: What role does the development person play in creating movies and pilots. What is your key purpose?

AT: We are sort of the invisible ingredient in the entertainment industry—we are a third point of view, creatively. Hopefully, we can bring sort of a stand-back overview to the project that a writer doesn't have yet. It doesn't matter if it's an original idea or a finished script. My job is to bring a fresh eye to it, to try and find what the heart of it is, what you, the writer, are saying—your passion, your vision. My job is to bring that out. Sometimes writers get very close to the material and they don't experience it as an audience would. Hopefully, that's what I can see. Usually it's structural. My job is not to tell you how to write—not to write it for you, not to tell you what's wrong, but to bring out what really speaks to people.

MD: It's sort of like buying a house: The structure already exists—now you make suggestions to the builder on what to bring out to enhance it, to show it at its best.

AT: Exactly.

MD: How did you get into development?

AT: I was teaching college working on my Ph.D. in anthropology and linguistics when I decided entertainment was a lot more fun. So I changed careers. It was a zigzag course like everybody's. I started out by developing television courses for college credit. Then I did production for a while and public affairs programming, then production and advertising for an advertising agency. I worked on the world telecasting of the Olympics for ABC. Then I heard about a management fellowship being offered by the cable industry, the Walter Kaitz Fellowship. I applied and I got it. It was a wonderful opportunity. A company hires you for nine months. I got a chance to learn the business that I would never have gotten any other way. At the end of the nine-month fellowship, if you've worked yourself into a job, they hire you permanently.

MD: Where were you at the end of the nine months?

AT: I started out reading scripts for the Original Programming Department at HBO. Then I moved up to a programming position. I stayed almost three years. My last title was Manager of Development for Original Programming. I was Director of Programming and Development at Paramount Television, and then I came to Shelley's company, Think Entertainment, where I'm Director of Development for Movies and Series.

MD: Alene, is your company looking for ideas or completed scripts?

AT: Right now I'm looking for completed scripts. When the material is written in a screenplay, you can see the writer's vision, you get a sense of what it is they want to say. The new writer must have a completed script. You absolutely have more leverage when it's down on paper.

MD: What if a new writer has a sensational pilot idea? Is it better to present a completed script or a bible?

AT: Pilots are almost nonexistent. People don't say the "P" word because they are such expensive propositions. If you want to write a spec pilot and show it to me, wonderful; then we can talk. Generally, cable does not follow a network model at all. They may be moving in that direction, but they don't, for instance, commission a lot of pilot scripts, produce a certain number of them, and then give a series order based on how the pilot comes out. They just don't have the money to do that, and they don't have that much time to fill.

MD: So, if you have an idea you'd be better off writing a "back-door" pilot? (A two-hour movie that sets up a series for television, i.e., the series is introduced through the back door as a movie first.)

AT: Very much.

MD: Test it as a two-hour movie to see if it has what it takes?

AT: Right. Although they're not looking that much for series in the first place. I do have something right now that's a two-hour back-door pilot at HBO.

MD: I've heard that cable relies heavily on packaging. This means projects need to be attached to established names. How does a new writer deal with this?

AT: A beginning writer came to me recently with an idea for a comedy series. He has some writing credits, but not in the area of series comedy. The writer was accompanied by his very savvy agent. She knew and I knew that we'd have to attach his idea to a heavyweight comedy writer. The writer understood that he would probably get

"Created By," and maybe the opportunity to co-write. That's how it happens.

MD: That's not such a bad place for that writer to be in. At least down the line if the series goes, he'll have the opportunity to write, not to mention the money he'll receive for "Created By."

AT: Exactly. I think it's good for new writers to understand that you are looking for that break. You must put ego aside—there's no room for it. This is a tough business on your ego. There isn't room for insecurity. I feel that writers and actors are the furthest removed from the decision-making process. It's very hard for them to find out what the hell is going on—why these decisions are made and what impact they will have on them. The fact is, the decision-making process in this town is not totally organized and it's not totally rational. Writers shouldn't perceive rejection as a personal insult, that it's a rejection of their talent or their ability to write.

MD: What is your advice to writers just starting out?

AT: You've got to know in the end what *you* want, and know as much as you can about this business, because it *is* a business. You have to learn when to say "yes," and when to say "no." You must know what is right for yourself. You can't think that an agent or anybody else is going to solve all your problems.

MD: New writers will often complain, "My agent is doing nothing for me." I respond by asking them what they have done for their agent lately. The fact is, ten percent of nothing is still nothing.

AT: Agents have only so many hours in a day. You're lucky if you can get one to do everything for you, but they'll do that only as long as it pays off. Writers should look for help, but shouldn't turn their career over to somebody else and think, "Thank God I don't have to do deals, I don't have to find people to pitch to, I don't have to sell my own scripts because my agent's going to do that." Wrong. People I've seen who are very successful, or are getting there, are those who really take their destiny into their own hands and make it happen for themselves.

15

The Most Frequently Asked
Questions in Marketing

Whether at speaking engagements or while teaching, when the subject turns to marketing, new scriptwriters have the same questions. I've made a list of those most commonly asked.

Can I Begin the Marketing Process Before My Script Is Complete? Don't ever attempt to begin marketing a script before you are finished writing it. Let's say someone wants to see your material immediately. You can't send it out. Instead, you must stop to complete it. By the time you are ready, your needed momentum along with your potential buyer is lost. What the writer can do while still writing is prepare the marketing strategy by reading the industry trades and journals, and accumulating the names of possible contacts.

What Is Meant By the Term Trades? The trades, as they are referred to by the industry, are *Daily Variety* and the *Hollywood Reporter.* Both journals are delivered five working days a week. Literally everything a writer needs to know is listed here—from Hollywood gossip and finances to what is in production, who is doing it, and where. Even productions scheduled for the future are listed. Since both journals cover the same information it is only necessary to order one (appendix A). It is crucial to be in the "know" where marketing is concerned. By subscribing to one of these publications the new writer is introduced and informed on every aspect of the industry.

Is It True You Need Contacts to Break into the Industry? There is no denying that contacts are a crucial part of breaking in. The good news is that contacts can be made. Your uncle does not have to own a studio. One of the best ways to meet industry contacts is through writers conferences, workshops, and film festivals. Keep on top of the trade papers and journals to find out who will be where, and when. Each year the May issue of *Writer's Digest* lists conferences throughout the country. Check to see if Hollywood agents, producers, staff writers, directors, or any executives in creative development will be attending. Once there, make a point of shaking hands and talking to them. Keep in touch. Once your script is complete, mention in your cover letter that you've made contact with them before.

Do I Have to Have An Agent to Sell My Material? No, but once the teleplay or screenplay is complete you should immediately go to work and find an agent who will represent your material. You should not, however, stop the marketing process while waiting for representation. Scripts can be sold without agents, and interest can be generated in the material that can eventually help you in finding an agent.

How Are Agents Paid? They receive ten percent of what the writer earns.

Do Agents Have Reader Fees? Film agents should never charge for reading scripts. They are looking at your material as a possible source of income for themselves. They have a personal interest at stake.

What Is Meant by the Term Franchised Agent? These agents have subscribed to the Writers Guild of American Artists Managers Basic Agreement. They deal with studios and producers who are signatories of the guild. Only look for a franchised agent.

How Do I Find a List of Franchised Agents? This list can be easily acquired by writing to the guild.

Do Agents Critique Your Work? Rarely. Their interest is whether or not they can market your material—not where the material went wrong. Don't look for a detailed analysis from an agent.

Which Is Better, to Sign with a Small Agency or a Large Agency? Don't worry about this. Go with the agent who wants you. If you are unhappy you can always change later. It is most likely in the beginning that you will end up at a smaller agency. This can be an advantage, since with the larger agencies it is easier to get lost in the shuffle.

Does an Agent Keep Me Informed? Yes. The writer should be made aware of each and every submission. If the agent does not offer this information, it is up to you to stay on top of the situation and call and ask.

What If I Already Have a Literary Agent? If this agent does not handle film, ask for a referral. Many literary agents have agreements with film agents and they receive a finder's fee. A reference from a professional works wonders in getting your material read.

Can I Use More Than One Film Agent? Once an agreement is made, you can only use that agent to represent the material.

Are There Agents Who Handle Both Film and Publishing? Yes. If you are interested in working in both mediums it might be advantageous for you to find an agent who deals in both. You can find these agents by simply calling the names on the list and inquiring. Talk to the receptionist. Let your motives be known and don't be afraid to ask questions!

Is An Agent/Client Contract Necessary? Not necessarily. Some agents require contracts with writers whereas others will simply operate on an oral agreement. It is important to remember that an oral agreement can be just as binding as a written agreement.

If I Am Unhappy with My Agent Can I Get Out of My Contract? Yes, you can fire your agent. If you are not employed in any field (including work outside WGA jurisdiction) for compensation of at least ten thousand dollars total, or you do not receive a bona fide and appropriate offer of employment for ten thousand dollars or more during any period of ninety consecutive days, then you can terminate your contract with your agent. However, the ninety-day clause works both ways. Your agent can terminate his or her contract with you on the same grounds. Termination requires prior written notice of ten business days.

Can I Submit My Scripts to Production Companies Without the Help of an Agent? Yes. But first you must identify these production companies, where they are, and how to reach them. A book I find invaluable is the *Pacific Coast Studio Directory* (appendix A). This handy publication comes out quarterly and lists hundreds of independent producers, their addresses, and phone numbers. Many independent production companies will read unsolicited material.

Once My Script Is Submitted Who Will Most Likely Read It? Many production companies, as well as the larger agencies, have a screening process. That process begins in almost every instance with a reader. The reader is the first stop along the road to a studio's or agent's acceptance. His or her role is to act as a filter for executives whose schedules prohibit them from reading every script.

What Is the Reader's Job? The reader, or story analyst, is the first screening process along the way. The reader's job is to read for executives who are too busy to do it themselves. A reader will average ten or more scripts per week.

How Does the Reader or Story Analyst Go about Evaluating My Script? Nearly all readers follow the same procedure. Their job is to supply coverage. That is, the front page of the reader's report lists the title of the property, who wrote it, the type of material, the length, and certain elements, if any, that stand out. In addition, a TV guideline, or a two-sentence Log Line, is included and whether or not the reader recommends the material. The reader attaches a two-page synopsis of the script.

When I Submit the Script Should I Include a Synopsis of the Story? No. This encourages readers not to read. You should only submit a synopsis when one is requested. In the event that it is asked for, the writing should be tight (no more than one page), and should entice the reader to dive into the script.

Before Submitting Material to Agents or Production Companies Should I Send a Query Letter? You will get varied answers on this one. I tell writers not to do this. It's better that your material lands on a pile somewhere than your getting a note back saying they are not interested in the subject matter. Let's suppose, for example, that Sylvester Stallone, before *Rocky* was purchased, sent a query letter asking producers if they were interested in a story about a down-and-out boxer who goes the distance. Many producers would reject this material simply because they were not interested in stories about boxing. The beauty of *Rocky* is its execution. Through the *read* we were made to care for the characters—not through its *log line.* Unless your story is unique and high-concept enough to warrant professional curiosity, I would not attempt a query letter.

Should I Submit My Teleplay or Screenplay with a Cover Letter? Yes. Keep it short and to the point. Remember, this is the production company's first sample of your writing. Unless you're wonderfully clever, don't try to be. Briefly introduce yourself, then go to work selling confidence in your material. Always try to come from a place of strength. If you've made previous contact with the individual, mention it. If you're an authority on the topic you choose to write about, mention that too (i.e., a police officer who has written a crime story or a physician who has scripted a medical mystery). Point out the strengths in the material. Is it a star vehicle (does it have powerful roles for a male or female lead)? Is it a fresh idea that has not been done yet? Is your story timely or controversial? Does it address an issue of crucial importance? Find powerful words to whet the appetite and pique interest. Don't be shy. Let the production company know it's well written and that you have confidence in yourself as a writer. Mention a follow-up phone call. This leaves the ball in your hands. Wait three weeks and call them. They probably won't have read it by then, but continue to call every couple of weeks until they do. Get to know the secretary's name and ask for him or her. Secretaries are some of the most powerful people in the business. They can provide you with invaluable information.

Do I Send a Self-Addressed Stamped Envelope with My Material? No. If no one reads your material, it will almost always be sent back on their dime. A screenplay costs about $2.40 to mail. Why double the cost and make it easy for your material to be returned? If there is no response you have the opportunity to call. And if your material is read, it will be so dog-eared by the time you get it back that it won't be reusable.

Do I Submit My Script to the Production Company or to an Individual Who Works for that Company? Never submit your script to a company. It could easily get lost in the mail room. By inquiring by phone or letter, get the name of the story editor or the development executive and address your material to one of them. This way, your script lands on a desk. At that point it may be referred to a reader. The trades will also mention individuals who work for production companies. Look up the company's mailing address in the *Pacific Coast Directory.*

If an Independent Producer or Company Is Interested in Making a Deal and I Don't Have an Agent, What Should I Do? Now is an ideal time to find an agent. You will have your pick once serious interest is generated in your material. Don't be greedy and say, "Why should I give up ten percent of my fee when I'm the one who got the job?" Never, and I repeat, never try to negotiate your own deal. A good agent is well worth ten percent when it comes to finding loopholes. Remember, the agent wants what's best for you because it means more for them as well. The only viable alternative is an entertainment attorney. Be weary of their fees—you may not be saving money in the long run!

How Do I Learn What Television Shows Are Open for Submissions? The *Writers Guild Journal,* a periodical sent to members once a month, provides a TV Market List detailing all the shows in production and their status as to availability for the season. Though this list cannot always be completely accurate, it is the best source available for information. The journal is forty dollars per year for nonmembers and can be ordered from the Writers Guild of America, West (see appendix B).

Do Episodic Television Shows Have Readers? No, this job belongs to the story editor. It is much more difficult to get a spec television script read than a two-hour movie read. Most television shows will not read unsolicited material. It is crucial, therefore, to write a few spec scripts for various existing shows, and on their merit find an agent who will go to bat for you. (Refer to the interview with agent Mitchel Stein, page 248.)

How Does a Writer Submit a Pilot? It is more important to submit the bible than the actual script (refer to chapter 10). A bible consists of in-depth character and format descriptions telling the reader exactly how the writer perceives his or her idea. Most bibles begin with a paragraph or two describing the overall concept of the show. This description should be lean and hook the reader immediately. Included next should be brief biographies on the main characters and secondary characters. It is important to keep the cast list down, and the writer shouldn't confuse the reader with excessive detail. The characters should reach our gut level. We, the audience, should somehow identify with them. Inner and outer conflict between the cast is crucial and implies to the reader the ongoing potential of the show. The character biographies are followed by four or five possible story lines or log lines. These should be no longer than a few sentences. Basically, they are TV line descriptions that again prove the potential of the show.

If the bible (developed concept) is purchased, the writer will get a "created by" payment, and if the show goes to air, the writer will subsequently get paid every time the show runs. It is highly unlikely that a newcomer will get a shot at writing a pilot script. Networks nearly always bring in a name or approved writer to do the job.

Do I Submit My Series Idea to the Major Networks? Absolutely not. The networks buy names, not ideas. They want writers with track records. In fact, ABC, CBS, and NBC all have "A-list" writers—that is, writers who have already been network-approved to write pilots and Movies of the Week. Instead, market your pilot ideas to independent producers who have track records of their own. Once you get them behind your project, you will go into the networks wearing their armor.

Can I Mail Only a Portion of My Script to Interest the Reader? Only when asked for. There are some agents who request only the first ten pages of your script to see if they are interested in your concept and to determine if you have the ability to execute a script. Never attempt submitting the first ten pages unless your script is complete, however. In the event that a reader or agent requests the rest of the material, be very certain you have it.

Should I Get a Professional Critique Before I Submit My Material? Yes. It is very important that you receive an in-depth critique before submission. Writers become too close to their material: They need an outside opinion. Also, a professional will help in making your presentation as slick as possible. In an industry as competitive as this one, you need an edge. The *Writers Guild Newsletter* and many industry periodicals will provide you with names of professional script doctors who will critique for a fee.

Are There Software Programs that Will Format My Scripts? Among the most commonly used are:

IBM-PC	MicroSoft Word WordPerfect WordStar	All can be used with SCRIPTOR, which provides the formatting for screenplays. It is suggested that MicroSoft Word works best as it has a built-in Spellcheck and Thesaurus.
	MovieMaster	Does screenplay formatting only, not a full-function word processing program.
MACINTOSH	MicroSoft Word	Again, the best program to use with SCRIPTOR.
	Scriptwriter	Like MovieMaster, this program is for formatting only, and is not a full-function word processing program.

Is It a Disadvantage Trying to Work and Sell While Living Away from the Los Angeles Area? Writers who do must make sacrifices. First, they must convince their agents that they are serious about their careers and accessible on short notice. Commuting is expensive, so of course there is a financial burden. Making contacts and developing social relationships are more difficult as well.

For those in episodic television, living in the area is almost a must because there are so many meetings. It can be done, however. I know some very successful writers who felt the sacrifices were worth it. For now, don't worry about where you live. Worry about the quality of your material. After you get a sale, then make a choice.

If I Sell My Script Can I Be Guaranteed the Movie or Television Show Will Get Made? No. Just because a sale takes place and money changes hands, there is no guarantee the television show or film will get made. Many reasons have nothing to do with the quality of the material. Don't fret—you have a legitimate credit anyway. You'll get paid, and it will pave the way to another job. It's disappointing, but at least you'll have made a hefty deposit.

How Can I Become a Member of the Writers Guild? First, you must sell to become eligible for admission into the guild. The guild works on a point system designed to measure as accurately as possible the nature and kind of writing done (see appendix B).

Once My Script Is Complete Should I Spend the Majority of My Time Marketing or Should I Begin Another Project? Begin another project! Under all circumstances you must continue to write. A well-written script is an excellent calling card but it's often not enough. Write! Write! Write! It's inevitable that production companies will want to see more.

What Is an Option? A fee paid by the studio or producer for movie or television rights to your script. In return, the writer promises not to shop the script anywhere else until the option period has expired. The average option runs one or two years. If, during this time, the studio or production company decides to make the film, they package, develop, bring the finances together, and do everything needed to get the movie into production.

What Is a Release Form? A release is the only protection a producer and the studios have against plagiarism suits. Just as there is writer paranoia, there is also producer paranoia. Try to understand their viewpoint. Ideas aren't that unique, and each week literally hundreds of scripts are pouring in. Suppose a studio is already developing an idea similar to yours at the time your script is received. When the movie is aired, if you could prove the production company had access to your material without signing a release form, you could accuse them of plagiarism. According to the legal department at the Writers Guild of America, West, release forms make lawsuits more difficult for writers—but they still can take legal action if they have to. Sign a release form if it is requested. It is the only way you will get your material read.

What Are Residuals? These are payments that writers receive every time the television show they scripted is rerun. The rate the writer receives is determined by Writers Guild of America contract and can be obtained by writing the guild and requesting a copy of the WGA Minimum Basic Agreement.

If My Script Sells, How Much Money Will I Make? The Writers Guild establishes set minimums for television and motion picture writing. Under the current contract the minimums are as follows:

Prime-Time Network Programs

30-Minute Script

Story	$ 3,883
Teleplay	$ 8,356
Story and Teleplay	$11,651

60-Minute Script

Story	$ 6,838
Teleplay	$11,272
Story and Teleplay	$17,134

120-Minute Script

Story	$12,199
Teleplay	$20,839
Story and Teleplay	$31,718

Screenplays (including treatment)

Low-Budget	High-Budget
(Theatricals costing less than $2,500,000)	(Theatricals costing more than $2,500,000)
$25,740	$47,867

It is important to note that for both Movies for Television and theatrical motion pictures, the fees are negotiable and can go much higher. For more detailed information, contact the Writers Guild of America, west, and ask for the current Theatrical and Television Basic Agreement.

16

A Final Note from the Author

Creativity does not stop once you write "The End" on the page. Now a whole new phase for the writer begins: the writer as salesperson. There is no getting around it. In the beginning you must sell yourself to break in. Once you're in, you must continue to sell yourself to get established.

For most writers, marketing ourselves is the toughest aspect of our work. Life would be so much easier if we could just hide behind our word processors and write. I tell students that marketing is like standing at the edge of a pool on a very hot day. The pool isn't heated, but you know if you could just let go, after that initial shock, you'd be glad you went in. If you stand there and overthink, if you focus on the discomfort instead of the end result, then you'll forego the experience altogether. Mental conditioning is half of everything in this business.

When I look back over my fourteen years in the industry, the high points in my career happened when I was in a good place, and the low points came when I wasn't. I remember being cut off once from an "Eight Is Enough" (this is not an unusual occurrence—it happens when a producer feels the writer did not deliver a satisfactory draft). I went out that day, bought new curtains for my house, and the next week went on to another job. Years later, when I was going through some difficult times, an executive commented that he didn't like my script, and I was so devastated that I didn't write again for a year. I was the same writer, and the quality of the script was good. The only thing that was different was my perception.

If you're serious about pursuing a career in television or film, it's important for you to find a way to detach yourself from your material. Run, meditate, say affirmations, stand on your head, or eat sausage. Find whatever it is that works for you and keeps you going. That way, when rejection comes, the disappointment won't deter you from your goal. In effect, you're under the wave instead of letting it hit you in the gut and pull you to shore.

Also remember, the most important part of writing is the process, not the sale. Of all the writers I have met who haven't sold, none of them have regretted writing a script. They find joy in the creative process. They get caught in the challenge, and they complete their projects, which is an incredible satisfaction in itself.

I wish you great luck in your writing.

APPENDIX A
Resources

PUBLICATIONS

American Film
American Film Institute (AFI)
P.O. Box 27999
2021 N. Western Ave.
Los Angeles, CA 90027

Monthly publication covering film, video, and the television arts. Timely interviews with a variety of industry professionals, as well as information regarding available instructional programs, etc. Subscription/Membership: $25 per year, includes *American Film Magazine.*

Daily Variety
Daily Variety, Ltd.
1400 N. Cahuenga Blvd.
Hollywood, CA 90028
213/469-1141

Daily publication that features news of the trade. Subscription fee is $97 per year; $87 for six months.

Hollywood Professional Directory
9601 Wilshire Blvd.
Beverly Hills, CA 90210
213/273-1101

A quarterly directory listing names, addresses, and phone numbers of agents, casting directors, personal managers, producers, production companies, commercial directors, print photographers, advertising agencies, and an industry reference guide.

Hollywood Reporter
6715 Sunset Blvd.
Hollywood, CA 90028
213/464-7411

Publishes daily industry news and information; some interviews and special issues. Subscription fee is $116 per year; $90 for six months.

Hollywood Scriptwriter
1626 N. Wilcox, #385
Hollywood, CA 90028
818/991-3096
Editor/Publisher Kerry Cox

Provides information on the film industry, agents, interviews, markets, workshops, and the "how to's" for writing good scripts. Monthly subscription is $39 per year; $20 for six months (discount when you renew; back issues available).

Pacific Coast Studio Directory
6313 Yucca St.
Hollywood, CA 90028-5093
213/467-2920

A directory published quarterly, which in alphabetical order (by state) lists names, addresses, and phone numbers of talent agencies representing writers and artists, film distributors, unions and guilds, film libraries, production companies, film commissions, and script services.

The Writers Guild Journal
Writers Guild of America, West
8955 Beverly Blvd.
Los Angeles, CA 90048-2456
213/205-2502

The *WGA's Journal* provides feature articles, industry news, writers services, phone listings for accurate subject information, and a Television Market List, which provides a listing of television series currently in production, their availability status, and the address and phone number of the producer and story editor. Subscription fee is $40 per year for nonmembers for the monthly publication.

ORGANIZATIONS

American Film Institute (AFI)
P.O. Box 27999
2021 N. Western Ave.
Los Angeles, CA 90027

Membership lends support to the nationwide preservation and advancement of the film and television arts. The organization sponsors workshops on just about every aspect of the industry.

National Writers Club
1450 South Havana
Aurora, CO 80012
303/751-7844

Provides national seminars on all types of writing including script writing. In addition, weekend conferences and special events are offered.

Sierra Writing Camp
18293 Crystal Street
Grass Valley, CA 95949
916/272-8047
Contact Karen Newcomb

Provides a summer school or camp which teaches participants how to write and sell all types of writing, including television and film scripts.

Sundance Institute
R.R. 3–B
Sundance, UT 84604

Sundance Institute is a nonprofit educational organization established to assist American independent filmmakers. They also offer playwriting, dance/film lab, and a composer lab. Write for further information (enclose self-addressed, stamped envelope).

Women in Film
6464 Sunset Blvd.
Suite 660
Los Angeles, CA 90028
213/463-0931

also Northern California Women in Film
415/431-3886

Promotes the recognition and contributions of women in film, television, and other media. Offers seminars, a monthly newsletter, and an annual film festival.

Writers Connection
1601 Saratoga-Sunnyvale Road
Suite 180
Cupertino, CA 95014
408/973-0227

Provides seminars on all types of writing including script writing, one-day and weekend conferences, and special events. Selling to Hollywood seminars are held on an annual basis. Write for further information.

SCRIPTS/MAIL ORDER

Script City
1765 N. Highland
760 W.D.M.
Hollywood, CA 90028

Film Analysis Series
5515 Jackson Dr.
Suite 246
La Mesa, CA 90230

SCRIPTS/TYPING SERVICES

Check industry periodicals and journals for advertisements. I have used the following two companies and find them highly professional:

Barbara Whitworth Taylor
Taylor'd Word Processing
P.O. Box 51897
Pacific Grove, CA 93950
408/384-2202

Barbara's Place
7925 Santa Monica Blvd.
Los Angeles, CA 90046
213/654-5902

Other typing services available include the following (write or call for further information):

On Word, Inc.
2434 Main St.
Santa Monica, CA 90405
213/399-7733

Scribe Secretarial Service
2288 Westwood Blvd., #201
Los Angeles, CA 90064
213/479-0729

The Script Center
7829 Melrose Ave.
Hollywood, CA 90046
213/651-2251

Starlite
8230 Beverly Blvd.
Suite 1
Los Angeles, CA 90048
213/651-0110

APPENDIX B
The Writers Guild of America

The Guild represents writers primarily for the purpose of collective bargaining in the motion picture, television, and radio industries. It does not obtain employment for writers, refer or recommend members for writing assignments, offer writing instruction or advice, or accept or handle material for submission to production companies.

Literary material should be submitted directly to the production company or through a literary agent. To obtain the current list of franchised agencies by mail, send your request with $1 to the attention of the Agency Department. The list is free if picked up at the Guild office. Guild office hours are 9:30 A.M. to 5:30 P.M., Monday through Friday.

For writing instruction or advice, the Guild suggests that you communicate with film schools, state colleges, universities, or with your local Board of Education. The Television Market List, featuring contact submission information on current weekly prime-time television programs, is published monthly in the *WGAW Journal* and is available to nonmembers at $5 per issue, or $40 for an annual subscription. Please send your request with a check or money order to:

WGAW Journal
Writers Guild of America, West
8955 Beverly Blvd.
West Hollywood, CA 90048

Guild policy prevents them from disclosing the address or phone number of any Guild member. First-class correspondence may be addressed to a member in care of the Guild and will be promptly forwarded to members without a referral address such as an agent. Please contact the Agency Department for further information.

A helpful book for accepted script format, entitled *Professional Writer's Teleplay/Screenplay Format Guide,* is available through the Writers Guild of America, East. The price, including postage, is $4.15. Please send your request with a check or money order to the Writers Guild of America, East, 555 West 57th Street, New York, NY 10019.

REGISTRATION

Writers Guild Registration Service
Registration Administrator: Blanche W. Baker
213/205-2541

Purpose

The Guild's Registration Service has been set up to assist members and nonmembers in establishing the completion date and the identity of their literary property written for the fields of theatrical motion pictures, television, and radio.

Value

Registration does not confer any statutory protection. It merely provides a record of the writer's claim to authorship of the literary material involved and of the date of its completion. The Registration Office does not make comparisons of registration deposits to determine similarity between works, nor does it give legal opinions or advice. Questions regarding copyright protection should be directed to an attorney specializing in that area of the law. *Registration does not take the place of registering the copyright on your material with the U.S. Copyright Office.*

Coverage

Registration with the Guild does not protect titles (neither does registration with the U.S. Copyright Office).

Procedure for Deposit

One 8½-by-11-inch unbound (no brads, staples, etc.) copy is required for deposit in the Guild files. When it is received, the property is sealed in a Guild Registration envelope, timed and dated. A receipt is returned.

Notice of registration shall consist of the following wording: REGISTERED WGAw NO. _____ and be applied upon the title page or the page immediately following.

Scripts specifically intended for radio, television, and theatrical motion pictures are registrable as are television series formats, step outlines, and story lines. The specific field of writing and the proper writing credits should be noted on the title page. Each property must be registered separately (exception: three episodes, skits, or sketches for an existing series may be deposited as a single registration). Be sure that the name under which you register is your full legal name. The use of pseudonyms, pen names, initials, or familiar forms of a proper name may require proof of identity if you want to recover the material left on deposit.

Fees

$5 for members of WGAw and WGAe, $10 for nonmembers. The fee must accompany the material that is to be registered.

Location of Registration Office

To register by mail only, material must be sent to:

8955 Beverly Blvd.
Los Angeles, CA 90048

To register in person:

9009 Beverly Blvd.
Los Angeles, CA 90048

Their business hours are: 10:00 A.M. to 12 noon, 2:00 P.M. to 5:00 P.M., Monday through Friday.

Duration
Material deposited for registration after September 1, 1982, is valid for a term of five years; material deposited for registration prior to September 1, 1982, is valid for a term of ten years. You may renew the registration for an additional ten-year or five-year term, whichever is applicable, at the then-current registration fee. You authorize the Guild to destroy the material without notice to you on the expiration of the term of registration if renewal is not made. The fee should accompany the request for renewal.

Procedure for Withdrawal
The registered copy left on deposit cannot be returned to the writer without defeating the purpose of registration, the point being that evidence should be available, if necessary, that the material has been in the Guild's charge since the date of deposit.

However, if the writer finds it necessary to have the copy returned, at least forty-eight hours' notice of intended withdrawal must be given to the Guild. A manuscript will be given up only on the signature(s) of the writer(s). If the registration is in the names of more than one person, the written consent of all is required to authorize withdrawal. In case a registrant is deceased, proof of death and the consent of his representatives or heirs must be presented. In no event, except under these provisions, shall any of the material be allowed to be taken from the Guild office unless a court order has been acquired.

If any person other than the writer named in the registration shall request confirmation of registration; the registration number and/or date of deposit; to see either the material deposited, the registration envelope, or any other material, such request shall be denied unless authorization from the writer(s) or a court order is presented in connection therewith.

Copyright
The Guild does not have a copyright service. For forms and instructions call 202/287-9100.

REQUIREMENTS FOR ADMISSION TO THE WGA, WEST, INC.*

An aggregate of twelve units of credit as set forth on the Schedule of Units of Credit, which units are based upon work completed under contract of employment or upon the sale or licensing of previously unpublished and unproduced literary or dramatic material is required. Said employment, sale, or licensing must be with a company or other entity that is signatory to the applicable WGA Collective Bargaining Agreement and must be within the

*Writers residing west of the Mississippi River may apply for membership in the WGA, West, Inc. Writers residing east of the Mississippi River are advised to contact:

WGA, East, Inc.
555 West 57th Street
New York, NY 10019

jurisdiction of the Guild as provided in its collective bargaining contracts. The twelve units must be accumulated within the preceding two years of application.

Schedule of Units of Credit

Two Units. For each complete week of employment within the Guild's jurisdiction on a week-to-week or term basis.

Three Units. Story for radio play or television program of less than thirty minutes in duration shall be prorated in five-minute increments.

Four Units. Story for a short-subject theatrical motion picture or for a radio play or television program of not less than thirty minutes or more than sixty minutes in duration.

Six Units. Teleplay or radio play of less than thirty minutes in duration, which shall be prorated in five-minute increments; television format or presentation for a new series; "Created By" credit given pursuant to the separation of rights provisions of the WGA Theatrical and Television Basic Agreement.

Eight Units. Story for radio play or television program of more than one hour but not more than two hours in duration; screenplay for a short-subject theatrical motion picture or for a radio play or teleplay of not less than thirty minutes but not more than sixty minutes in duration.

The Following Shall Constitute Twelve Units

Story for a feature-length theatrical motion picture or for a television program or radio play of more than two hours in duration; screenplay for a feature-length theatrical motion picture or for a teleplay or a television program or a radio play for a radio program of more than one hour in duration.

Bible: Long-term story projection as used herein shall be defined as a bible, for a specified term on an existing, five times per week non-prime-time serial.

A rewrite is entitled to one-half the number of units allotted to its particular category as set forth in the schedule listed above.

A polish is entitled to one-quarter the number of units allotted to its particular category as set forth in the schedule listed above.

Sale of an option earns one-half the number of units allotted to its particular category as set forth in the schedule of units listed above, subject to a maximum entitlement of four such units *per project* in any one year.

Where writers collaborate on the same project each shall be accorded the appropriate number of units designated in the schedule of units listed above.

In all cases, to qualify for membership, if the writer's employment agreement or purchase agreement is with a company owned in whole or in part by the writer or writer's family, there must be an agreement for financing, production, and/or distribution with a third-party signatory producing company or, failing such agreement, the script must be produced and the writer must receive writing credit on screen in the form of "Written By," "Teleplay By," "Screenplay By," or "Radio Play By."

The applicant writer is required to apply for membership no later than the thirty-first day of employment.

In exceptional cases, the Board of Directors, acting upon a recommendation from the Membership and Finance Committee, shall have the power and authority to grant membership based on work done prior to two years before the applicant has filed an application for membership.

For purposes of the credit requirements in the foregoing provisions, audio credit for a writer employed to write radio or a writer who sells literary material for radio programming will suffice.

The initiation fee of $1,500 is payable only by cashier's check or by money order. No personal or corporate checks will be accepted. All membership applications are to be supported by a copy of executed employment or sales contracts or other acceptable evidence of employment or sales.

Index

About the Author

Madeline DiMaggio's experience in the field of screenwriting includes over thirty hours of episodic television, five television pilots, in the half-hour and one-hour formats, and over a half-dozen screenplays, for both Movie of the Weeks and feature films, including "Belly Up," and her latest, "If The Shoe Fits" (co-written with Academy Award winner, Pamela Wallace—*Witness*). Madeline was formerly a contract writer for Paramount Studios. While under contract to Paramount and NBC, she worked as a creative consultant and story editor. She has just optioned a TV movie, and is currently writing an episode of a half-hour sitcom entitled "13 East" for NBC. A popular lecturer, Madeline conducts writer's workshops and speaks at writer's conventions throughout the country. For information regarding her workshops and audio and video tapes, please write to:

Screenwriting Workshop
P.O. Box 1172
Pebble Beach, CA 93953